WORDS NOT
REQUIRED

WORDS NOT REQUIRED

A Father's Legacy of Honor, Grit, and Quiet Strength

DON P. MARTONE

First printing. Published and printed in 2026.

ISBN: 979-8-90057-194-2 - Ebook
ISBN: 979-8-90057-195-9 - Paperback
ISBN: 979-8-90057-196-6 - Hardcover

DEDICATION

To my beautiful wife, whose unwavering love, patience, and wisdom have been both my anchor and my compass. You remind me daily that true legacy is not built in titles, numbers, or accolades, but in the quiet rhythms of devotion—in shared laughter, hard-earned peace, and the grace of walking through every season hand in hand. You are the living proof that purpose is not found—it's practiced. And your steady belief in me gives meaning to every word on these pages.

And to my father, whose calloused hands and unrelenting spirit taught me that a man's worth is not measured by what he gains, but by what he gives, what he endures, and what he builds in silence. Though you began with little, you gave me everything that mattered—the grit, humility, and quiet conviction that love is best spoken through labor and presence. Your life was your message, and I am still learning to live it well.

This book is for both of you because what I've written here is not theory or philosophy, but the living truth of your example—that legacy is not what we leave behind, but how faithfully we show up, love deeply, and live it every day.

What we inherit shapes us.

What we carry forward defines us.

CONTENTS

PART IV

THE COURAGE TO LOVE WITHOUT WORDS

A Note From The Author

"What you do speaks so loudly that I cannot hear what you say."

—Ralph Waldo Emerson (1803-1882), American essayist, lecturer, and poet

---

There are books that begin with an idea, and then there are those that begin with a person. This one began with my father. He was not a man inclined toward long explanations or grand pronouncements. He did not speak often about his dreams or philosophies, nor did he offer guidance in the form of formal lessons. Instead, he lived in a manner that rendered words almost unnecessary. His life itself became the instruction, and only years later would I realize how completely he had been teaching all along.

I did not grow up in a house filled with long conversations. Ours was not a family that lingered around the table, dissecting the day or sharing great reflections about life. My father, especially, was a man of few words. He didn't sit me down to offer his philosophy, and he never rehearsed any great lessons for the moments when I needed direction. He wasn't withholding anything—he simply believed that a life was meant to be lived, not narrated.

As a boy, I sometimes mistook that quiet for distance. I didn't yet understand that silence can be a form of presence, and that some men communicate through steadiness rather than speech. Children look for language because it's the easiest thing to grasp. But a father—especially a father like mine—speaks in a far older language, one shaped not by articulation but by example. He taught me in the way he moved through a room, the way he set down his tools at the end of a long day, the way his shoulders settled into the evening with equal parts exhaustion and acceptance. Even before he spoke, his life was already speaking. And for years, I was too young to know how to listen.

There were patterns to how he lived—rhythms I didn't recognize when I was young. A kind of internal gravity drew him back to what needed doing, without drama and without delay. He tied his boots the same way every morning, slowly and deliberately, as though preparing himself to shoulder responsibility one more time. There was something sacred in it—that small, familiar moment when a man gathers himself to carry the weight he never asked to escape. He had a way of setting his jaw when confronted with a problem—not in frustration, but in acceptance, as though he believed every obstacle had already been measured and found manageable. Watching him face work was watching a man face life. He didn't flinch. He simply stepped forward.

I didn't know it then, but I was learning in silence. And silence, I've come to realize, is its own kind of teaching. There were no lectures about perseverance—only the sight of him returning to a task until it was done right. No speeches about humility—only the quiet example of him giving more than he kept. No sermons about faith—only the bowed head before a meal, the unspoken gratitude of a man who believed thankfulness was something you practiced, not performed. For most of my youth, I assumed these were ordinary gestures. They were not. They were the shape of character forming itself in front of me.

When I was younger, I misunderstood that quiet. I took it as reserve, perhaps even distance. I thought love required language, and that the absence of words meant something was missing. But time has a way of translating what youth cannot comprehend. As I grew older, I began to see what had always been there—the eloquence of his restraint, the dignity in his labor, and the deep generosity in his endurance. His silence was not withdrawal; it was focus. His lack of explanation was not withholding; it was wisdom born from a belief that the best truths are meant to be lived, not spoken.

There were times I wondered why he didn't share more of himself in words. I wanted to know what he thought as he came home exhausted from work. I wanted him to explain the weight he carried—the financial strain, the long hours, the sacrifices that had become the unseen foundation of our family. I wanted access to the inner world he rarely revealed. But wanting something doesn't mean you're ready for it, and understanding doesn't always come when you ask for it. Looking back now, I realize that even if he had tried to explain his heart, I might not have understood. I needed time—time to work, to fail, to carry weight of my own. Only then could I begin to grasp the message he had been sending all along. That is the beauty and the ache of a quiet father's love—you understand it in hindsight, when experience finally gives you the ears to hear what life had been saying.

It is only now, as a husband, and a man responsible for others, that I fully grasp the magnitude of what he gave. My father built a life with calloused hands and quiet faith. He built without applause, led without titles, and loved without ceremony. He taught me that strength is not loud and that influence does not require visibility. Real strength, he showed me, lives in the unseen— in the hours before dawn, in the choices no one witnesses, in the constancy of doing what must be done without complaint.

As I reflect on his life, I realize how much of what endures in us is formed not by what we are told, but by what we observe. We become fluent, often unconsciously, in the language of those who raise us. The rhythm of their days becomes the cadence of our own. Their reactions to hardship become our instincts. Their restraint becomes our measure of control. My father wrestled with patience his whole life, and in that struggle, he taught me more about endurance than any calm example could have. From him I learned that peace is not the absence of agitation, but the decision to stay present through it. He never told me to be humble; I learned humility in the way he deferred credit.

He never told me what love required; I learned it in the way he came home each night, tired but unwavering, choosing presence over comfort. Every lesson that mattered was woven into the fabric of his living.

We live in a world that prizes expression—where we are taught to articulate, brand, and broadcast our thoughts to prove they matter. But I've come to believe that the greatest wisdom still resides in quietness. It is born not from analysis, but from living with integrity long enough that your life speaks for itself. My father's life did exactly that. It spoke in the language of faithfulness, in the grammar of endurance, and in the punctuation of small, repeated acts of devotion. I didn't hear it clearly as a boy; I only recognized its music once I began to live my own version of it.

There came a time when I wanted to tell him everything I had come to understand—to thank him for the example he set, to name the ways he had shaped me. But when I tried to imagine that conversation, I realized it was unnecessary. He already knew. Our relationship was not built on exchanged words, but on mirrored actions. I had spent a lifetime responding to his unspoken lessons simply by trying to live up to them. And that, I now see, was the conversation that mattered most.

What I've written in *Words Not Required* is not a eulogy, nor a philosophical treatise. It is, at its core, an act of recognition—a way of saying that the life he lived still echoes in mine. It is also an invitation, because I believe many of us were raised by quiet men and women whose influence has outlasted their voices. Their strength wasn't in speeches, but in the way they kept showing up when life demanded it most. Their love wasn't in sentiment, but in sacrifice. They weren't always understood in their time, but their example continues to steady us long after they're gone.

My father's way of living has also shaped how I understand my marriage, my work, and the legacy my wife and I now hope to create together. She teaches me daily that purpose is not a future goal—it is a daily posture. Through her patience and insight, I've learned that legacy doesn't have to be monumental to be meaningful. It happens in the quiet rituals of partnership—the morning coffee, the shared laughter, the forgiveness after long days, the small acts of generosity that become the architecture of a life well lived. Where my father taught me how to endure, she continues to teach me how to renew. Her grace is the complement to his grit. Between them, I've learned that love and legacy both require presence, and presence is built through choice.

In writing this book, I've come to understand that legacy does not begin at the end of life—it begins in the middle, in the details, in the moments when no one is keeping score. It is written in the way we face uncertainty, how we handle responsibility, and how we treat those who depend on us. My father's legacy began long before he realized he was leaving one. It began the moment he chose integrity over ease, service over self, faith over fear. I suspect most legacies begin that way—invisible to the one living them, but unmistakable to those who come after.

When I think of him now, I don't hear his voice as much as I see his life. I see his shoulders, stooped but strong. I see his hands, rough but capable. I see his eyes, steady and unflinching. Those images say everything that words cannot. They remind me that love, when it is real, does not always announce itself. Sometimes it simply endures.

This book is about understanding what it means to live richly—not through possessions or achievements, but through purpose and love that endure. The truest kind of wealth is not stored in accounts or accolades; it is found in character, in devotion, and in the quiet grace of doing what matters most without the need for recognition. My father left no material inheritance behind, yet he left me everything that lasts—an example of how to live with steadiness, humility, and unwavering care. His life taught me that a man's value is revealed not in what he earns, but in how he carries himself when no one is looking, and how faithfully he keeps showing up when it matters most.

So, this book is not just for him. It's for everyone who has been shaped by the quiet influence of someone who lived with integrity and humility. It is for the sons and daughters who are only now realizing that the lessons they inherited were already being lived out in front of them. It is for those who have discovered that the deepest truths are rarely spoken, and that the most powerful love stories are often the ones without dialogue.

My father's life taught me that legacy isn't defined by what we leave behind, but by how we live—how we show up, how we persevere, and how we keep faith when life gives us reasons not to. And so, these pages are my attempt to pass that truth forward. To honor the life that formed me. To give voice to the silence that raised me. To say, finally and simply—"I saw you. I learned from you. And I am still learning now."

— *Don P. Martone*
Houston, Texas

For the quiet men whose lives still speak louder than their words ever did.

WHY THIS BOOK?

"Legacy is not leaving something behind for people.
It's leaving something behind in people."

— Peter Strople, entrepreneur and philanthropist known
for his work on leadership and legacy

Every story, whether spoken aloud or carried quietly within us, begins with a moment of decision—a crossing from what was known into what is not yet understood. For my father, that moment arrived when he chose to leave behind the familiar and begin again. For me, it came when I realized how much of who I am was formed in the shadow of his willingness to endure what could not be controlled and to keep moving forward anyway. This book is, in many ways, about both journeys—the courage to start over and the faith to keep going when strength alone no longer feels sufficient.

Words Not Required is not just a reflection on one man's life. It is an invitation—to remember the people whose quiet endurance made our own lives possible, and to rediscover the sacred work of resilience that defines every generation. It is about the unseen strength that carries ordinary people through extraordinary change—the kind of courage that rarely announces itself, yet holds entire families together. We often imagine legacy as something we plan for later, but legacy begins now, in the middle, in the decisions made under pressure, and in the quiet perseverance that sustains us through uncertainty.

When my father left behind the world he knew, he carried little except faith, discipline, and a conviction that he could build something better through honest work and belief in God's provision. His story, though deeply personal, is not unique. It belongs to anyone who has ever stood at the edge of what's next—unsure, unready, but willing. It belongs to the immigrant like my dad who steps onto unfamiliar soil, to the family that rebuilds after loss, to the man who must reinvent himself after years in one trade, and to the woman who shoulders what was never meant to be hers but carries it with grace anyway. It belongs to all who learn, often the hard way, that starting over is less about leaving something behind and more about learning to trust what still endures.

We tend to speak of beginnings as clean slates, but they never truly are. We carry the remnants of where we came from—the fears we inherited, the wisdom we absorbed, the quiet determination of those who came before. My father's life taught me that starting over is not an act of erasure; it is a continuation. Every act of rebuilding begins with memory—with what was worth preserving, and with the faith that the same God who guided yesterday will meet us again tomorrow.

This book exists because I have come to believe that strength and faith are born from the same soil—hardship. The men and women who shaped me did not speak about resilience or courage as ideals. They simply lived them. They worked through the storm rather than around it. They gave more than they kept. They stayed when leaving would have been easier. They endured because their faith told them endurance mattered. Their strength was not performative, and because of that, it was unbreakable.

In our world today, noise has become the currency of attention. We are told to speak quickly, to move faster, to always be seen. But the lessons that last still come quietly—through presence, patience, and prayer. The deepest wisdom still grows in silence, and the greatest acts of faith still happen without fanfare. My father's generation understood this. They lived their lives as testimony, not performance. They measured worth not by applause, but by consistency—the willingness to keep showing up, to keep doing what's right even when no one was watching.

The first section of this book, "The Strength to Start Over," begins in that spirit. It begins with faith—the kind that compels a person to leave the known for the unknown, to plant again in barren ground, and to trust that meaning and provision will reveal themselves one step at a time. "Faith Enough to Brave the Unknown," the opening chapter, begins where every life of substance begins—in uncertainty. It is there, in the crossing, that faith becomes more than belief. It becomes movement.

Each chapter that follows will close with three simple companions— "Sacred Waypoints," "Anchors of the Word," and "Legacy Notes."

In "Sacred Waypoints," you will find invitations to pause—moments for reflection, prayer, or gratitude drawn from the story just told. They are spaces for stillness, designed not as commentary but as conversation—between the reader and the lessons stirring within their own life.

"Anchors of the Word" sections offer brief reflections drawn from Scripture— passages that reveal the timelessness of what my father lived and what this book seeks to affirm. They are reminders that the stories of quiet endurance, sacrifice, and faith are not new. They are woven through the history of God's people, through men and women who trusted more than they could see and kept walking when the outcome was unclear.

"Legacy Notes," at the end of each chapter, are left intentionally blank—a private space for the reader to capture what the story awakened in them, what memories surfaced, what questions rose, and what truths they feel called to carry forward. These are the beginnings of their own legacy work—the handwritten intersections between what they've lived and what they hope to pass on.

Together, these three companions—reflection, revelation, and response—are not separate from the story but essential to it. For this is not only a son's tribute to his father. It is a meditation on what it means to live a life anchored in faith and guided by purpose. It is about rediscovering the sacred in the ordinary, the holy in the habit of showing up, and the divine wisdom in the act of beginning again.

Words Not Required is for those who have endured long seasons of silence, who have worked without recognition, who have loved without needing to be heard. It is for those who now look back and see, perhaps for the first time, how much of their strength they inherited from another's quiet faith. It is for the fathers who labored in obscurity, the mothers who prayed without ceasing, and the sons and daughters who now realize that the lessons that mattered most were never spoken aloud.

This is not a book about nostalgia; it is a book about renewal. About faith that is lived, not declared. About the sacred continuity between generations. And about the truth that beginnings and endings are rarely opposites—they are often the same act of courage seen from different sides of time.

If there is one message I hope endures after these pages, it is this: Courage is not always loud. Sometimes it sounds like a whisper. Sometimes it looks like patience. Sometimes it takes the shape of a man tying his boots before dawn, or a woman bowing her head in prayer over an uncertain tomorrow. Sometimes it is faith enough to brave the unknown.

That is where this book begins—and where each part ultimately leads. It begins with the strength to start over, the grit to withstand the storm, the grace to build what lasts, and the courage to love when words fall short. It begins with a man who lived the lessons I now write about, and with the generations who continue that work in their own quiet ways.

I hope that as you read, you will see yourself somewhere within these pages—in the work, in the waiting, in the silence that speaks—and that you will pause at the "Sacred Waypoints," "Anchors of the Word," and "Legacy Notes" not as detours but as resting places. They are the places where reflection deepens into understanding, and understanding blossoms into renewal.

And when the final chapter closes, you will find one last section—"Legacy Notes to Carry Forward"—a gathering place for all that has been stirred in you throughout the journey. A space to name what you now know, what you want to remember, and what you hope to carry into the next chapter of your own story.

THE STRENGTH TO START OVER

ONE

Faith Enough to Brave
the Unknown

"Never be afraid to trust an unknown future to a known God."

— *Corrie ten Boom (1892-1983),*
Dutch Christian watchmaker, author, and Holocaust survivor

Every journey worth remembering begins with a leaving. Not the kind that shouts or celebrates, not the kind marked by speeches or certainty, but the kind that unfolds in silence—one decision, one prayer, one trembling step at a time.

Leaving, in the truest sense, begins long before anyone packs a bag. It begins in hunger. In longing. In the quiet ache that whispers "there must be more than this." It begins in the unmistakable pull toward a life not yet seen.

My father's leaving began in a house that had no running water, no furnace, and no sense of ease—only the slow burn of a fire that smoked its way through the stones of the wall. In the Italian town of Bella, Potenza, winters were short but damp, the cold burrowing into clothes and bones in a way that never fully left. The hills surrounding the village were beautiful from a distance, but up close they were unforgiving—fields carved into slopes that produced more stones than food. The outhouse stood a few steps from the door. Water had to be carried in metal pails from the well until the shoulders ached. That wasn't a chore; it was the cadence of survival.

That house, humble and hard, shaped my father long before he knew he was being formed. It taught him what endurance looked like — not as a virtue to admire, but as a skill he developed because the alternative was hunger. He grew up in the soil of want, in a world where nothing came easily and everything took work. Days did not unfold according to preference. They followed a script written by necessity. Rise with the sun, tend the land, feed the animals, mend what is broken, and pray the next season will be kinder than the last.

He never spoke much about dreams, at least not in the way we use that word now. Dreams, in his world, were for people whose stomachs were full and whose futures were stable enough to let them imagine something different. When survival is the question, aspiration feels like a luxury. And yet, even in a life that left little room for imagination, something in him was listening.

He listened to the land and its thin generosity. He listened to his parents' quiet sighs and the fatigue that settled into their shoulders. And, in time, he listened to the stories carried across an ocean in fragile envelopes.

Letters arrived from his brothers who had gone ahead to Canada. At night, in the dim light of a single bulb or a flickering lamp, the family gathered at the kitchen table to read them aloud. The words traveled slowly, but the images they painted moved quickly. The clang of factory lines instead of the creak of oxen, the steady rhythm of paydays instead of the guessing game of harvest, the possibility that a man's labor might finally build something that would last.

Those letters were like sparks. Fragile. Flickering. But enough to set something burning inside him.

When he met my mother, that distant spark found a face, a companion, and eventually—direction.

She lived in Baragiano, the next town over, which was connected to Bella by a ridge and generations of shared festivals, faith, and habits. Her family worked the land just like my father's, but the land had been kinder to them. Their farm was more prosperous and reliable. They had steady work, a modest but well-kept home, and the sort of stability that allowed Sunday meals with enough food for everyone and new clothes at Easter.

If his childhood story was scarcity, hers was modest sufficiency. Yet she never looked down on what he came from. If anything, she admired what that life had created in him. She admired the grit carved into him by years of doing without, the steadiness he carried in the face of uncertainty, the resolve hardship had quietly forged.

Where he brought determination, she brought grace. Where he brought endurance, she brought hope. Together, even before they had words for it, they began to imagine a life beyond the hills that had defined their families for generations.

By then, his brothers were already in Canada. One worked long days in the factories. The eldest had taken a different route—using the only skill he knew—electrical work—to start a small contracting business. They were part of a growing pattern. Many Italians had begun making Guelph, Ontario their new home, drawn by the same promise that Canada held: steady work, a reliable wage, and a future that could be built instead of merely endured.

The letters home were filled with this new world—streets lined with factories, work that was hard but consistent, paychecks that could support not just bodies but possibilities. My father read them and heard opportunity. My mother heard them and felt both fear and faith tug at her heart.

Hearing these stories—the reliable jobs, the wages that could support a family, the sense that Canada offered a wider horizon—she didn't ask for guarantees. She simply believed. She shared my father's willingness to trade the familiar for the promise of something they could not fully imagine but deeply hoped for. So, when the chance came to join his brothers in Guelph, she said yes.

They were newly married when they left in 1965. My mother was young and brave, carrying in her chest the ache of leaving her parents and the faint hope of return visits that never truly came. My father packed a small suitcase, a handful of lire, and a quiet conviction that hard work and faith could build a new beginning.

He never talked much about the voyage, but I have learned to picture it clearly. The restless sway of the ship that cut through cold northern waters, the wind on the open deck sharp enough to sting the skin, the hopeful chatter of families who had bet everything on a future they could not yet see, the smell of salt and diesel and sweat rising together, and fear pressing up against excitement, neither strong enough to swallow the other.

My mother once told me she prayed every night on that crossing. She prayed that God would give her husband strength to build whatever life lay ahead, and that she would have enough courage to follow him wherever that life required them to go.

They arrived in Canada in winter, stepping into a world shaped by snow and steel. The air was so cold it made their lungs ache. The sky sat low and heavy, colored like iron. For two people from the warm, sunlit slopes of the Basilicata region of Italy, it might as well have been another planet. But new worlds rarely introduce themselves kindly. They demand courage from those who enter.

My father did not understand the language, but language is only one way of reading a place. He understood tone. He understood the speed of life here— the determined gait of people who had somewhere to be, the confidence of those who had never known what it meant to go to bed hungry. His brothers met them at the station in coats too thin for the cold but with faces brightened by reunion. They led my parents through streets lined with factories, where chimneys exhaled steam and the hum of machinery filled the air. In that sound, my father heard more than noise. He heard survival.

They settled in an upstairs apartment in a narrow house not far from the factory gates—just big enough for two adults and, soon after, a newborn. Me. The rooms were small, the ceilings low, and the floors creaked under every step. The walls were thin enough to catch the muffled soundtrack of other lives rising and falling above and below.

Those early years, my mother later told me, were a blur of diapers, laundry strung in cramped spaces, soups simmering on the stove, prayers whispered over a crib, and waves of homesickness that came without warning. The stairwells hummed with the sound of Italian women's voices—dialects from Calabria, Sicily, Abruzzo, and our own Potenza—stitched into a fabric of familiarity laid gently over an unfamiliar world. My mother never learned much English. She didn't have to. The neighborhood was its own village, held together by shared memory, shared struggle, and the comfort of hearing your own language in a land that often felt indifferent to your presence.

Nearly three years later, my brother was born, and our family took its final shape. His arrival added new joy and new weight—another mouth to feed, another life to protect, another future to build one shift, one paycheck, one sacrifice at a time. My mother's days grew fuller, her arms rarely empty, her prayers stretching wider to cover the growing life inside those narrow walls. My father's shoulders squared a little more, as if each child added a new line of responsibility drawn quietly across his back.

That little apartment—cramped, drafty in winter and overheated in summer—became our first true home in Canada. It was in those tight rooms, crowded with a young couple and two small boys, that the earliest threads of our story were woven. Sacrifice, faith, endurance, and love expressed not through big speeches, but through the stubborn, daily act of showing up— repeatedly, no matter the cost.

My father, meanwhile, went to work.

His brothers found him a job in a gray factory with dingy windows, the kind of place where daylight seeped through in dull, colorless stripes. The building produced electrical transformers—heavy, industrial boxes he never fully understood. He didn't know exactly where they ended up or what machines they powered, and he never pretended to. Understanding their destination would not have changed what mattered most. This was honest work, and it paid.

He learned the job the way he had learned everything else in his life—by watching, listening, and doing. He studied how others moved, how the foremen pointed, how the pieces fit together. Words failed him, but gestures did not. In his world, work didn't need to be inspiring; it needed to be consistent. Work was obedience—to duty, to responsibility, to the promise he had made to my mother and, in his own quiet way, to God.

He admired both his brothers, but there was something almost reverent in the way he spoke of the eldest. Even as a child, long before I understood anything about business or risk, I could feel the air in the room change when my uncle's name came up. Children notice that kind of thing. They may not understand the reasons, but they feel the weight.

While one brother took a factory job much like my father's, the elder had chosen a different path. He had carried his trade—an electrician's skill learned back in Italy—across the ocean and, instead of waiting for someone to hire him, started his own small electrical contracting business. In a foreign country. In a foreign language. With no guarantee except his own willingness to work and trust.

My father never used grand language to describe what his brother had done. There were no lectures about entrepreneurship or courage. There was just a tone—a softness when he mentioned him, a hint of pride that slipped through in simple phrases, an almost invisible lift in his posture when we pulled into his brother's driveway on Sundays.

I didn't understand business, but I understood pride. I understood that my uncle had done something that mattered. And somewhere in the quiet corners of my childhood, that realization began to settle into me like silt in a riverbed.

On those Sunday visits, I would trail behind my father into the garage. The space felt different from other places I knew. Tools lined up neatly. Coils of wire stacked with intention. Work orders clipped to a board. A truck with my uncle's business name painted on the door sitting in the driveway like a declaration: "I made something where there was nothing."

I watched my father watching all of it. He studied not out of envy, but out of respect. He was not the kind of man who wanted attention. He didn't long for his own name on a truck. But he honored the courage it took for his brother to step beyond simply taking a job and instead create one.

In those visits, something in me was learning without my knowing. I saw the difference between taking whatever life hands you and daring to shape it. I saw the difference between surviving and building. I saw, most of all, the way one man's risk could become another man's quiet inspiration.

My father never tried to follow his brother's path. His calling was different. It wasn't reinvention, but responsibility. He stepped onto the factory floor each morning with the weight of our family on his shoulders—my mother, my brother, and me. He worked six days a week, sometimes seven. Always on time. Never complaining. Never asking for anything except the chance to keep providing.

Over the years, the factory changed names and ownership several times, switched machines, reorganized lines, and weathered labor strikes. But my father stayed. He did not chase opportunity; he built endurance. He measured his life not by promotions, but by his children having what he did not, his household never being unsure of its next meal, and his wife staying home and raising us in a way his own mother never could.

I remember how he looked when he came home. Tired, his hands were stained with grease that no soap could fully erase, his clothes were heavy with the smell of metal and oil. He would hang his coat, wash his hands in silence, and sit at the table with the calm presence of a man who had given everything the day demanded and still managed to bring something of himself back through the door.

The sounds I grew up with were my father's boots on the wooden steps, my mother's pots simmering, the steady hum of perseverance filling the spaces between words. And somewhere in that soundtrack, without my realizing it, my understanding of love, courage, and faith was taking shape.

The first winters in Canada were not merely seasons; they were tests—quiet, unrelenting initiations that confronted every immigrant who arrived believing that hard work alone could carve a new beginning. For my parents, those early years were something deeper than adaptation. They were the slow, often harsh work of becoming—becoming part of a new country, becoming a new kind of family, becoming the people God was shaping them into long before they understood the purpose behind the hardship.

They stepped into that new life with almost nothing—no English, no savings, no roadmap, not even the comfort of familiarity. What they carried instead was a conviction that years of scarcity had carved into them: "We will work, and God will do the rest." Faith didn't remove the difficulty. It steadied them inside it.

My father confronted language, the first and most unforgiving barrier. He had grown up speaking dialect, a regional blend of Italian shaped by hills, villages, and centuries of local tradition. In Canada, every sound felt sharp-edged and impossibly fast. Conversations in the street blurred together like wind carrying syllables he couldn't catch. Instructions at work arrived in words he didn't grasp—only tones, hands pointing, eyebrows tightening.

His earliest vocabulary in the new world was not made of sentences but of nods—small affirmations offered in silence with the hope they matched what was being asked of him. He relied on instinct, context, and prayer. Each mistake felt like a tiny wound, not because anyone scolded him, but because he held himself to a standard forged in necessity: "If I fail here, I fail my family."

The factory floor became his first classroom. He learned not by listening, but by watching. Where to place his hands. How the metal should feel when it locked correctly. How to interpret urgency through the tilt of a foreman's head or the tightening of a jaw. Each day demanded a humility that strips a man down to who he really is. My father never showed frustration. He simply endured. To him, endurance, was not resignation; it was obedience to the life God had placed before him.

During lunch breaks, he sat with other Italian men—some from Calabria, others from Sicily, a few from the north—men who were also building a new life one word, one paycheck, one mistake at a time. Their accents differed, their stories differed, but their burdens did not. They shared sandwiches wrapped in wax paper, fragments of English, warnings about foremen to avoid, tips on surviving the cold, and the unspoken recognition that they were all beginners again. Terms like *'payday,' 'foreman,' 'overtime,'* and *'good job'* became the fragile building blocks of belonging, assembled one syllable at a time.

While my father learned the world outside, my mother faced her own battle inside the walls of our small apartment. She spent her days caring for my brother and me, surrounded by other Italian women who had also left their families behind. They spoke in dialects stitched together by memory—snippets from Calabria, Puglia, Basilicata—each voice carrying a thread of home. English wasn't needed among them. They could barter, comfort, and confide in the only language that felt like theirs.

But loneliness doesn't require translation. Displacement sits quietly in corners, in the long afternoons when the house is too still, in the moments after a letter is read and folded back into an envelope that can't hold what has been lost. My mother fought that loneliness with routine. Morning prayers were whispered before we woke, soups simmering gently on the stove, laundry hung with precision. Letters home were written slowly as if careful pen strokes could close the distance between continents.

Before they had that apartment, my parents lived briefly in a boardinghouse run by another Italian family. The home was narrow, its rooms carved into cramped quarters where every footstep reverberated. Men left for work before sunrise, returning long after dark. On weekends, the women crowded the kitchen, turning simple ingredients into meals that tasted like memory— tomato sauce thickened with patience, bread kneaded with longing, coffee brewed strong enough to quiet the homesick heart for a little while. For families that had left everything behind, these rituals weren't luxuries; they were lifelines.

They saved every dollar they could, stretching wages that had to cover rent, food, coal for the stove, diapers, stamps, and dreams they rarely spoke aloud. Some evenings, after a long day at the factory, my father and mother would sit side by side at a small window, watching snow gather silently on the rooftops. They didn't say much. They didn't need to. Their shared silence became its own kind of prayer: "We are still here. We are still trying."

In time, they moved from the boardinghouse into a modest apartment of their own. Eventually, after years of saving, they bought a small house — nothing grand, but theirs. I still remember the day we moved in. My father was standing at the threshold, his hand resting for a moment on the key before turning it. A simple motion, but full of meaning. He didn't speak. His silence said everything: "We made it this far."

Looking back now, I see that those first winters were not about only survival; they were about formation. In the cold, in the labor, in the isolation, my parents were becoming. Hardship did not harden them; it refined them. It taught them who they were, what they valued, and who they hoped to be. Becoming is rarely visible in the moment. It reveals itself later, when you realize that the deepest parts of your character were shaped in the places you once mistook for emptiness.

Those years were not only their beginning. They were also mine.

The sound of my father's boots on the stairs.

The scent of my mother's cooking.

The murmur of dialects seeping through thin walls.

These became the soil of my earliest understanding of sacrifice, purpose, and faith. They were the years no one else saw, the years the world never applauded, the years that built everything that came after.

When my younger brother was born, the shape of our family widened in ways my parents could not have fully imagined when they first stepped into the Canadian cold. His arrival brought not only new joy but new responsibility—another life depending on their courage. For me, he was more than a sibling. He was my companion in the unfamiliar, my partner in the quiet work of growing up between two worlds.

We shared a small bedroom that barely held two beds. The closeness made us inseparable. On the coldest winter nights, when the radiator clanged in protest and the wind pressed against the window like an unwelcome guest, he would shuffle across the narrow strip of floor and climb into my bed. We fell asleep pressed together for warmth. I didn't think of it as protection. It was simply what brothers did—leaning toward each other the way our parents leaned into their faith.

While my father worked and my mother tended the home, my brother and I carved out our own small world inside the larger one they were trying to understand. We played with whatever we had—tin cups, wooden spoons, scraps of fabric turned into makeshift capes. We invented games that required nothing but imagination because imagination was the one thing the cold could not take from us.

We were too young to understand what our parents carried, but we felt the atmosphere of our home—the mix of struggle and devotion, of worry and warmth—and we absorbed it together. Sometimes, when adult voices in the kitchen lowered into tones that suggested concern, my brother and I sat shoulder to shoulder on the floor, sensing tension without context. Our presence didn't solve anything, but it softened the room. Children don't know they are doing this. They simply exist, and in existing, they give their parents a reason to endure.

Looking back now, I can see that my brother and I were not just along for the ride. We were part of the architecture of our parents' resilience. We were their reason to keep walking into unfamiliar winters. And in turn, they taught us by example how to carry weight together, how to lean without shame, and how to build a life on faith when certainty is in short supply.

The older I get, the more I realize that the beginning of my father's story did not stay contained in his life alone. It stretched across decades like a long, patient shadow—quiet, consistent, impossible to outrun—and shaped who I would become long before I had the language to name its influence.

As a child, I saw my father's life as a series of dependable actions. He worked. He provided. He came home with the slow, deliberate steps of a man who carried more than he said. He rarely talked about his fears or desires. Silence in our home was not absence; it was its own form of presence. Only later did I begin to understand what stood behind that silence, and how much courage it takes to keep walking when the path ahead is unclear and the cost of each step is counted privately.

For many years, their sacrifices didn't look like sacrifices. They looked like the natural choreography of family life—my father leaving before dawn, returning after dark; my mother tending the home with a devotion so steady it became almost invisible; the two of them stretching every paycheck as though it were elastic; the quiet ritual of reading letters from home, each one carrying both comfort and ache. These moments passed through my childhood like weather—present, constant, unexamined.

But adulthood gives you a second lens. It returns you to those scenes with a clarity you didn't possess the first time. What once appeared ordinary becomes extraordinary. What once seemed like "the way things are" reveals itself as the sacred architecture of a family.

I began to see that what looked like routine was actually resilience. What looked like survival was, in truth, formation. What looked like silence was a form of communication that spoke louder than any words.

My father never called himself courageous. He would have laughed off the idea. To him, responsibility, was simply "what had to be done." But courage often hides inside such simplicity. It lives in the decision to act without applause, to endure without certainty, to press forward without knowing how the story will end. It is the courage of a young man boarding a ship for a land he has only read about. The courage of a young woman leaving her mother's kitchen for a life shaped by unfamiliar cold and unfamiliar hope. The courage of two people standing in a foreign city with a suitcase, a baby, and the belief that hard work will be enough.

It took me years—decades, really—to see that my parents' beginning in Canada was not simply a story of hardship. It was the lens through which I would come to understand faith. Not faith as sentiment or inspiration, but faith as embodied obedience. Faith as daily practice. Faith as the willingness to move forward even when every step is taken in the dark.

My father trusted God without flourish. His faith lived not in language, but in motion. He did not preach. He did not correct. He did not quote Scripture at the table. He simply lived in a way that made belief visible. Show up, endure and remain steady. Faith was built into hands that worked until they cracked. It was woven into footsteps that always came home. It was etched into the lines of a face that learned to carry both hope and exhaustion with dignity.

My mother's faith was different—gentle, persistent, almost musical. She prayed over everything. Meals were cooked from scratch, she raised her children without nearby family, and her husband labored in noise and danger. Her prayers were not frantic pleas for rescue. They were offerings of gratitude that God had carried them through another day, and quiet trust that He would do it again tomorrow.

Together, without ever naming it, my parents gave me my first understanding of legacy. Not legacy as wealth or achievement, but legacy as foundation. Legacy as the shape of character passed from one life into another. Legacy as the slow, faithful work of two people building something that would outlive them.

As I moved from childhood into adolescence and then into adulthood, I began to notice pieces of my father showing up in me—his discipline, his steady way of carrying responsibility, his instinct to make sure others were taken care of before tending to himself, his belief that life's purpose is not found in noise or notoriety, but in quietly fulfilling the duties entrusted to you.

Those traits didn't appear all at once. They accumulated slowly, like sediment at the bottom of a river, creating a bedrock I didn't realize I was standing on.

I didn't think of it as legacy then. I simply thought, "This is what it means to be a man." Only later, when life tested me in ways I could not have anticipated, did I realize how much of my strength I had borrowed from theirs.

What my parents carried in those first winters became the quiet architecture beneath my own choices. Their endurance shaped my instincts. Their courage shaped my convictions. Their faith shaped the way I came to understand God—not as an abstraction, but as a presence that carries us through seasons we would never have chosen.

In time, I came to see that legacy does not end with understanding. It asks for response. My parents did not build a foundation for me to admire; they built one for me to stand on. They didn't endure hardship simply for their own survival; they endured so my brother and I could step into lives shaped more by opportunity than scarcity. Honoring that inheritance does not mean repeating their story, but living with the same courage, integrity, and faith that made it possible.

Now, when I look back at their beginning—the cold, the work, the loneliness, the prayers whispered into dim rooms—I feel the weight of it differently. It is not merely our history; it is our spiritual DNA. It is the truth that steadies me when life becomes uncertain. It is the reminder that every important journey begins without clarity, and that God's presence is often clearest not in the warm seasons, but in the cold ones.

Their beginning became my compass. Their endurance became my inheritance. Their faith became the anchor I return to again and again.

And so, this first chapter does not close where their struggles eased. It closes where understanding begins—at the point where I can finally see what those first winters truly were. They were not merely seasons of survival, but seasons of formation, shaping their lives, shaping mine, and shaping the generations that will follow.

Long before I knew the language of faith, my father lived it. Long before I understood legacy, my father built it. Long before I recognized how deeply their story would shape mine, their beginning had already become the truest part of my foundation.

Their beginning is my first sacred waypoint.

Their endurance is the anchor of my understanding of how faith works— quietly, steadily, one unseen step at a time.

And long before I was aware of it, their beginning had already become the first chapter of my own legacy.

SACRED WAYPOINTS

The Quiet Ache of "More Than This"

Where in your life have you felt that quiet ache that whispers, "There must be more than this?"

- Sit with that memory for a moment.
- Was it born from pain, boredom, frustration, or holy discontent?
- What, if anything, did you do with that ache—or what have you been afraid to do?

Ask God to show you whether that ache was (or is) an invitation, not an irritation.

Houses That Shape Us

Think about the home you grew up in—the sounds, the smells, the routines.

- What unspoken lessons did that house teach you about work, love, and God?
- Which of those lessons were life-giving?
- Which ones might have taught you scarcity, fear, or self-reliance instead of trust?

Offer a simple prayer of gratitude for what was good and gently name before God what needs healing.

Letters from Another World

In Chapter 1, the letters from Canada were sparks of possibility—stories that stretched beyond the hills of home.

- What "letters" have reached you in your life—stories, people, books, or opportunities that hinted at another kind of future?
- Did you lean in, ignore them, or file them away for later?

Ask God: "What invitations to a different future have I treated as background noise? Show me what I need to hear again."

The Decision to Leave (Even If You Stayed)

Not everyone crosses an ocean, but everyone faces moments when staying exactly where you are would mean slowly shrinking.

- When have you had to leave something familiar—a job, a role, a version of yourself—to be faithful to what God was calling you into?
- Did others see it as courage, or simply "doing what had to be done?"
- Are there places today where God may be nudging you to leave certainty for trust?

Ask for the same quiet courage your parents or grandparents might have carried without ever naming it.

Work as Obedience, Not Identity

My father's work in the factory was not glamorous or self-expressive. It was obedience to a promise.

- Where in your life has work felt more like a duty than a calling—and yet, looking back, you can see how God used that season to shape you?
- Are there "gray factory" places in your story you've only ever resented, but never honored?

Pray a simple, honest prayer: "Lord, help me see the holy in the ordinary work I have done and still do. Show me where You were with me on the factory floor of my own life."

The Faith of Those Who Never Preached

My father rarely spoke about faith; he lived it. My mother wove it into prayers and daily routine.

- Who in your life modeled faith without many words—someone whose steadiness spoke louder than any sermon?
- What specific habit, posture, or decision of theirs shaped what you now believe about God?

Take a moment to thank God for that person by name—and, if possible, consider how you might honor them with the way you live.

Brothers in the Cold

In the chapter, my brother and I learn to lean on one another in a small, drafty room caught between two worlds—the new country we were born into and the old ways of the one my parents left in hopes of a better life.

- Who has stood "shoulder to shoulder" with you in your winters—literally or figuratively?
- Did you let them carry some of the weight, or did you try to shoulder it alone?

Ask God: "Lord, show me the people You placed beside me in the cold. Help me be that presence for someone else."

Legacy as Foundation, Not Finish Line

By the end of Chapter 1, it becomes clear that my parents' beginning was not just their story—it became my foundation.

- What foundations were quietly laid beneath your life—by parents, grandparents, mentors, or others?
- What part of that foundation do you want to carry forward?
- What part, if any, do you need to rebuild differently in this generation?

Pray a simple, honest prayer: "Thank You Lord for the people who built what I now stand on. Give me wisdom to carry forward what is faithful, and courage to change what is not."

ANCHORS OF THE WORD 

The Call to Leave What Is Known

"The Lord said to Abram, 'Go from your country, your people and your father's household to the land I will show you.'" (Genesis 12:1 NIV)

Abram was not given a map, a timeline, or a guarantee—only a direction and a promise.

This verse captures the essence of my parents' departure, that is the bravery of stepping into a life they had not yet seen, trusting that God would meet them along the way.

My father did not hear God in thunder or vision; he heard Him in opportunity. My mother heard Him in the quiet conviction that love must sometimes travel far to become what it was meant to be.

Leaving is not always dramatic. More often, it is the simple obedience of ordinary people taking the next faithful step.

Reflection: Where is God asking you to trust Him without a full picture of what lies ahead?

Faith in Motion

"By faith Abraham, when called to go to a place he would later receive as his inheritance, obeyed and went, even though he did not know where he was going." (Hebrews 11:8 NIV)

Faith, in Scripture and in life, often looks like movement—like stepping forward before clarity arrives.

My father lived this verse long before he knew it. He boarded a ship not because he was fearless, but because obedience outweighed uncertainty.

He trusted that the inheritance God had for him was not land, but legacy—something his children and grandchildren would one day stand on, even if he never fully saw its fulfillment.

Reflection: How might God be inviting you to move—even if you cannot yet see the destination?

God Who Keeps Watch

"The LORD watches over you—the LORD is your shade at your right hand;

The LORD will keep you from all harm—he will watch over your life; the LORD will watch over your coming and going both now and forevermore." (Psalm 121:5-8 NIV)

This is a psalm for travelers, immigrants, and anyone stepping into unfamiliar ground. My parents walked into a land of strange accents, harsh winters, and unspoken fears—but Scripture reminds us that no one steps into a new place alone.

God was in the cold apartment.

God was in the noisy factory.

God was in the boardinghouse and in the quiet moments where homesickness and hope collided.

His protection was not the absence of hardship—it was His presence within it.

Reflection: Where can you look back and see God's keeping, even in places that felt uncertain or overwhelming?

The Promise in Hard Places

"When you pass through the waters, I will be with you; and when you pass through the rivers, they will not sweep over you. When you walk through the fire, you will not be burned; the flames will not set you ablaze." (Isaiah 43:2 NIV)

This was the quiet truth beneath the first winters in Canada.

The waters were cold.

The rivers rushed fast.

The fire of fear and loneliness burned hot. But my parents were never consumed.

God did not remove the difficulty. He carried them through it.

This verse affirms what they lived. We don't produce endurance alone. It is the faithfulness of God meeting the faithfulness of ordinary people who refuse to quit.

Reflection: What "waters" or "fire" of your life has God carried you through?

Courage for the Ordinary Days

"Be strong and courageous. Do not be afraid or terrified…for the Lord your God goes with you; He will never leave you nor forsake you." (Deuteronomy 31:6 NIV)

Courage is often misunderstood as bold action or fearless declaration. But Scripture defines courage as presence—God's presence with us, and our presence within the life He's given.

My parents' courage was quiet, unpolished, almost invisible. It lived in daily bread, in early mornings and late nights, in routines that held more faith than emotion.

They did not feel strong, yet they lived strongly. They did not feel courageous, yet their lives displayed courage in every step.

Reflection: Where is God calling you to be courageous in the ordinary, unseen rhythms of life?

The House God Builds

"Unless the Lord builds the house, the builders labor in vain." (Psalm 127:1 NIV)

My father helped build a small farmhouse with his hands in Italy and transformers in Canada, but the true house he built was spiritual—one of character, endurance, faith, and love expressed through presence.

But even his labor was never his alone. God was building alongside him — quietly shaping a family, a legacy, a foundation that would one day hold the weight of our lives.

Their efforts were human.

The outcome was divine.

Reflection: What is God building beneath the surface of your life—something you cannot yet see but can sense taking shape?

Stones of Remembrance

"In the future, when your children ask you, 'What do these stones mean?' tell them…" (Joshua 4:6-7 NIV)

This verse perfectly captures the heart of Chapter 1—remembrance, ancestry, and legacy.

The winters, the work, the sacrifice—these were the stones my parents laid without knowing it. Stones my brother and I now stand upon.

Our family story is a living memorial to God's faithfulness through two ordinary immigrants who trusted Him enough to start over.

Reflection: What "stones" has God placed in your story—moments meant to be remembered, passed down, and built upon?

LEGACY NOTES

TWO

The Making of a Man in an Unfamiliar World

"All true journeys begin in fear, and end in becoming someone new."

— Mario Puzo (1920-1999), best known for writing The Godfather

---

All true journeys begin in fear—and my father's was no exception.

The first chapter of my parents' life in Canada closed with their becoming, the slow formation wrought through cold winters, long shifts, whispered prayers, and quiet endurance. But the next chapter opened on a different note. In that moment, the world around them revealed its unfamiliarity, showing just how foreign it truly was.

The early days in a new country do not ask for understanding; they demand surrender. They demand that a man release the life he once knew so he can begin, however unwillingly, to inhabit the life he has entered. And in those first disorienting days, my father stepped across an invisible threshold— moving from a life shaped by familiarity to a world that insisted he remake himself from the ground up.

For my father, this confrontation with the unfamiliar began the second he stepped off the train platform into the piercing Canadian winter. The cold was so sharp it felt alive, a creature whose breath stung the skin and seized the lungs before a man could take his second inhale. Snow blew sideways, not as soft flakes drifting from the sky but as shards of ice hurled by a wind that carried no familiarity. The sky hung low, thick and metallic, pressing down on the streets with a weight that felt almost personal.

If Basilicata's hills had been shaped by sun and stone, Canada felt carved from iron.

The streets moved differently here. People walked fast, shoulders squared, their faces set with purpose. Doors opened and closed with the efficiency of a city that had no patience for hesitation. Cars passed in bursts of motion my father could not predict. Even the rhythm of the streetlights felt foreign—an order and speed that did not match the wandering cadence of village life he had always known.

He felt, in those first hours, like someone watching life through a window, able to see its motion but unable to belong to it.

Nothing prepared him for how quickly a man could feel small in a world that owed him nothing.

His own language—his anchor, his heritage, his proof of identity—meant almost nothing here. The moment he tried to speak, the realization hit him with a force colder than the winter air. The words he had always trusted no longer carried meaning. The dialect shaped by generations of his village dissolved into useless syllables in this place. English surrounded him like a fast-moving river—rushing, relentless, impossible to grasp.

He tried to listen, but everything blurred. Conversations flowed too quickly, each phrase clipped, sharp-edged, indifferent to a newcomer's ears. When someone addressed him directly, he could catch neither the words nor the meaning—only the impatience underneath.

A simple greeting—something he had given thousands of times in Italy— became a trial. He offered a nod when a word was expected. A half-smile when a question was. He responded with gestures that felt childish to him, as though he had been reduced back to boyhood in an instant.

This loss of language was more than communication; it was identity slipping away. It was the humiliation of being unable to defend himself, to clarify a misunderstanding, to assert even the smallest piece of who he was. He felt himself shrinking—not because others made him feel small, but because he could no longer speak the world into focus.

Silence became both shield and prison. A shield, because silence could not be misinterpreted. A prison, because silence kept him from entering the life happening all around him.

He understood quickly that in this country, words were currency, and he had arrived without any to spend.

And inside that silence, loneliness began its slow work. Loneliness is not dramatic. It is subtle, patient, and thorough. It begins in the gaps—moments when instinct reaches for something familiar and finds only emptiness. It settles into the pauses between one sound and the next. It lingers in the spaces where language once stood.

Each evening, after the noise of the day receded, he felt it pressing against him. Home was not just far away—it was unreachable. Loneliness grew in the knowledge that he could no longer walk outside and hear voices he recognized, dialects that felt like skin against bone. In the ache that no letter, no matter how warmly written, could quiet.

He missed the land—not just its contours, but its generosity of familiarity. He missed knowing who he was in the eyes of others. In his village, he had been Carmine—known by name, by family, by reputation, by history. Here he was simply "the new guy," "the Italian," "the one who doesn't understand."

His old world had known him completely. This new world asked him to earn the right to belong.

The internal shift came slowly, subtly—first as frustration, then as humility, then as recognition. He understood that this place would not bend for him. He would have to bend for it. The country did not care who he had been back home. It was up to him to decide who he would become here.

Yet somewhere inside him—beneath the fatigue, beneath the fear, beneath the quiet humiliation—something resolute awakened. The same endurance that had carried him through the thin generosity of the Italian soil rose again, reshaped now for a different landscape. The determination that had once survived scarcity began to adapt itself to language, to cold, to the strange, urgent rhythm of Canadian life.

Canada felt, in those early days, like a test he had never prepared for.

But instinctively, he understood something vital. Passing the test was not optional. Too much depended on it. His wife. His sons. His future. The promise he carried inside him when he left Italy.

He would not allow failure to touch the people he loved.

So, he stepped forward—not boldly, not confidently, but faithfully. He showed up each day in a world that did not yet know his name. He endured the cold, the silence, the uncertainty.

He faced the unfamiliar with the only tools he could trust—his work ethic, his humility, and his faith.

He did not yet know it, but these early days—these moments of disorientation and quiet resolve—were shaping the man he would become in Canada. They were chiseling away the parts of him that belonged to a past life and building the foundation of a future he could not yet imagine.

A man is often made not in the moments of triumph, but in the moments when he must learn to stand in a life that feels nothing like the one he left behind. And in those first days, walking streets that moved too fast and hearing a language that cut sharper than the winter air, my father began the long, faithful work of becoming.

That work did not arrive in dramatic gestures. It arrived in small, stubborn decisions—one of which I remember vividly, even though I did not understand its significance at the time. My father realized that he could not remain a visitor in the country he had promised to build a life in. He could no longer rely on gestures alone, or trust that tone would carry him where words could not. If he wanted to stand fully in this unfamiliar world, he would have to learn its language.

And so, after long shifts on the factory floor, after hours spent lifting steel, soldering wires, and absorbing instructions he barely comprehended, he would wash up, change his clothes, and catch a bus to the local community college. The building was old, the classrooms dim, the chalkboards worn by a thousand hesitant hands. But to him, it was a doorway.

He sat at a desk surrounded by other immigrants—men with tired eyes and heavy boots, women who whispered questions in accents thick with their homelands, people who knew that survival required not just endurance, but understanding. My father held a pencil awkwardly, as though it belonged more naturally in a child's hand. He traced letters slowly, carefully, as if each one were a step toward a future he could not yet see.

At home, he practiced at the kitchen table. He sounded out words under his breath, repeating them until they settled into his tongue. He wrote his name over and over again, not because he had forgotten how to shape the letters, but because he wanted to claim it in a new language, in a new life. Sometimes he would ask me to help read a note or a form aloud, and I would watch him lean over that piece of paper as if deciphering a secret message.

I did not grasp the magnitude of what he was doing—not then. I only knew that my father, who seemed to understand everything with so few words, was now pursuing words with more determination than I had ever seen in anyone. There was a seriousness in the way he held his pencil, a quiet fire in the way he repeated phrases, a humility in the way he erased mistakes and began again.

Only years later did I understand the full weight of it. My father had finished only the fifth grade in Italy—not because he lacked ability, but because boys born into farming families were not raised for classrooms. They were raised for the land. They were needed in the fields at dawn, in the stalls at dusk, helping coax survival out of soil that rarely cooperated. School was not a pathway; it was an interruption. And so, like countless boys of his region and generation, he traded notebooks for shovels, pencils for calloused hands, lessons for labor. The world he knew required strength, not sentences. Work, not words.

But even with so little formal education, he carried a kind of practical intelligence that always amazed me. He could do arithmetic in his head with astonishing speed—the type of math farmers learned out of necessity, not textbooks. He could calculate measurements, weights, seed ratios, and livestock feed faster than most people with years of schooling. Numbers, somehow, obeyed him. They made sense to him in a way English did not. Watching him add, subtract, and estimate with quiet confidence, I often wondered how someone with only a fifth-grade education could see solutions so clearly.

Which is why, looking back, the sight of him hunched over a workbook carries a weight I could not have seen then. He was not just trying to learn English. He was challenging the boundaries of the life he had been born into—the story that circumstances had written for him before he ever had a chance to choose one of his own. Every letter he traced, every word he sounded out, every sentence he pieced together was an act of defiance against the limits of his upbringing and an act of devotion to the life he hoped to build for us.

And then there was the pride—my pride—rising in me before I even knew the word for it. I watched him, night after night, sit at that table with aching hands and a tired body, working to grasp this new language, and refusing to let the unfamiliar world remain impenetrable. He did not want luxury. He did not want ease. He wanted to belong. He wanted to stand on equal ground with the people whose language shaped the world he now lived in. He wanted to be able to speak for himself, for his family, and for the life he was trying to build in a place that demanded more than hard work alone.

Years later, when I think about what makes a man, I do not picture achievements or accolades. I picture my father at that small kitchen table, shoulders rounded from a day's labor, brow furrowed in concentration, tracing letters that would one day give him a voice in a world that had once felt too sharp, too fast, too foreign. I picture a man who refused to be defined by what he lacked in education or opportunity, and who quietly rebuilt himself one word at a time.

This was when it began to take hold—when he stopped merely being present in this new world and started taking his place in it. Not as a visitor, but as a participant. Not as an outsider, but as a man claiming his voice.

And in that small classroom, under fluorescent lights and with a pencil worn down from repetition, my father was not just learning English. He was learning how to inhabit the life he had crossed an ocean to create. He was stepping into a world that had once overwhelmed him—and slowly, faithfully, he was making it his own.

That is the moment—though I did not know it then—when his becoming became unmistakable.

When my father sat at the kitchen table with his workbook, it was only the beginning. English gave him a small foothold in an overwhelming world, but when he stepped back onto the factory floor the next morning, nothing around him had changed. The machines still roared with the indifference of metal. Men still moved at a pace that suggested they had long ago made peace with this demanding world. Foremen still barked instructions that sailed past him like wind cutting through narrow alleys. Canada did not soften simply because he tried to meet it halfway. The world does not pause for those who are learning; it demands that they catch up.

And yet, something in him had shifted. The unfamiliar life that had once felt like a wall slowly began to feel like a threshold. He did not cross it easily, but he crossed it faithfully. This was the life he had chosen—the life he had sailed toward through cold northern waters—and now it required that he stand inside it, however unsteady his footing felt.

The factory became his first true teacher. Back in Italy, the rhythms of his days had been dictated by the land—the crow of roosters, the burn of the sun rising over the hills, the quiet patience of animals waiting to be fed. Here, the rhythm was mechanical and merciless. Machines did not care about exhaustion. They demanded precision, speed, and obedience. My father learned not through instruction—there were no lessons suited to a man with limited English—but through imitation. He studied the way foremen pointed when a line was too slow or when a mistake threatened to ripple down the conveyor belt. He noticed how seasoned workers adjusted their grip, how they tightened bolts with the confidence of men born into this world of metal.

Sometimes he misread gestures. Sometimes his hands moved more slowly than expected. Sometimes he reached for the wrong part or misunderstood the urgency in a foreman's eyes. He felt each error as a sting—not because anyone scolded him harshly, but because each mistake reminded him of the distance between the life he had known and the life he was trying to enter. But then, just as quietly, the small victories came. A foreman's approving nod. A co-worker offering him a thermos of hot coffee. A slightly more difficult task placed in front of him—a sign that someone believed he could handle it. These small gestures were invisible to the outside world, but monumental to a man who had arrived with nothing but faith and determination.

Responsibility found him faster than confidence did. Bills gathered on the table like unwelcome guests — rent, heat, food, clothing for a growing child. My brother would be born in a few years, and even before he arrived, the idea of another life to protect pressed invisibly into the atmosphere of our home. My father did not have time to wait until he 'felt ready.' Manhood does not always arrive through preparation; sometimes it arrives through necessity. For him, it arrived the moment he understood that every hour worked meant stability for the people he loved. He carried that weight with a kind of dignity that made it seem effortless, though nothing about it was easy.

At home, in that tight apartment, fatherhood took shape in the smallest of ways. I remember the way he would lift me after work, his clothes still smelling of oil and metal, and hold me just a little longer than needed—as if grounding himself in the one place in this new world that felt certain. The space was small, barely enough for two adults and a child. But within those walls he learned the softer half of responsibility. Exhaustion did not erase tenderness. If anything, it refined it. Even small gestures—a hand on my back, a nod to my mother, a brief smile at something trivial—revealed a man who was learning how to anchor himself in a world that kept unmooring him.

Beyond our apartment, the immigrant community threaded itself into his becoming. During breaks at the factory and on weekends, men from Calabria, Sicily, Abruzzo, and our own region gathered like tributaries flowing toward the same river. They shared thick slices of bread wrapped in cloth, olives brined in memories of home, jokes that crossed dialects, and warnings about supervisors who favored speed over safety. One of the older men once told him, *"Qui, siamo tutti bambini di nuovo."* "Here, we are all children again." My father laughed, but those words settled into him. In this place, everyone was beginning again. No matter what they had been in Italy, here they were starting from the same ground. That truth, oddly enough, brought comfort.

His brothers became mirrors, each showing him something different about the man he could become. One worked in a factory much like the one my father worked in—steady and predictable. In him, my father saw endurance—proof that dignity could exist in routine. The elder brother lived another kind of story—a man who had taken his trade, carried it across an ocean, and built a business from nothing. My father admired him deeply, not with envy but with respect. Even as a child, I could feel the air change when my father spoke of him. His voice softened, and his posture shifted slightly, as though acknowledging the courage it took to carve one's own place in a foreign world. My father did not desire entrepreneurship, but he drew inspiration from the possibility it represented. If his brother could shape a new life from skill and risk, perhaps my father could shape one through work and faith.

From where I sat as a boy, the details blurred into impressions—the smell of machinery on his clothes, the creak of the stairs as he came home, the slow exhale he made as he lowered himself into a chair, the quiet gratitude in his eyes as he looked at the small world he was building for us. I did not understand then that I was witnessing transformation. I only knew that my father was somehow expanding—steadier, deeper, more rooted than before.

But he wasn't perfect. No man is, especially one learning to live inside a world that does not yet feel like his own. The frustration of it—the strain of a language he could not command, the pressure of bills that arrived faster than confidence, the exhaustion of days that seemed to take more than they gave—sometimes wore straight through the surface. There were evenings when impatience flared, his voice tightening, rising, not in anger but in the raw ache of a man trying to will his life into place more quickly than time allowed.

Those shouts did not frighten me. Even then, I sensed they were not the storm themselves but the sound of a man trying to outrun the storm, a man who was terrified of falling short of the promise he had carried across the ocean.

And yet, every time, he found his way back. The frustration would move through him like weather, sharp and brief, and then he would settle again— quieter, softer, remorse flickering through his eyes even if no apology was spoken. He was learning how to build a life at the same time he was learning how to hold one together. It was not an easy balance.

Canada stripped him down at first. It took his language. It took his confidence. It took the familiarity that had once settled around him like a well-worn coat. It exposed the edges of his limitations and forced him to confront the parts of himself that had never been tested this way. But through work, responsibility, and the quiet determination not to quit, it rebuilt him—not into someone new, but into someone truer.

There was dignity in that rebuilding, even in the imperfect moments. Each passing day, each shift worked, each mistake corrected, each problem faced without retreat became part of a slow, faithful reconstruction. He was learning to stand in a life built on uncertainty, one where nothing was guaranteed and everything had to be earned. He did not speak about this inner struggle, but it lived in the set of his jaw, in the heaviness of his footsteps, and in the way he woke each morning with resolve rather than fear.

Some evenings, long after my mother had finished cleaning the kitchen, he would sit alone at the table, staring at papers or bills or simply nothing at all. I realize now that this was not defeat—it was recalibration. It was the moment when a man lays his burdens down just long enough to gather himself for the next day. It was the soundless intermission between effort and effort again.

Looking back now, I see those years for what they truly were—the forging of a man who did not yet realize he was becoming the anchor his family would one day depend on. His imperfections, far from diminishing him, made him more real, more human, more heroic in a quiet way I couldn't see then. The unfamiliar world that once overwhelmed him was shaping him, strengthening him, preparing him. And through it all, despite the strain and stumbles and sharp edges, he remained faithful to the promise he had carried across the ocean: to build a life worthy of the people he loved, no matter the cost.

His frustration did not define him. His perseverance did. And in the tension between the two, a man was being made—slowly, painfully, beautifully—in an unfamiliar world that was becoming, piece by piece, his own.

In time—slowly, almost imperceptibly at first—the unfamiliar world that had once pressed so heavily against him began to loosen its grip. English, the language that had once felt like an impenetrable wall, started to reveal its edges. It arrived not in dramatic breakthroughs but in small, steady moments. A word understood in the factory. A phrase he could repeat without stumbling. A sentence that landed exactly as it had been spoken. These were not small victories to him. They were proof that the world he lived in was no longer entirely foreign.

He carried each success quietly, almost shyly, as though naming it might cause it to disappear. But I could see it—the subtle lift in his shoulders, the slight ease in his movements, the new light in his eyes whenever understanding arrived. The ability to respond, even imperfectly, gave him footing. Not mastery, but belonging. Not fluency, but voice. For a man who had spent months speaking mostly in nods and gestures, that voice mattered more than anyone around him could have known.

Competence at work followed close behind. At first, he had been watched the way newcomers often are—evaluated with caution, measured by results, tolerated out of necessity. But in time, foremen began to trust him. They handed him tasks and walked away. They stopped hovering behind his shoulder. They started speaking to him not as someone who might slow the line, but as someone who could steady it.

Coworkers noticed, too. Some would ask for his help when a part wouldn't align or when the line's rhythm sped up. They saw the way he studied the work, how seriously he approached each step. They recognized something in him—a blend of reliability, resilience, and the quiet confidence of a man who understood that shortcuts rarely save time and often create more trouble than they solve. With each moment of trust, he shed one more layer of the insecurity that had weighed him down. The factory, once overwhelming, began to feel like a place where he belonged.

But belonging in Canada required more than English and work. It required learning an entirely different language—one not spoken, but written. Numbers, bills, statements, checks, credit forms. A financial system he had never encountered in Italy, where everything was paid in cash or bartered, where credit did not exist and banks were for people with money, not families clawing their way through scarcity.

In this new world, money was not simply earned; it had to be managed. Paid on time. Sent through the mail. Tracked. Saved. Documented. Bills arrived in envelopes he couldn't read. Forms asked for information he didn't yet have words for. A wrong signature or a missed payment could unravel weeks of work. It was an invisible maze, one as foreign as the language itself.

This is where I entered his story in a way I wouldn't understand until much later.

I loved helping him. Even as a boy, I wanted to learn. I wanted to stand beside him the way he stood beside us. So, I watched him write checks—slowly, carefully, copying the letters from the examples the bank had given him. I watched him sign his name again and again on scratch paper until the loops felt natural, the motion confident. I sat with him as he spread bills across the kitchen table, smoothing them flat, turning them over, trying to understand what each one meant.

Together, we deciphered the language of survival in a new country.

I learned to read the envelopes. I learned which numbers mattered. I learned how to explain due dates, balances, interest, minimum payments—concepts he had never encountered in the hills of Potenza, where life was measured by seasons, not statements. I loved being needed. I loved being able to help him stand a little straighter in a world that still felt dangerous in its unfamiliarity.

And slowly, something remarkable began to happen. The money started to stretch further than the bills. Not always. Not steadily. But occasionally—just enough to breathe. There were weeks when the payments were made on time, the pantry was full, and something small—just a few dollars—remained. Those moments felt like miracles. Not because the amount was large, but because it meant the tide was beginning to shift.

In those moments his dreams began to find shape. A reliable car. A home of our own. A small cushion in the bank. A future that wasn't defined by fear of the next envelope arriving in the mail. He was learning to not just work in Canada, but to function in Canada—to participate in the financial world that governed everything from mortgages to utility bills. And I, unknowingly, was learning alongside him—learning responsibility, discernment, and the quiet privilege of being trusted by a man who trusted very few.

As English began to land and financial systems began to make sense, competence at work deepened. He was no longer being trained; he was being relied upon. He no longer felt like the last one chosen; he had become a man others sought out. And with each recognition—each nod of respect, each small advancement, each difficult task completed well—his confidence thickened into something sturdier.

At home, the small accomplishments multiplied. Groceries that once felt like luxuries became affordable more often. Bills were paid not with dread, but with order. The idea of a house—once a fragile hope—became a plan. I could see pride taking root in him, not the boastful kind, but the quiet pride of a man who knows he is moving his family forward one step at a time.

Through it all, faith remained the compass that guided him. His faith lived in motion—in showing up, in enduring, in offering effort instead of excuses. My mother's faith lived in prayer—soft, persistent, unwavering. Together, their faith had no need for spectacle. It moved in only one direction, forward. And somehow, that was enough.

My brother and I learned more from watching them than from anything they ever said. We learned to read silence as strength. We learned the weight of responsibility without being told it was heavy. We learned that a man's character does not erupt suddenly—it accumulates, decision by decision, sacrifice by sacrifice, day by quiet day.

And somewhere in those years—those long shifts, those kitchen-table lessons, those whispered prayers—Canada stopped being foreign. It became the ground on which my father stood fully, not as a visitor or a man merely surviving, but as a man growing into himself.

He had mastered not the life he once imagined, but the life he chose to embrace. And in doing so, he gave us more than stability. He gave us a model of what becoming truly means.

As the early years in Canada found their rhythm, something in my father began to settle—not into comfort, but into conviction. The unfamiliar world around him still demanded more than it gave, still tested the limits of his endurance, still reminded him at every turn that belonging was something earned slowly. But through work, repetition, and responsibility, he began to inhabit the life he had once entered with nothing but hope and determination.

Each small victory marked a quiet shift. The day he understood a full sentence in English and answered back without shrinking. The moment a foreman trusted him to work unsupervised. The week the paycheck covered the bills with just enough left over for my mother to buy fruit that felt like a luxury. These were the milestones no one else saw—no celebrations, no applause—yet they were the victories that slowly stitched confidence into the seams of his life.

I can still see the day we moved into our first real home in Canada. My father stood in the doorway with the key resting in his palm, holding it as though it carried the weight of every sacrifice that brought him there. He lingered before turning it, just long enough to absorb what it meant. This was not simply shelter. It was proof that hardship had not emptied him; it had revealed him. It had clarified something essential and enduring inside him.

He didn't speak. He didn't need to. His silence carried a pride formed not from what he had gained, but from what he had overcome.

Looking back as an adult, I understand those years differently. As a child, I mistook steadiness for ease. I assumed consistency came naturally. I believed a parent's presence was simply what parents did. Only later did I understand the cost behind all that constancy—the strain hidden beneath exhaustion, the quiet calculations of risk and responsibility, the weight of the bills spread across the kitchen table as he learned how money moved in a country where nothing came easily.

He learned to write checks, track expenses, understand credit, and set aside enough to keep the future from feeling like a threat. None of this had been part of the world he came from. On the farm in Italy, survival depended on instinct, strength, and the rhythms of the land. In Canada, survival depended on systems and structures he had never been taught to navigate. And so, he learned them the only way he knew how—slowly, steadily, with humility and persistence.

I watched him long before I realized I was watching. I listened long before I understood what I was hearing. I studied the way he bent over the table, pencil in hand, working through numbers that once intimidated him, claiming the knowledge piece by piece until it could no longer threaten his dignity. In time, I began to help—reading forms, sounding out words, double-checking arithmetic. I didn't know then that I was being shaped just as much as he was. But I was. Responsibility was being passed to me one small moment at a time.

His life was becoming a blueprint—a quiet, steadfast pattern that would one day become my own internal compass. I saw that manhood was not announced; it was demonstrated. Strength was not loud; it was reliable. Faith was not declared; it was lived.

Canada had stripped him bare, but it was also building him back—not into someone different, but into someone truer. He became the man his past had required and his future demanded. And in becoming that man, he made it possible for his children to imagine lives larger than the one he had left behind.

Only with age did I grasp the fullness of that legacy. The scenes I once overlooked—the tightening of his jaw when money was scarce, the quiet sigh before he rose for another shift, the rare but unmistakable moments when frustration cracked through—now reveal the depth of the weight he carried. His silence was not emptiness. It was discipline. It was fear held firmly enough to keep from breaking through. It was love so committed it rarely paused long enough to articulate itself.

These years were not just the story of my father's becoming. They were the beginning of mine. Long before I understood the language of faith, he lived it in front of me. Long before I understood the meaning of legacy, he built it with his bare hands. Long before I understood who I would become, his becoming shaped the outline of my life.

And yet, for all the strength that emerged in him, those years also carried something else—something quieter, deeper, and far more complex. Beneath the victories, beneath the slow mastery, beneath the expanding confidence, there was a current that ran through everything he did—a constant, steady hum of worry and want.

He wanted more for his family than he had been given. He worried that his strength might not be enough. He wanted to secure a life he could barely imagine but would spend his entire youth trying to build. He worried that the sacrifices he made might not carry us far enough. These wants and worries became the tension that shaped his manhood—and the tension that would shape my understanding of him.

His becoming was not simply a story of triumph. It was a story of carrying fear without letting it define him. It was a story of wanting more without being swallowed by the ache of what he lacked. It was a story of learning to live with worry as a constant companion, yet never allowing it to dictate the choices he made.

Which is why, as the narrative of this book turns toward the next chapter, the truth becomes clear.

My father's life was shaped not only by the hope that drove him forward, but by the worry and want that followed him everywhere.

And it is there, in the space between those two forces—hope pulling, worry pressing—that Chapter 3 begins.

A life shaped by worry and want.

A life built in the tension between fear and faith.

A life forged in the quiet spaces where a man learns what he is truly made of.

SACRED WAYPOINTS

Crossing the Threshold of the Unknown

My father stepped into a world that felt sharper, colder, and faster than anything he had known. Belonging was not offered; it had to be earned.

- When have you entered a season where nothing fit—not the pace, not the language, not even your sense of self?
- What did you cling to in those moments?
- What did you eventually have to surrender to move forward?

Response: Take one honest inventory. Ask "Where in my life am I resisting a threshold God is asking me to cross?" Write down one next step you sense emerging.

When Silence Protects—and Restricts

My father's silence sheltered him from humiliation, but it also kept him outside the life unfolding around him.

- Where has silence protected you?
- Where has it held you back from relationship, courage, or belonging?
- What truth, question or confession longs to find your voice again?

Invitation: Speak one sentence today—to God, to yourself, or to someone you trust—that breaks the silence gently.

The Humility of Beginning Again

In a night-school classroom full of tired hands and hopeful eyes, my father learned that starting over does not diminish dignity—it deepens it.

- Where are you being asked to become a beginner again?
- What pride or fear makes that beginning feel risky?
- What doorway might humility be unlocking in this season?

Practice: Choose one area where you feel inadequate. Take one small action toward learning—a conversation, a question, a step.

Work That Shapes the Worker

The factory floor became my father's teacher—not through instruction, but through endurance, repetition, and the quiet example of others.

- What work—visible or invisible—has shaped who you are?
- Where did routine become the refining fire of your character?
- Who showed you how to work with integrity?

Gratitude: Name (privately or aloud) one person whose quiet example formed you. Offer thanks for them by name.

Learning the Hidden Language of Survival

At the kitchen table, deciphering bills and checks, my father learned the unspoken language of a new country—and I learned beside him.

- What unspoken lessons shaped you—especially the ones no one noticed you were absorbing?
- Who sat beside you in your own seasons of learning-to-survive?
- What part of that early formation still guides your decisions today?

Reflection: Consider what you inherited (wisdom, habits, disciplines). Ask, "Which of these serves me now—and which ones need to be released?"

The Tension That Forms a Man

Beneath his progress ran a quiet hum of worry and want—not failure, but love carrying more weight than one life seemed built to hold.

- What tensions shape you now—the hopes that pull you forward and the fears that slow your steps?
- How do these tensions form, stretch, or deepen you?
- What desire or worry do you hold so tightly that it exhausts you?

Release: Open your hands—literally—and imagine placing one burden into God's care. Sit with the relief that follows.

ANCHORS OF THE WORD 

Strength When the World Feels Too Big

"From the ends of the earth I call to You… lead me to the rock that is higher than I." (Psalm 61:2 NIV)

When my father stepped into the bitter Canadian winter, everything felt larger than his strength—the cold, the language, the pace, the expectations. Yet Scripture reminds us that God meets us precisely in the places that exceed our capacity. Strength does not begin with our readiness. It begins with our need.

My father's first prayers in that unfamiliar land were not eloquent. They were quiet pleas for grounding, for steadiness, for a place to stand. And the God who hears us "from the ends of the earth" answered by becoming the rock beneath his feet.

Reflection: Where do you feel small in the face of something new? Ask God to lead you to a rock higher than your fear.

New Tongue for a New Life

"The Sovereign Lord has given me a well-instructed tongue, to know the word that sustains the weary." (Isaiah 50:4 NIV)

Learning English was more than a skill for my father—it was a reclaiming of voice, dignity, and place. Scripture speaks of God giving a "well-instructed tongue," not simply for eloquence, but to sustain life. My father's efforts at that kitchen table were an act of hope—a belief that God could teach him what he had never been taught, and restore what fear had taken.

He began with awkward pencil strokes, whispered repetitions, and a courage so quiet it barely made a sound. But heaven heard it.

Consider: Where do you need God to instruct your tongue—to help you speak, learn, apologize, forgive, or begin again?

Work Done Unto the Lord

"Whatever you do, work at it with all your heart, as working for the Lord…" (Colossians 3:23 NIV)

The factory became my father's teacher not because it was noble work, but because it demanded everything of him—focus, endurance, adaptability, humility. Scripture does not separate sacred work from secular work; it dignifies all labor done with a faithful heart.

My father's competence didn't blossom overnight. It came through repetition, mistakes, and small victories no one else celebrated. But God saw every unspoken prayer in every shift, every task done with integrity even when no one thanked him.

Reflection: What work—visible or hidden—is God asking you to approach "with all your heart" in this season?"

Wisdom in the Daily Stewardship of Life

"Be sure you know the condition of your flocks, give careful attention to your herds." (Proverbs 27:23 NIV)

In Italy, stewardship meant tending livestock and land. In Canada, it meant managing bills, budgets, credit forms, and the mysterious arithmetic of survival. Scripture's wisdom applies to both worlds—steward what is in front of you with care, clarity, and intention.

At the kitchen table, my father learned a new form of stewardship. He learned how to manage a life that required planning, numbers, and systems he had never been taught. And without realizing it, he was teaching me the same.

Prompt: What area of your life needs renewed attention or stewardship right now—finances, relationships, rhythms, health, or faith?

A Faith That Does Not Quit

"Let us not grow weary in doing good, for at the proper time we will reap a harvest if we do not give up." (Galatians 6:9 NIV)

My father's progress did not arrive through inspiration, but through persistence. He got up each day when he felt inadequate. He stayed when everything felt foreign. He tried again when frustration broke through. Scripture names this not merely endurance, but sowing—and God Himself promises the harvest.

His harvest was not immediate. But it came—in belonging, in language, in competence, and in the home we eventually opened with trembling gratitude.

Reflection: Where are you tempted to give up? What small act of perseverance today could become tomorrow's harvest?

Quiet Trust in the Midst of Worry

"Be still before the LORD and wait patiently for him; do not fret when people succeed in their ways, when they carry out their wicked schemes." (Psalm 37:7 NIV)

Beneath all my father's progress ran a steady undercurrent of worry and want—the fear of not being enough, the desire to build what he had never been given. Scripture does not shame worry; it invites us to rest in One who carries what we cannot.

My father never found perfect stillness, but he found something close—the discipline of showing up, the patience of trusting slow progress, and the quiet surrender of placing his life in God's hands even when fear hummed beneath the surface.

Invitation: Sit in silence for sixty seconds. Let your breath slow. Let one worry loosen its grip. Whisper, "I trust You here."

LEGACY NOTES

THREE

A Life Shaped by Worry and Want

"Worry does not empty tomorrow of its sorrow; it empties today of its strength."

— Corrie ten Boom (1892-1983),
Dutch Christian watchmaker, author, and Holocaust survivor

By the time my father began to find his footing in Canada, it might have appeared to anyone looking in from the outside that he had finally "arrived." English no longer sounded like a wall he couldn't climb. The factory foremen trusted him. He could follow instructions, anticipate problems, even step in to help others who were struggling. Paychecks covered the bills with a little room to breathe. There were days when my mother could buy meat without calculating whether it would jeopardize the week's budget. There were evenings when my father sat at the table not in confusion over a form or a statement, but in quiet acknowledgment of a day well spent.

It was easy, from a distance, to mistake these small victories for certainty.

But inside him, fear never left. It simply changed shape.

Where the early days in Canada had brought fear thick and immediate—the fear of misunderstanding, of being misunderstood, of not belonging—the years that followed carried a thinner, more persistent kind. A quieter fear. A companion he did not invite but learned to walk beside. Worry moved with him like a second shadow, present even in moments of progress. If anything, the more he gained, the more he feared losing it.

He had grown up in a world where scarcity wasn't a concept—it was the air his family breathed. Hunger was not a metaphor but a memory that lived under his skin. In his home region of Basilicata, food had seasons, and even in good seasons, it was never abundant. Rain could ruin crops, a broken plow could mean a week of hunger, and a sick animal could unravel an entire family's stability. Those early uncertainties carved themselves into him, shaping instincts that did not disappear simply because he now lived in a country of supermarkets and paychecks.

The fear of "not enough" followed him across the ocean.

Even when bills were paid and a small amount remained, he waited for the moment it would vanish. Even with steady work, he imagined the foreman calling him in to say there was no more job. Even with food in the pantry, he glanced twice at the shelves, checking what might run out.

Scarcity, once it enters a man, does not leave quietly.

And so, while his outward life began to stabilize, his inner world was still learning how to trust abundance.

He lived with a vigilance that seemed, to others, unnecessary. But to him, it was survival. He scanned for threats without realizing he was doing it. A rumor at work about possible layoffs tightened something deep inside him. A passing winter cough made him consider how the family would function if he missed even one week's wages. Rising grocery prices or an unexpected repair could turn an ordinary day into one that required silence and recalibration.

Stability felt fragile, like glass that could shatter with the wrong kind of pressure.

Even as a child, I knew this. I didn't know the word worry, but I recognized its presence—the way a child senses a storm before ever seeing the clouds. It lived in the air of our home, not as tension, but as alertness. As if at any moment something might shift, and we would all need to brace ourselves without understanding why. That atmosphere settled into me quietly, long before I had language for it, and it would become a part of me in ways I am still unravelling even now.

I remember watching my father sit at the table with the bills spread before him. His shoulders rounded slightly—not in defeat, but in concentration. He studied each amount the way a man studies a map, tracing where the dangers might be hidden. He counted and re-counted, his lips moving, his pencil tapping in a steady rhythm that felt almost like a heartbeat echoing through the room. Those evenings carried a silence that was not the quiet of rest but the weighted quiet of responsibility tightening its grip.

I understood the silence of fatigue. Fatigue was soft, familiar, predictable. It faded with sleep. But this other silence—the silence of worry—felt taut, like a thread pulled too tightly across the room. It changed the way I moved. It made me sit still without being told. It made my mother soften her footsteps, as if even sound itself might tip the balance of a fragile equation my father was trying to solve.

Some nights he exhaled deeply, the kind of breath a man releases only when the day has taken something from him that he cannot put into words. Sometimes he leaned back and rubbed his forehead, not in pain but in thought. And sometimes, he simply stared at a single envelope, holding it longer than necessary, as though it contained a truth he had not yet gathered the strength to face.

He never said, "I'm worried."

He never said, "I'm afraid we might not make it."

He never said, "This feels heavy."

But a child does not need words to understand the weight a father carries. Some things are absorbed simply by being nearby.

And the truth is, I absorbed more than I realized. The alertness that filled our home—the readiness for something to go wrong, the instinct to keep watch even in moments of calm—wove itself into me. What began as a child's sensitivity became, over the years, a quiet anxiety I still battle at times today. Not the dramatic kind, but the subtle kind—the persistent hum beneath the surface, the reflex to anticipate what might fall apart, the habit of bracing for impact even when life is steady.

Worry became part of the rhythm of our home—not dominating it but threading through it. It lived behind my father's steadiness, behind the effort he gave to his work, behind the discipline he brought to each day. His progress brought relief, yes, but not release. Want still whispered. Worry still pressed.

And though he rarely spoke of it, a truth began to settle into me as I grew older. What shaped him most during those years was not only the world he was building, but also the fears he carried while building it. His strength was real, but so was his worry, and both lived side by side inside him.

Only later did I understand how deeply those unseen battles formed me. The anxiety I felt as a child—the quiet alertness, the instinct to watch the room, the sense that stability could shift without warning—didn't disappear as I grew. It stayed with me, emerging at times even now. But it also forged something unexpected in me, a quiet but relentless drive to achieve, to bring order where there had once been uncertainty, and to build a life for my family that felt secure and deliberate.

His fears became part of my foundation. Not as burdens, but as fuel. Not as limitations, but as the quiet fire that pushed me to rise, to prepare, to work harder than I understood at the time.

In ways I could never have grasped then, the worries he carried shaped him— and the echoes of those worries shaped me too.

As the years passed, my father moved through Canada with a steadier rhythm. He understood more, hesitated less, and carried himself with a hard-won confidence. On the factory floor, he no longer seemed like a man trying to keep pace. He had become someone others depended on, someone whose presence brought order to the noise around him. To the outside world, it appeared he had settled into the life he had crossed an ocean to build.

Inside our home, the truth was more complicated.

He returned each evening carrying a second life that few ever saw. It was the life shaped by quiet fear, by vigilance that never fully loosened its grip, by the weight of responsibility that remained long after the factory doors had closed behind him. He loved us fiercely, but that love came wrapped in a kind of tension that settled into the air long before he took off his boots.

There were small signs, almost imperceptible at first, that revealed the worry he tried so hard to hide. I watched him count and re-count the money in his worn leather wallet, flipping through the bills as if confirming they were still there, as if the simple act of touching them might keep them from disappearing. At the grocery store, he stood longer than most fathers in front of shelves, comparing prices, calculating totals in his head with the same quiet precision he used at the factory. Sometimes he put items back. Sometimes he hesitated with something small I wanted, weighing not the price itself but the margin it would leave for the week ahead. Even then, I sensed the tension beneath the surface—not embarrassment, but pressure. A man trying to provide enough in a world where "enough" always felt like a moving target.

The pressure grew even more visible each December. Christmas shopping was supposed to feel magical, but I often saw the storm gathering behind his eyes. He wanted to give us what he saw other children receiving—the toys displayed in store windows, the skates and sleds my friends talked about, the gifts that made me feel, for a moment, the pull of "keeping up with the Joneses." He never said it out loud, but I could feel the heaviness in him, the ache of a man who wanted to give generously while living inside the tight limits of a budget he could not allow to break. He would pick up a gift, study it, turn it over as if weighing more than cost—weighing his own hope of giving me a childhood that did not feel less than the ones unfolding around me.

I did not understand the language of those moments, but I understood the look on his face. It was the same one he wore at the kitchen table when the bills were spread out before him. The same one he carried when unexpected expenses arrived, or when winter heating costs rose, or when a friend at work mentioned layoffs. His worry lived in these glimpses—in the pause before choosing groceries, in the silence between one Christmas toy and the next, in the careful movements of a man trying to stretch possibility without breaking reality.

At home, the rituals continued. He tugged on doorknobs to be sure they were locked. He pressed his palm briefly against the stove to confirm it was cool. He paused at the thermostat as if the numbers might shift the moment he turned away. These habits were not rooted in fear; they came from something deeper—the belief that vigilance was the only defense in a world that had never offered him anything without cost. These small acts gave him a sense of control, as if he could hold instability at bay through sheer attentiveness and discipline.

Looking back, I see that every gesture was the outward sign of a man who carried responsibility like a second skin. A life built from scarcity had trained his senses to stay alert. Even progress, even belonging, even moments of abundance could not fully quiet the part of him that feared how easily it might all slip away.

As a child, I absorbed all of it—not through conversations, but through watching him move through the world. The grocery aisles. The store shelves at Christmas. The way his brow tightened at prices. The long, slow breath before he placed something in the cart. I didn't yet understand that this was worry, or that the same worry would imprint itself on me, shaping the vigilance, over-preparation, and relentless drive to achieve that I still wrestle with today.

Now, as an adult, I see those moments for what they were. My father wasn't merely providing; he was protecting. He was trying to build possibility out of limits, trying to ensure his children never carried the hunger or scarcity that had shadowed his own youth. And in his effort to shield us from those burdens, he unknowingly passed down something else—a sensitivity to instability, a determination not to fall behind, an inner push to create the security he chased for so long.

Responsibility never intimidated him, but it carried an emotional cost. He feared disappointing us, feared failing the promise he had whispered to my mother on the journey across the ocean, feared that one misstep might undo the fragile progress he had fought so hard to build. Every gain felt like solid ground, yet he stepped as if it could collapse beneath him.

My mother carried part of that weight as well. She absorbed the emotional overflow of those years—steady, gentle, tired in ways she rarely revealed. Her prayers deepened, shaped by both hope and heaviness. She prayed for his strength, for God's provision, for a softness in him that worry sometimes hardened. When he fell into silence at the table, she sat with it. When frustration flared, she tended to the fracture with quiet patience.

Worry seeped into the fabric of our home. It surfaced in raised voices that came not from anger but from accumulated strain. It showed itself in the shift of his mood when an unexpected expense arrived or when rumors of layoffs moved through the factory like an unwelcome wind. It tightened the emotional atmosphere just enough to remind us that stability was still fragile and that he felt an urgent responsibility to protect it.

None of this diminished him. If anything, it made him more human—complex, tender, quietly heroic. Worry never defeated him. It never kept him from showing up or fulfilling his duties. It simply moved beneath the surface of everything he built, shaping his decisions, his temperament, and the atmosphere of our home.

And without realizing it, I was learning from that worry too—learning its shape, its presence, its cost, and the ways it formed a man who was willing to give everything he had to keep his family safe.

Worry shaped the rhythm of his days but want shaped the direction of his life. And where worry revealed what he feared losing, want revealed what he longed to build.

Want, for my father, was never about ambition or accumulation. It was not tied to ego or status or the desire to impress anyone. His want was quieter, older, shaped by memories of scarcity that had marked his childhood long before he ever imagined setting foot in Canada. It lived beneath the surface of everything he did—not as greed, but as yearning. Yearning for security. Yearning for permanence. Yearning for a life that could not be undone by a single bad season or a single lost shift.

He wanted a home that no landlord could take away. He wanted work that would not vanish without warning. He wanted his sons to have choices he never did, choices not dictated by the thin generosity of the land or the weight of family necessity. His longing wasn't for things, but for stability—a future built on solid ground rather than trembling uncertainty.

There is a profound difference between desire and greed, though the two can look similar from the outside. My father's want was rooted in memory—the ache of missed meals, the sound of his mother stretching ingredients that refused to stretch any further, the winters when shoes wore thin before spring arrived. He carried those memories not as wounds but as warnings. Want, for him, was not about more; it was about enough. Enough warmth. Enough food. Enough certainty to sleep without listening for the storm.

In many ways, his want functioned like a prayer. Not the kind spoken aloud, but the kind lived out quietly through effort and persistence. Imagining a future with abundance—even modest abundance—felt almost sacred to him. Every small goal carried a kind of reverence—a reliable car, a bit of savings in the bank, a down payment on a house. These were not purchases. They were expressions of hope. Each one marked a step toward a life where fear no longer sat at the edge of every decision.

And that want shaped the way he worked. He said yes to overtime when his body begged for rest. He endured difficult supervisors because the alternative threatened the stability he was fighting to build. He worked through pain, through illness, through exhaustion because stepping back felt too dangerous. The want he carried did not push him upward—it pushed him forward. It kept him moving when everything in him longed to stop.

That same want seeped into our home, forming patterns that would shape my brother and me in ways we didn't recognize until adulthood. He encouraged us to study, to strive, to excel—not out of pride, but out of protection. He believed education was armor, opportunity was safety, advancement was insurance against the life he had known. The message beneath his encouragement was subtle but unmistakable: "Build what I could not. Secure what I could only imagine."

Want, for him, was not about accumulation; it was about redemption—not for himself, but for his children. He wanted to lift the next generation above the circumstances that had shaped his own youth. He wanted us to begin where he had never been allowed to start.

Looking back, I can see how worry and want lived side by side within him. Worry defined what he feared losing; want defined what he dreamed of giving. One tightened his jaw. The other kept him moving. Together, they formed the quiet engine of his life—and in ways I did not understand at the time, they also shaped the engine of mine.

Want carried my father forward, but something else steadied his steps. The further he walked into the life he was building, the more he leaned on a force that had always been present but had never felt as essential as it did in Canada. Fear pressed from one side. Want pulled from the other. And between them, faith rose as the one thing that kept his world from tilting too far in either direction.

Faith, for my father, began to shift from something inherited to something applied. In Italy, faith was woven into the rhythm of village life—feast days, processions, the steady tolling of church bells marking time. It was a tradition, a comfort, a backdrop. But in Canada, faith became something more elemental. It became the quiet tool he reached for when worry tightened his chest or want stretched further than his strength. His prayers were not poetic. They were necessary. They were whispered under his breath before he walked into work, spoken silently as he studied the stack of bills, breathed out at night when fatigue settled into his bones. They were the simple pleas of a man who understood he could not carry everything alone, even if he tried.

My mother's faith carried its own strength. She absorbed the emotional overflow of those years with a steadiness that still astonishes me. Her prayers softened the rough edges in our home, smoothing the atmosphere when strain threatened to fray it. She prayed with expectation—not for ease, but for God to meet them in the middle of their effort. She believed that heaven bent toward persistence, that God honored the work of hands as much as the words of prayers. Her faith became the quiet scaffolding that held our small family upright.

My father's faith looked different. It lived in motion. He attended church even on Sunday mornings when exhaustion wrapped itself around him like a heavy coat he could not take off. He blessed the food quietly, not as ritual but as gratitude. And often, at the end of the day, he would sit for a moment in stillness—not defeated, not discouraged, but surrendered. It was the posture of a man acknowledging both his limits and his hope. Faith did not erase the weight he carried, but it gave the weight direction.

I have come to realize that my parents' faith was part of a broader psychology that many immigrants shared. When the world shifts beneath your feet, when nothing around you resembles the land that shaped you, faith becomes the one familiar anchor. Immigrants pray differently. They pray not for comfort but for strength. Not for escape but for resilience. Not for a miracle, but for enough—enough endurance, enough clarity, enough courage to keep going when everything inside you whispers that you are far from home.

This blend of fear, want, and faith formed the spiritual atmosphere of my childhood. It shaped my earliest understanding of God. Faith, as I absorbed it, was not primarily about emotion. It was effort. It was the decision to rise each morning. It was the whispered prayer before opening an envelope. It was the quiet trust that God stood beside those who carried heavy things.

Even now, as an adult, that understanding remains with me. My father taught me—without ever explaining it—that God does not remove the weight; He strengthens the shoulders. He does not erase uncertainty; He walks with the uncertain. He does not promise ease; He promises presence.

And in that presence, my father found the courage to keep building. His faith did not silence his worry, and it did not diminish his want. But it gave meaning to his want and courage to his worry. It became the thread stitching together the fragile, determined fabric of his life.

Faith steadied him, but it did not silence the worry he carried. Instead, it lived beside his devotion like a quiet companion, shaping not only the way he worked, but the way he loved. And nowhere was that influence more evident than in his fatherhood.

His protectiveness grew out of the same soil as his fear. When he warned us sternly about crossing streets, talking to strangers, or wandering too far at the park, it was not the voice of an authoritarian man—it was the voice of someone who had seen how quickly life can turn on those who are unprepared. His caution was not control; it was a shield he forged with whatever tools he had. In public, he watched us closely, eyes scanning for risk the way he scanned his workstation for hazards. He wanted to be sure nothing caught him off guard, nothing took from us what he had worked so hard to give.

And though he loved deeply, affection rarely came through words. His tenderness arrived in indirect ways—tightening the straps of my winter boots before school, checking that doors to our home were locked at night, repairing toys late into the evening so they would be waiting for us by morning. He provided more than he hugged. He showed up more than he spoke up. For him, love was a verb measured in consistency, not language. It was the roof over our heads, the heat in the winter, the groceries neatly arranged on the table, the bills paid before anything else.

And yet, there were moments when worry loosened its grip.

Bursts of laughter at the dinner table. Small celebrations—a slice of birthday cake he insisted we eat first, a proud smile over a good report card, the way he admired a new winter coat as if it were armor he had earned for us. These flashes of joy were brief but unmistakable, like sunlight breaking through a heavy cloud. They revealed the father he longed to be beneath the layers of responsibility he carried.

Some of those moments unfolded at the rink.

After long days at the factory, he would stand along the boards at cold community arenas, hands tucked into his coat pockets, breath visible in the air, watching my brother and me chase the puck across the ice. He rarely spoke much during practice. He didn't shout instructions or offer analysis. He simply watched—steady, attentive, fully present. When we skated well, when we improved, when we played with confidence, his face softened. A quiet smile would appear, one that didn't need words.

On the ice, effort mattered. Progress was visible. Excellence earned its reward immediately. And for a few moments at a time, the weight he carried loosened. The bills were not on the table. The future was not pressing in. There was only the sound of blades cutting ice, the rhythm of movement, and the quiet pride of a father watching his sons grow stronger in a world that finally felt, if only briefly, generous.

Those hours at the rink were not escapes from responsibility; they were reminders of why he carried it. Watching us excel gave shape to the sacrifices he made. It affirmed that the vigilance, the restraint, the endless calculations were building toward something real. In those cold arenas, standing silently among other parents, he allowed himself moments of satisfaction—not because life was easy, but because his effort was working.

Those moments mattered more than I understood at the time. They revealed a tenderness that responsibility often concealed. A man who could rest, briefly, in the sight of his children thriving. A man whose joy did not announce itself loudly, but arrived quietly, honestly, and without pretense.

They were small moments. Fleeting ones. But they were enough to show me who he was beneath the worry—and why he carried it so faithfully.

From him, I learned the lesson of presence long before I understood its power. Even when he was emotionally stretched thin, he never left. He was home every night. He stood in the doorway when we came in from school. He sat at the dinner table even when exhaustion blurred the edges of his face. His presence was unwavering, and in that presence lived the deepest expression of his love. He might not have spoken it freely, but he lived it fully.

As a child, I interpreted all of this through the limited vocabulary of youth. I did not know that love could arrive wrapped in tension. I did not know that affection could hide itself inside vigilance. I did not know that a father could be terrified and devoted at the same time. I only sensed that life felt serious, the world required attention, and joy had to be earned and protected. I absorbed those messages quietly, letting them imprint themselves on me long before I understood their origin.

Worry shaped not just how my father lived, but how he loved. It created a home where affection was measured in effort, where safety was guarded with intensity, where love was steady even when life was not. And without realizing it, I learned to read love through that lens — through presence, through provision, and through the quiet acts that hold a family together even when the man at the center carries more than he ever says.

As the years passed and my world widened, something in my understanding began to shift. The father I had known in childhood—steady, vigilant, often quiet—slowly came into clearer focus, not as the symbol I once saw, but as a man shaped by forces I was only beginning to comprehend.

His silence, which I had once interpreted simply as temperament, revealed itself to be something far more complex. It was not emptiness. It was effort. It was the quiet space a man creates when he is carrying more than he can say aloud. When I look back at old photographs now—him standing in front of our first house, or holding me in a winter coat two sizes too big—I see the strain beneath the smile. I see the questions behind his eyes. I see the ways fear and hope lived side by side inside him, even in moments meant to feel triumphant.

With adulthood came a new lens through which to revisit my childhood memories. I can picture him at the kitchen table long after the rest of us had gone to bed, pencil in hand, balancing numbers as if our safety depended on the outcome—because in his mind, it did. I can hear the soft movements of his footsteps in the early morning, when he rose before dawn despite the exhaustion that clung to him from the day before. I can recall the rare moments when his composure cracked, when worry broke through despite his effort to keep it contained. As a child, those moments felt like weather—sudden, unexplainable, passing. As an adult, I understand them as the cost of a life lived under persistent pressure.

It took years to recognize how much of that inheritance found its way into me. Worry wove itself quietly into my own wiring, shaping the way I anticipated challenges, the way I prepared for uncertainty, the way I scanned the horizon even when things appeared calm. Want—the yearning for something safer, something more secure, something sturdier—became the engine behind my ambition. His burden, though never intentionally handed down, became one of the forces that drove me. It sharpened my instincts. It fueled my discipline. It created in me a determination to build the life he had once only imagined.

And somewhere along the way, without ceremony or announcement, I stopped seeing him solely as 'my father' and began seeing him as a man — a man who carried his history into every decision, who tried to build a new world while still healing from the old one, and who loved fiercely even when fear reshaped the expression of that love.

Seeing him through the wider lens of adulthood did not change the past, but it changed me. Memories that once felt sharp began to soften. Moments that once confused me found their meaning. I came to understand something children seldom grasp but adults eventually learn. Our parents are not the myths we imagine in childhood. They are real people whose unseen struggles, private fears, and quiet acts of devotion shape the very lives we grow into.

Understanding him in this fuller way did more than soften the past. It opened a door. It revealed the quiet truth that the inner world my father carried—with all its tensions, hopes, and fears—had already begun shaping the outer world I would one day build for myself. His life did not simply influence mine; it left an imprint, a blueprint traced in habits, instincts, and longings I did not recognize as inherited until much later.

I can see now that I absorbed his awareness of risk long before I knew what the word meant. I learned to scan the edges of situations, to anticipate what might go wrong, and to prepare earlier and more thoroughly than others. It felt natural, but it was not. It was learned. It was the echo of a man who believed safety came not from luck, but from vigilance.

I inherited his hunger for stability as well. The desire to build something solid, something lasting, something immune to the fragile unpredictability that shaped his early years. I understand now why I plan so carefully, why I construct systems that hold under pressure, why I guide others toward security with such conviction. I was raised by a man for whom stability was not a luxury. It was salvation.

I inherited his drive to provide too—the impulse to fill gaps before anyone else notices them, to make sure the people I love feel safe, protected, and supported. It is the instinct that wakes before dawn, the instinct that stays until the work is done, the instinct that refuses to leave needs unmet. To me, this has always felt like responsibility. Only in adulthood did I understand it as legacy.

And woven through all of this was his faith in motion. Not spoken, not dramatically displayed, but lived through effort, sacrifice, and constancy. His faith taught me that strength is measured not by what a man declares but by what he carries, what he shows up for, and what he builds when no one is watching.

His worry became my vigilance. His want became my ambition. His burdens became the architecture of who I would become.

This was not a burden he intended to pass on. It was a blueprint formed quietly, almost accidentally, through the way he navigated the world. And I, watching him from rooms where I barely understood the stakes, took it in piece by piece until it became the scaffolding of my own life.

In understanding him, I began to understand myself.

As I look back on those years, I see a paradox woven through the heart of my father's becoming. He built a life stronger than the worries that shaped it. He created stability out of scarcity, dignity out of labor, and hope out of days that offered him very little in return. Yet the very worries he worked so hard to outrun became threads in our family story, stitching themselves into the fabric of who we were and who we would become.

A life shaped by worry and want is often misunderstood. To some, it might look like fragility. To others, like hardship or limitation. But for my father, worry sharpened his awareness and want deepened his resolve. These forces did not weaken him; they refined him. They created vigilance where carelessness might have lived. They created devotion where indifference could have taken root. They created a relentless hope, one that insisted on pushing forward even when fear tugged hard in the opposite direction.

He carried these forces with a kind of quiet strength that rarely showed itself in words. I can see it in the way he rose each morning, in the steadiness of his hands, in the long exhale he took before stepping out into another day of responsibility. I can feel it in the atmosphere of our home, a blend of gravity and grace that shaped us more than any lesson could. He did not speak about resilience or perseverance. He lived them in a way that left no room for doubt.

And as he navigated those early decades in Canada, he began to embody a truth he never would have claimed for himself. He was becoming a man defined not by what he lacked, but by what he refused to stop striving for. He worked through exhaustion, fear, and uncertainty with the same quiet conviction that had carried him across an ocean. In each effort, he was building more than a life. He was building the foundation for the lives that would follow.

But there was a cost to such striving. The emotional toll of vigilance. The spiritual fatigue of living with both fear and hope that pressed against the same heart. The constant tension between wanting to provide more and fearing that one misstep could take everything away. These forces shaped him as surely as the work he performed with his hands. And as the years went on, they began to reveal another layer of his story—the weight that even the strongest men cannot carry without consequence.

This is where the next chapter and section begins. In the space where strength meets strain. In the quiet places where a man's efforts run ahead of his rest. In the moments when the life he built with unwavering determination begins to show him the limits of even his endurance.

Worry sharpened him. Want drove him. Faith steadied him.

And the strain of holding all three would become the next terrain he had to cross.

SACRED WAYPOINTS

When Fear Changes Shape

In this chapter, my father begins to "arrive" in Canada—competence grows, English becomes familiar, bills get paid on time. Yet even then, fear does not disappear. It simply changes shape, becoming quieter but more persistent.

- Where in your life has fear softened its voice but not its presence?
- Is there an area where progress brought relief, but not release?

Sit with this truth: Fear that changes shape often invites deeper strengthening, not deeper running.

Scarcity That Follows You Across Oceans

Scarcity became part of my father in childhood—born into the thin margins of Basilicata where harvests failed and hunger lingered. Even in Canada, abundance did not immediately rewire those early instincts.

- What memories of "not enough" still influence the way you move through the world today?
- Do those memories guide you wisely, or do they confine you?

Ask God for clarity: Reveal what comes from wisdom, and what comes from old wounds.

The Atmosphere Children Absorb

As a boy, I sensed worry in the air long before I understood the word. It shaped my nervous system, my instincts, and some of the anxieties I still carry as an adult.

- What emotional atmosphere formed you long before you understood its meaning?
- What did you absorb simply by being near it?

Hold this gently: Sometimes healing begins by naming what we once breathed in without question.

Worry as a Form of Love

My father's vigilance—checking stoves, counting bills, tugging on locks—was not obsession. It was devotion. He feared failing his family more than he feared exhaustion or embarrassment.

- Where in your life is worry flowing out of love rather than fear?
- And where is it flowing out of fear disguised as love?

Practice a simple act: Offer gratitude for someone whose vigilance once protected you, even if imperfectly.

The Want That Redeems, Not Consumes

My father's longing for "more" was not greed; it was hope. A house to call his own. Work that lasted. A future where his sons had choices he never did. His want was a prayer written in effort.

- What do you long for that is not about status, but about safety, dignity, or redemption?
- What hope keeps you moving even when you're tired?

Journal one line: "The future I quietly long for is…" Let the sentence finish itself.

The Blueprint Passed on Quietly

My father's worry became my vigilance. His want became my ambition. His burdens became the architecture of whom I would become—long before I realized any inheritance was being handed down.

- What unspoken lessons shaped the way you work, plan, parent, or pray?
- Which of those lessons do you want to carry forward, and which are asking to be released?

Ask God for discernment: "Lord, help me keep what formed me well, and gently set down what I no longer need to carry."

ANCHORS OF THE WORD

Grace for the Unseen Tomorrow

"Therefore, do not worry about tomorrow, for tomorrow will worry about itself. Each day has enough trouble of its own." (Matthew 6:34 NIV)

My father never lived a day without thinking of tomorrow. Worry became the quiet rhythm beneath everything he built—not because he lacked faith, but because life had taught him how fragile stability could be.

Yet even in that vigilance, God met him in the present. In the work of his hands. In the protection he offered his family. In the breath he finally released at night.

Reflection: Where might God be inviting you to rest—not in the absence of responsibility, but in the presence of His sufficiency for today?

Deliverance in the Middle, Not the End

"I sought the Lord, and He answered me; He delivered me from all my fears." (Psalm 34:4 NIV)

Deliverance, for my father, didn't look like fears evaporating. It looked like strength arriving in the very places fear lived.

God did not remove his worries about layoffs, bills, or the uncertainty of a new world—but He steadied him inside those storms, shaping courage from the inside out.

Reflection: Where has God strengthened you long before your circumstances changed?

The Secret of Enough

"I have learned to be content whatever the circumstances… whether in plenty or in want." (Philippians 4:11-12 NIV)

My father carried both plenty and want across his lifetime.

He knew hunger as a boy, responsibility as a young immigrant, and the fragile security of working-class life in Canada. Contentment for him was never passive. It was chosen, practiced, and earned through discipline and gratitude. He knew what it meant to stretch possibility without losing hope.

Reflection: What practices help you cultivate contentment even when life feels uncertain?

Rest for the Overworked Heart

"In vain you rise early and stay up late, toiling for food to eat—for he grants sleep to those he loves." (Psalm 127:2 NIV)

My father rose early, worked late, and bore the weight of anxious toil daily.

Yet even in the long stretches of strain, there were evenings when peace slipped quietly into our home—through my mother's prayers, through shared laughter, through a moment of stillness after the day's labor.

Reflection: Where might God be offering you rest that you have not yet allowed yourself to receive?

Strength That Stands with Us

"So do not fear, for I am with you; do not be dismayed, for I am your God. I will strengthen you and help you; I will uphold you with my righteous right hand." (Isaiah 41:10 NIV)

When worry tightened its grip, my father did not collapse under its weight.

His steps sometimes slowed, his voice sometimes sharpened, his breath sometimes caught—but he kept going. God upheld him not by removing fear, but by enabling him to move through it with steadiness and resolve.

Reflection: What fear do you need God to walk *with* you through, rather than take away?

Legacy as Provision and Presence

"A good person leaves an inheritance for their children's children, but a sinner's wealth is stored up for the righteous." (Proverbs 13:22 NIV)

My father's inheritance was not money.

It was vigilance, devotion, and the unwavering desire to build a life stronger than the one he came from. His worry became my awareness. His want became my drive. His life shaped the architecture of my own.

Reflection: What part of your inner world—your habits, longings, or fears—is becoming part of the legacy you are building?

LEGACY NOTES

PART II

THE GRIT TO WITHSTAND THE STORM

FOUR

The Heavy Weight of Doing What Must Be Done

*"When we are no longer able to change a situation,
we are challenged to change ourselves."*

*— Viktor Frankl (1905-1997),
Holocaust survivor and author of Man's Search for Meaning*

There comes a moment in every life when effort becomes identity, when the work a man performs shifts from something he does to something he is. My father reached that moment not through dramatic choice, but through accumulation—small victories, quiet progress, and the steady mastering of a world that had once left him trembling in uncertainty. And like many men shaped by necessity rather than ambition, he did not realize that the strength he was building would soon become the very reason more weight was placed upon him.

The early years in Canada had demanded adaptation. Later they demanded endurance.

Progress did not give my father ease. It gave him expectation. Strength, once others notice it, becomes a language. It signals capability. It signals reliability. And for a man like him, it signaled something else entirely, something unspoken but deeply ingrained. When others trusted him, he believed it was his duty to justify that trust, even at the expense of his own rest.

In the beginning, my father's progress felt like relief. He understood enough English to function without fear. He could read most of a paycheck stub without having to ask anyone for help. He moved through the factory with a quiet ease that had been unimaginable during those first months of confusion and cold. His foremen noticed. His coworkers noticed. It was as though the man who had once stood on unfamiliar ground now carried a gravity that belonged to him.

But with recognition came responsibility.

As he grew more confident, more was placed on his shoulders. It happened subtly, almost invisibly. A supervisor asked him to stay late one night because he trusted his precision. A coworker requested help on a task that required steadiness. A new hire was told to watch how he worked. None of these were burdens on their own, yet together they created a shift he could feel deeply.

Competence transformed into expectation. Reliability became obligation. His progress, instead of lightening his load, increased it.

At first, he took pride in this. Pride born not from ego, but from knowing he was becoming someone others could depend on. That mattered to him more than anything—the assurance that his efforts carried weight in the world. But the very thing that lifted him also began to press down. The more he proved himself, the more he believed he had to keep proving himself. The more he carried, the more he felt that dropping even the smallest piece would risk everything he had built so far.

Strength, for my father, did not come with applause. It came with responsibility. And responsibility came with its own kind of exhaustion.

The expectation to show up became constant. Illness felt like a luxury he could not afford. Fatigue became something he learned to ignore. Doubt became something he swallowed before it reached the surface. This was the psychology of an immigrant father—the belief that progress was fragile, temporary, easily undone. Rest felt dangerous. Hesitation felt like risk. He had no margin for missteps. No cushion if he faltered. No inheritance to fall back on.

Everything depended on him. He believed this with a conviction that ran deeper than logic. The family's bills, the future of his children, the security of a home they fought to hold, the dignity of not slipping backward—all of it rested on his ability to rise each morning and give more than he had given the day before.

And as his responsibilities expanded at work, they expanded at home as well. My brother was born, adding new joy and new pressure. Two children meant more meals, more clothing, more everything. Meanwhile, across the ocean, his own parents were aging, and though my father could not help them financially in any significant way, the worry of distance added another layer of weight he carried in silence.

Then came the mortgage. The house he had fought so hard to purchase was a triumph, yes, but also a tether. Every payment was a reminder that progress had a price. A roof meant security, but it also meant that failure no longer affected only him. It would affect all of us. Stability, once imagined as freedom, now felt like something he had to defend every day.

What once felt like hope began to feel like duty.

He no longer simply wanted to succeed—he needed to. The dream of a better life for his sons, the promise whispered to my mother on the ship, the expectations of a family counting on him across two continents—these were not aspirations. They were obligations. He carried them with reverence, but reverence has weight too, and it rests on a man long after others have stopped noticing the effort required to hold it.

Outsiders might have seen a man rising. Inside, another truth lived quietly. Progress brought pride, but it also brought pressure. Each step forward required more of him. Each gain increased the fear of loss. And each sign of strength invited more weight onto shoulders already stretched thin.

This is the story of many fathers who build new lives in unfamiliar lands. Their success becomes the reason no one asks if they are tired. Their reliability becomes the reason no one thinks they might break. Their endurance becomes the expectation that they will endure always.

My father lived inside that silent expectation. And though he carried it with dignity, even dignity can grow heavy over time.

This is where the next part of his journey begins. Not in weakness, but in the increasing weight of doing what must be done—day after day, year after year, even when strength begins to thin.

The world saw a man standing tall.

Only he knew the cost of holding himself upright.

There comes a point in a man's life when the weight he carries stops being something he picks up and becomes something he simply is. By the time my father had settled into a rhythm of work and responsibility, the expectation placed upon him from the outside had fused with an expectation he quietly placed upon himself. Strength became habit. Habit became duty. And duty soon became a burden he believed he had no right to put down.

From the outside, he appeared to be handling it all. But inside, a heavier truth lived unspoken.

My father carried within him an unspoken contract of fatherhood, a belief shaped long before he ever stepped foot in Canada. In his mind, a man's worth was measured by the stability he created for others, not by the ease he created for himself. Everything he provided had to be visible and reliable. Everything he suffered had to be hidden. In the cultural world that shaped him, men did not confess fear. They did not share burdens. They endured in silence, trusting that their effort would be understood even if their struggle remained unseen.

It was as if he believed the entire family's wellbeing rested solely on his back. And in many ways, he was right. One lost workday could throw the budget into disarray. One missed paycheck could unravel the fragile equilibrium he was fighting to maintain. Whether anyone said it or not, he felt responsible not just for the roof over our heads but for the emotional atmosphere inside the home, the future unfolding in front of his children, and the dreams my mother had carried with her from Italy.

He internalized all of it. And he spoke of none of it.

The fear of failing the people he loved was not dramatic or loud. It was quiet, persistent, and deeply rooted. A setback at work did not register in him as a simple inconvenience. It felt existential. Any hint of layoffs, any mistake during a shift, any technological change he did not yet understand made him feel as though the ground beneath us might shift. He lived with the memory of what it was like to have nothing. And that memory made every small misstep feel like the first step toward collapse.

Finances carried the same weight. A bill that was larger than expected, a car repair that arrived at the wrong moment, even a small miscalculation in the grocery budget could bring a shadow over the evening. Not because the numbers were catastrophic, but because he interpreted every surprise as a warning. A man who has lived through scarcity does not see a setback as temporary. He sees it as proof that the past is always waiting to reclaim him.

To him, provision was not only practical. It was emotional. It was identity. Every time he succeeded, he felt like he was keeping a promise. Every time something slipped beyond his control, he feared that promise was at risk.

My mother saw this long before I did. She recognized the strain in his movements, the quiet in his voice, the way his shoulders carried tension even when his hands were still. She understood the weight he refused to name. And because he would not voice his fears, she absorbed them. She held space for the heaviness he carried. She listened without needing explanation. She prayed the prayers he could not form. She became the quiet place where his burden could soften, even if only for a moment.

Her interventions were never dramatic. They were small, steady, and threaded with grace. A gentle reminder that they had survived harder seasons. A soft word when she sensed his worry tightening. A touch on his arm when silence pressed too heavily. A prayer whispered while folding laundry or stirring sauce, asking God to meet him where she could not. She understood his fear without needing to hear it. She saw the cost of his devotion even when he did not.

In these years, something profound unfolded. Provision, for my father, became more than a responsibility. It became the core of who he believed himself to be. And once a man's identity fuses with what he must produce, he begins to live in a world where failure feels personal, rest feels undeserved, and need feels like weakness.

He did not resent this burden. He accepted it as the shape of his life. But acceptance does not make weight lighter. If anything, it made it heavier.

Provision became identity. Identity became pressure. Pressure became quiet suffering.

And because he carried it silently, no one knew to help him lift it. Not because we were unwilling, but because he believed the burden was his alone.

This is where the deeper strain of his journey begins. Not in the weight itself, but in the silence that wrapped around it—a silence that made him stronger in the eyes of the world, yet more vulnerable in the quiet places no one else could see.

The burden he carried at home did not dissipate when he stepped into the factory. If anything, it intensified there, meeting him each morning in the clang of metal, the rush of machinery, and the knowledge that his body was the only tool he could not afford to have fail. Responsibility lived in our home, but the factory was where it collected its toll.

The work demanded more from him than he ever said aloud. Piece by piece, it began to take from him in ways no one could see.

The physical strain arrived first. The early mornings started before dawn, on days when cold seeped into his bones before he had even left the house. He braced himself against the wind, stepping into a world that seemed determined to test what remained of his strength. Inside the factory, the air was thick with metal dust that clung to his skin, his clothes, and sometimes even his breath. Hours of repetitive motion tightened the muscles in his back until every bend felt heavier than the last. His joints stiffened. His hands grew thick with calluses. His shoulders carried not just weight, but fatigue that settled deeper each year.

There were no sick days in his mind. Illness felt like a luxury he could not afford. A missed shift meant a smaller paycheck. A smaller paycheck meant instability. And instability—even the whisper of it—was a threat he refused to allow anywhere near our home. So, he worked through colds, through pain, through mornings when getting out of bed felt like lifting a stone that had grown heavier overnight. He believed rest was dangerous. He believed stopping, even briefly, might cause everything he had built to collapse.

The emotional strain found him next. The factory floor was not unkind, but it was unyielding. Supervisors demanded more, not less. And as his competence grew, so did the expectations placed on him. He became the man they turned to when a machine jammed, a line slowed or someone else was falling behind. His reliability, admired by others, quietly became a burden he could not set down. There was no room for mistakes. No space for hesitation. No understanding of the invisible pressure he carried.

The culture of the immigrant worker deepened the weight. The rules were simple: Say nothing. Work harder. Do not complain. Do not draw attention. Do not risk the job that keeps the family afloat. He lived those rules so consistently that they became part of his posture—shoulders forward, head slightly lowered, pace steady, breath controlled. The world he came from had taught him scarcity. The world he worked in taught him silence.

And beneath the physical and emotional strain was something quieter and harder to name. A spiritual fatigue that crept in slowly, softening the edges of the faith that had carried him across an ocean. His belief in God never wavered, but exhaustion dulled its brightness. His prayers grew shorter. They became quieter, whispered in a breath rather than spoken in sentences. Sometimes they were little more than a word—*strength, help, mercy*—uttered as he walked into the factory or sat with his head bowed at the kitchen table.

His faith remained, but the weight he bore pressed against it daily.

He was not broken. But he was being bent. Bent by responsibility that never let him stand fully upright. Bent by fear that whispered of how easily progress could unravel. Bent by the relentless demand of work that took far more from him than it ever returned.

And yet, he never considered walking away. In his mind, endurance was not a choice. It was the only path that honored the sacrifices already made. It was the cost of providing for the family he loved. It was the quiet vow he kept to himself every time he tied his boots and stepped into another day that asked everything of him and offered almost nothing in return.

Still, something was shifting inside him, almost imperceptibly. A man can carry weight for years, even decades, but every burden has a point where it begins to shape the man who bears it. The next part of his journey—the part he never spoke of and perhaps never fully understood—began in this space where strength met strain, where devotion collided with sheer exhaustion, where doing what must be done started demanding more from him than he knew he had.

And it is in that space that the next movement of his story begins.

The weight he carried at the factory did not stay there. Even though he tried—even though he believed a man's duty was to leave his burdens at the door—strain has its own way of traveling home with you. It rides in silence, in tightened muscles, in the small gestures a child notices long before he can name their meaning. And despite my father's best efforts, the life that bent him during the day began to leave faint cracks in the armor he wore at night.

There were rare moments when his composure slipped, brief but unmistakable. A sharp reply that startled the room into stillness. A drawer closed with more force than needed, the sound echoing louder than the act itself. A sigh that lingered too long, heavy enough to settle over the dinner table before anyone dared speak again. These were not tantrums or tempers; they were the quiet overflow of a man who had no other outlet. Pressure, when contained too tightly for too long, escapes through whatever seams it can find.

As a child, I did not understand these moments. I only felt them. I felt the tension in the air. I felt the shift in his posture. I felt the way my mother moved gently, as if soothing the very atmosphere. Children are sensitive to emotional weather, even without language for it. I did not know the word stress. I did not know the concept of strain. I only knew that sometimes the house felt heavier, my father seemed distant, and I wondered if something I did had caused the change.

It's a strange truth of childhood. When the world feels unsettled, a child assumes he is the cause. So, I learned to tread lightly on those evenings. I learned to listen for the tone of his footsteps, the cadence of his breathing, the small cues that revealed whether the day had taken more from him than usual. I didn't resent him for this; I simply didn't understand him yet. I mistook his quiet for disinterest, his tension for displeasure, his weariness for distance. I couldn't see the weight that bent him—only the way it changed the air around him.

Only years later, with an adult's eyes and a fuller understanding of the world he came from, did I begin to reinterpret those moments. What I once saw as sharpness, I now see as overflow — the release valve of a man who had spent an entire day holding himself together so his family would never see how close he sometimes felt to unraveling. What I once took as withdrawal, I now see as fatigue so deep it had no language. I once feared anger, I now understand it as fear—fear of failing, fear of falling behind, fear of the fragile stability he fought so hard to maintain.

Strong men are often those who cannot afford to crumble.

My father was one of them.

He carried his world on his shoulders—not because he wanted to, but because he believed no one else should have to bear the weight of it. And sometimes that weight pressed too hard. Sometimes it leaked into the room in the form of a slammed drawer or a lingering sigh. Sometimes it showed up in the silence that followed a long day. But these moments did not reveal weakness. They revealed the cost of being unshakeable in a world that never stopped shaking him.

The myth of the unshakeable man—the man who never falters, never bends, never aches — is just that. A myth. My father was steady, yes. Reliable, unquestionably. Strong in ways that shaped the very structure of our lives. But he was also human. He felt strain. He felt fear. He felt the weight of every expectation placed upon him.

And the truth that Chapter 4 begins to uncover is this.

The weight of doing what must be done does not disappear simply because a man refuses to speak of it.

It settles in his bones. It alters his breathing. It becomes part of the story he carries silently, hoping no one notices the cracks forming beneath.

Those cracks did not diminish my father. They made him real. They made him knowable.

And in time, they made him even more heroic.

Growing up, I sensed things long before I understood them. Children don't need explanations to feel the temperature of a home change; they simply absorb it. And in our house, there were evenings when the air felt heavier, as if something unseen had entered the room with my father the moment he stepped through the door. It wasn't dramatic. It wasn't loud. It was something subtler—a shift in atmosphere that told me the day had taken more from him than he had to give back.

I noticed it when the bills arrived. The way an envelope seemed to alter the room before it was even opened. The pause he took before sitting down, the quiet exhale, the way he studied the numbers with a concentration that bordered on strain. I noticed it at dinner, too—the silences that stretched just a little too long, the moments when he nodded but didn't quite respond, the faraway look that told me his mind was still wrestling with something he couldn't put down. Sometimes he lingered in the hallway after coming home, standing there as if adjusting to the shift between the world he carried and the world he was entering. Even then, before I knew words like *pressure* and *responsibility*, I knew something was heavy inside him.

And like many children growing up under the quiet gravity of an overburdened parent, I reacted instinctively. I behaved better. I became more cautious, more polite, more aware of the smallest cues. I watched his expression the way some children watch the weather, reading the signs of what the evening might hold. I learned when to speak and when silence mattered more. I learned to put my toys away before being asked, to help with small tasks, to step lightly through the house when I sensed he needed quiet.

I didn't do these things out of fear. I did them out of love—a child's early attempt to lighten a burden he could not lift. I believed, without knowing I believed it, that if I behaved well enough, contributed in small ways, brought home good grades or made myself helpful, it might ease the heaviness I saw in him. It was a tender misunderstanding—the idea that a child's goodness could soften the weight of a man's responsibility. But that misunderstanding planted seeds that would shape me for decades.

Those early instincts grew with me. What began as a child's caution evolved into hypervigilance—the need to anticipate problems before they surfaced, to scan for emotional shifts in a room, to ensure nothing I did added strain to anyone else. Wanting to help became people-pleasing. Wanting to avoid adding to his stress became an instinct to avoid disappointing anyone. Wanting to contribute became a drive to achieve—not out of ambition, but out of a deeply rooted belief that achievement created safety.

Achievement, in those early years, felt like armor.

Responsibility felt like belonging.

Excellence felt like protection—not just for me, but for the people I loved.

I did not know then that I was responding to his weight. I only knew that the heaviness in our home had a way of settling into me too. It shaped the way I moved through the world, the way I interpreted silence, and the way I braced for uncertainty even when none was present. His silence became my listening. His vigilance became my awareness. His worry became my readiness.

Looking back now, I see those years with far more clarity. My father never asked me to carry anything for him. He never burdened me intentionally. But the weight he bore—the weight of providing, of protecting, of pushing forward through exhaustion and fear—had a way of spilling into the spaces around him. And children, by nature, pick up whatever falls.

His weight began shaping my weight. His inner world began giving shape to mine.

And though I could not name it then, those early impressions would become some of the deepest contours of my character—the foundations of empathy, responsibility, and drive that would define me long before I understood their origin.

The heavy weight of doing what must be done was not his alone. Even in childhood, I was already beginning to feel its outline.

The more I began to sense the heaviness in my father, the more I realized there was another force shaping the atmosphere of our home—one that steadied us at times and shook us at others. If my father carried the weight of what must be done, my mother carried the weight of emotions that often overwhelmed her, and both realities left their imprint on our lives.

She had a gentleness that could soften an entire room. A calm voice. A warm plate of food waiting on the table. The quiet rhythm of order she created in the home. When the strain in my father tightened the air, she often loosened it with a soft word or a small act of care. Her faith was part of that gentleness—whispered prayers over laundry, quiet pleas offered while stirring a pot on the stove, a steady belief that God saw effort even when the world felt unforgiving. In those moments, she was the stabilizer, the one who kept our small family from tipping too far in one direction.

But the truth beneath that gentleness was far more complex.

My mother also carried storms inside her—storms she did not choose and often could not control. Looking back, I can see the early signs of the bipolar tendencies that shaped so many of her moods and reactions. One day our home would feel warm, predictable, and held together by her soft presence. The next, tension would rise without warning, sharp and bewildering, sending tremors through the walls and through the child I was, who never knew what might come next.

There were nights when arguments escalated into scenes no child should witness. I remember the police arriving—flashes of blue and red lights outside our window, the sound of voices too loud for the hour, the look on my father's face, not angry but weary and wounded. I remember moments when she struck out at him, not out of malice but out of an inner chaos that had no language of its own. I remember my father absorbing the blows—physical, emotional, spiritual—as if he believed that endurance was the only way to protect all of us. And in many ways, it was.

Some of my earliest memories include visiting her in psychiatric homes. Walking down hallways that smelled of antiseptic and uncertainty. Seeing her behind a door or at the end of a corridor, fragile and distant, yet still my mother. I didn't have the words then to understand mood cycles or mental illness. I only knew that she could be both the gentlest and the most unpredictable force in my world—and that both versions of her shaped me.

For a child, these contradictions became the landscape of home.

My father worked to keep the ground beneath us steady, while my mother—through no fault of her heart—sometimes shook it. Her episodes added a layer of tension that deepened the anxiety already forming inside me. The atmosphere in our home could shift without warning, so I learned early to read rooms, scan faces, and brace for changes I couldn't predict. Hypervigilance was not a trait I developed; it was a survival instinct I absorbed.

Yet even in all this, my mother was not defined by her storms. She was also the one who softened my father's edges, interpreting his silence for us, steadying him when worry hardened him, absorbing emotions he didn't know how to express. She loved with a tenderness that was unmistakable in her stable moments. She believed in God with a sincerity that gave shape to the spiritual atmosphere of our home. She protected us in ways she could, even as she struggled against forces within her that neither she nor we fully understood.

Her life added weight to my father's burden, yes—but she also helped him carry the parts of himself that he didn't know how to hold alone. Their lives were intertwined in a way that was both beautiful and deeply painful, a bond forged in shared hardship and a stubborn kind of love that survived more than it should have.

And through it all, I watched. I watched my father absorb both the demands of survival and the volatility of the woman he loved. I watched my mother shift between gentleness and chaos, trying to find equilibrium in a world that offered her few places of rest. And I watched the tension between them shape the emotional weather of our home and, unknowingly, of my own future.

As the years pressed forward, something quiet but unmistakable began to happen in my father. The responsibilities he carried no longer sat beside him; they fused with him. What began as obligation slowly became identity, until the roles he performed each day were no longer duties he fulfilled but definitions of who he believed himself to be.

He saw himself through the lens of responsibility.

Provider. Protector. Worker.

These were not tasks he completed. They were the framework through which he understood his value in the world. And once they settled into him, they left very little room for anything else.

The man he might have been — the young boy from Bella, Potenza who once ran through olive groves, who laughed easily, who might have dreamed of something beyond the horizon of his village—faded beneath the weight of necessity. The life he lived in Canada demanded so much that personal dreams became luxuries he could no longer afford. He stopped imagining a future for himself that did not revolve around his wife and children. His desires became irrelevant compared to the towering need to ensure that our lives would not mirror the scarcity that had shaped his own childhood.

It is one of the great paradoxes of immigrant fatherhood. A man crosses an ocean searching for a better life, only to give his own life to build that better life for everyone but himself. The striving becomes relentless, unquestioned, almost holy. Rest feels dangerous, indulgent, or simply impossible. A man tells himself he will slow down "one day," but one day never arrives. The hope that once fueled the journey becomes replaced by duty, obligation, and the unshakeable belief that his worth is measured by what he carries.

My father embodied that paradox without ever naming it. He pushed through pain because stopping felt like failure. He worked overtime because progress always seemed fragile. He rarely voiced a desire, because desire felt selfish when survival had once been uncertain. Sacrifice became not only his instinct but his identity—the unquestioned truth that shaped how he loved, how he lived, and how he saw himself.

And somewhere in the middle of all that effort, the man beneath the roles grew quieter.

Not gone. Not diminished.

Just hidden beneath layers of purpose that never left him.

He carried his duty the way others carry identity. It was woven into his posture, his silence, his steady presence, and the way he rose before dawn, no matter how tired he was. He did not perform duty. It was someone he had become.

As the years unfolded, my father continued moving through life with the same unwavering resolve that had carried him across an ocean. He worked. He provided. He held our home steady even when storms rose inside it. To anyone watching from a distance, he appeared unshakeable—the kind of man who absorbed more than he ever released, who endured without complaint, who met each day with a steadiness that seemed almost invincible.

But beneath that steady surface, a quiet unraveling had begun.

A deeper exhaustion settled into his bones, one that sleep could not undo. This was not merely the fatigue of long shifts or physical strain. It was the weariness of a man who had been vigilant for too many years, a man who carried responsibility like a weight strapped to his chest, a man who believed that rest was something he had to earn—and never quite did. His body kept its rhythm, but his spirit began to show the signs of a life lived with no margin for collapse.

He laughed less. His conversations thinned. His silences lengthened. Even joyful moments seemed to pass him with less vibrancy than before. He often lingered at the table after dinner, not in leisure but in depletion. The spark in his eyes—once lit by hope, duty, and sheer determination—grew softer, subdued by the strain he carried alone.

And subtly, quietly, wine began to take on a new role in our home.

Wine had always been part of our Italian table. It was cultural. Familial. A familiar comfort that connected him to the land and people he had left behind. But as the pressures mounted, wine shifted into something more than tradition. It became a softening agent, a brief cushion against the heaviness of the day. One glass held longer than usual. A second poured a bit too easily. Never enough to impair him, never enough to disrupt the home—but enough to signal that he needed something to take the edge off the life he carried.

For him, wine was not indulgence. It was release. A way to exhale the burdens he held too tightly for too long.

And yet—here lay the beautiful dichotomy—wine was also one of the purest ways he showed up for me.

Because making wine together at home was something entirely different. That ritual belonged to joy, not escape. It was where he pulled me into his world, where his hands taught mine how to crush grapes, siphon liquid, seal barrels, and test aroma. These were moments when he was present, engaged, and invested. Moments when the weight slipped from his shoulders and he simply became my father—not the provider, not the protector, not the worrier. He was just a man teaching his son an art older than both of us.

The wine we made together was never about numbing life. It was about preserving something sacred from the life he had left behind. It was heritage. It was bonding. It was the language he spoke fluently when words failed him.

I did not understand then how both truths could coexist—that wine could be the tool he leaned on when his burdens pressed too heavily, and the craft that gave us some of our most tender, connected moments. Only later would I see how both belonged to the same man. How both were expressions of his humanity.

All the while, the consequences of his unrelenting load continued to surface. He grew quieter, more inward. Fatigue settled into his face in ways I could not name as a child. And without intending to, I began to mirror him. I took on responsibilities too young. I watched the emotional weather of our home with a precision far beyond my age. I learned to adjust myself to the atmosphere, to behave better, move carefully, and anticipate needs long before they were spoken.

His weight began shaping my weight, long before I recognized its form.

These were consequences no one saw coming—not even him. They arrived gently, quietly, in the soft erosion of joy, in the lengthening of his silences, in the extra glass of wine that eased him through a long day, and in the small boy who absorbed more than anyone realized.

As the rhythms of our life settled into place, it became clear that my father was living inside a paradox.. With every responsibility he met, he grew stronger in ways that inspired me. Yet with every new burden added to his shoulders, something inside him stretched thinner, quieter, more fragile than anyone could see from the outside. Strength and strain lived side by side within him, each shaping the contours of the man he was becoming.

He carried so much silently. The weight of providing for a family in a country he was still learning to navigate. The weight of meeting expectations—his own more than anyone else's—to never falter, never fall behind, and never let the people he loved feel the uncertainty that lived inside him. And the weight of wanting more than simple survival, yearning for a life where his children could move freely without fear of scarcity's shadow. These burdens rarely showed themselves in words, but they lived in his every gesture, every sigh, every careful step he took through the world.

Yet the truth revealed itself slowly, first at the edges, then in the center of everything he did. Doing what must be done demands strength. But sustaining that strength—year after year, season after season — demands grace that no man can generate alone. Even the strongest shoulders eventually feel the gravity of what they carry. Even the most determined hearts grow weary beneath the invisible load of constant vigilance and unspoken fear.

It took me years to see that the very qualities that made him dependable also made him vulnerable to collapse. He would never name it, never confess it, never pause long enough to acknowledge its presence. But the signs were there, quiet yet insistent. A man can rise through grit, but he cannot sustain himself on grit alone.

So, the questions began to form—not in him, but in me, as I looked back on those years with adult eyes.

Where does a man turn when duty exceeds his strength?

What happens when the weight he carries begins to shape the way he bends—or breaks?

And how does a life built on relentless responsibility begin to reckon with the limits of the human heart?

These questions form the next terrain of his becoming—the shadowed landscape of Chapter 5.

The heavy weight he carried so faithfully would soon reveal the limits of even the strongest man's endurance—and the cost of a life lived without room to rest.

SACRED WAYPOINTS

When Strength Turns into Expectation

My father's competence—slowly earned through hardship—became the very reason more weight was placed upon him. What began as progress transformed into pressure.

Reflection: Where in your life has someone mistaken your strength for limitless capacity?

Where have you allowed expectation to replace intentional choice?

Invitation: Name one place where you need permission to be human rather than heroic.

The Silent Contract of Provision

My father believed the family's stability rested solely on him. His worth became tethered to what he could provide, not who he was.

Reflection: Have you ever tied your identity to your productivity? What unspoken contracts have you inherited—or created?

Practice: Write down one burden you carry that was never meant to be your identity.

The Cost of Being the Steady One

My father helped at work because others depended on him. He endured at home because he believed collapsing was not an option. His strength became a language others relied on but rarely questioned.

Reflection: Who assumes you will always hold the line? Who have you taught—intentionally or not—to depend on your steadiness?

Invitation: Share with someone you trust one place where you feel stretched thin.

The Weight That Cannot Be Spoken

My father's heaviest burdens were the ones he never named. Fear of failure. Fear of slipping backward. Fear that one misstep could unravel all he had built.

Reflection: What fears do you carry quietly because naming them feels like weakness? Which of them lose power when spoken aloud?

Practice: Take ten minutes and write down the fear beneath the fear—the one that drives the others.

The Blend of Strength and Strain

The outside world saw a man standing tall. Only my father knew the cost of holding himself upright. His strain showed in small moments: a lingering sigh, a slammed drawer, the soft erosion of joy.

Reflection: What subtle signs reveal that you are carrying more weight than you let on?

What do your "cracks" look like—and what are they trying to tell you?

Invitation: Allow yourself to pause long enough to feel what you normally outrun.

When Duty Becomes Identity

Over time, what my father did became who he was. Provider. Protector. Worker. He never questioned the burden, because he believed the burden was the measure of a good man.

Reflection: Where has duty blurred into identity in your own life? What dreams went quiet because responsibility spoke louder?

Practice: Revisit one desire you set aside in the name of duty. Ask whether it still deserves a place in your life.

The Unseen Inheritance

My father's weight shaped my weight. His vigilance became my awareness. His worry became my readiness. His striving became my drive.

Reflection: What parts of your inner life were formed by watching someone carry more than they could say? Which of those inheritances have served you—and which have silently exhausted you?

Invitation: Name one inherited burden you are ready to transform rather than transmit.

When Effort Outpaces Grace

A man can rise through grit, but grit alone cannot sustain him. My father lived in the tension between the strength he showed and the grace he rarely received.

Reflection: Where are you trying to meet impossible expectations with your own effort? Where do you need grace—from yourself, from others, or from God?

Practice: Offer yourself one act of grace today that you normally deny.

ANCHORS OF THE WORD

Strength in the Strain

"So do not fear, for I am with you; do not be dismayed, for I am your God. I will strengthen you and help you; I will uphold you with my righteous right hand." (Isaiah 41:10 NIV)

The world demanded from my father work that often exceeded his strength. Yet he kept going— believing he had no choice. This verse speaks into the very places where human endurance begins to thin. God does not ask us to carry loads alone; He upholds the weary even when they cannot feel the support.

Reflection: Where in your life are you mistaking endurance for isolation?

The Weight Not Meant for Your Shoulders

"Cast your cares on the LORD and he will sustain you; he will never let the righteous be shaken." (Psalm 55:22 NIV)

My father believed every burden was his to bear—the bills, the future, the fears, the expectations. Scripture offers a different model. Burdens are to be shared, not hidden; weight transferred, not hoarded. God sustains what men cannot.

Reflection: What burden do you continue to carry because you believe no one else should?

Rest for the Overworked

"Come to me, all you who are weary and burdened, and I will give you rest." (Matthew 11:28 NIV)

My father worked through pain, illness, exhaustion—convinced rest was dangerous. Jesus names rest as sacred, not optional. The invitation is not to stop working, but to stop believing that work holds the world together.

Reflection: Where have you denied yourself rest because you fear what will happen if you stop?

The Call to Shared Loads

"Carry each other's burdens, and in this way you will fulfill the law of Christ." (Galatians 6:2 NIV)

My father never believed his weight was meant to be shared, yet Scripture frames burden-bearing as communal. In the kingdom of God, strength is not proven by carrying alone, but by allowing others to carry with you.

Reflection: Who has God placed around you to help lift what you have been holding in silence?

Renewal Beneath Exhaustion

"Therefore we do not lose heart. Though outwardly we are wasting away, yet inwardly we are being renewed day by day." (2 Corinthians 4:16 NIV)

The work my father performed took more from his body than it ever returned. Yet even in exhaustion, God offers renewal that reaches deeper than muscle or bone—renewal of spirit, perspective, hope, and identity.

Reflection: Where do you need inner renewal more than external relief?

Strength Beyond Human Limits

"My flesh and my heart may fail, but God is the strength of my heart and my portion forever." (Psalm 73:26 NIV)

This verse speaks directly into the core truth of the chapter. Even strong men bend; even steady men tire; even devoted men come to the end of themselves. God's strength meets us at the precise point where our own runs out.

Reflection: What part of your strength is beginning to thin—and what would it look like to let God meet you there?

Guidance When the Path Is Heavy

"Trust in the LORD with all your heart and lean not on your own understanding; in all your ways submit to him, and he will make your paths straight." (Proverbs 3:5-6 NIV)

My father walked a path shaped not by option but by obligation. This proverb reframes duty—not as something carried alone, but as something directed by God when we release our white-knuckled grip on control.

Reflection: Where are you leaning on your own understanding instead of God's direction?

Strength for the Weary Hands

"Therefore, strengthen your feeble arms and weak knees." (Hebrews 12:12 NIV)

This is not a reprimand but a compassion-filled charge—God sees the tired arms of the ones who hold families together. He names them. He strengthens them. He dignifies the fatigue. He doesn't dismiss it.

Reflection: What part of your life feels like tired hands holding up more than they were designed for?

LEGACY NOTES

FIVE

How Sacrifice and Duty Forged His Purpose

"Action springs not from thought, but from a readiness for responsibility."

— Dietrich Bonhoeffer (1906-1945), author of The Cost of Discipleship

---

There are moments in a man's life when responsibility stops feeling like weight and begins to feel like meaning. My father never announced such a turning point, and perhaps he never realized it fully himself. But somewhere between the long shifts at the factory, the early mornings that arrived too soon, and the constant vigilance of providing for a family in a new world, the burden he carried began to transform. What once bent him became the very thing that steadied him. What once felt heavy began to feel necessary. And what once seemed imposed on him slowly became the place where he discovered who he was.

In the early years, duty pressed against him like a weight he had no choice but to shoulder. Every bill, every shift, every unexpected expense carried the anxiety of someone who had climbed out of scarcity and feared falling back into it. But over time, something subtle began to change. The pressure did not disappear, but the meaning beneath it deepened. Instead of asking, "Why must this be mine to carry", he began moving through the world with a quiet conviction that whispered, "Of course it is mine."

He no longer saw responsibility as something placed upon him. He saw it as something he was meant to lift.

This evolution did not arrive in dramatic fashion; it surfaced in small, unspoken shifts. Sacrifice, which had once felt like necessity, began to shape his identity. He found meaning not in ease—which was rarely available—but in endurance. Each day became an act of devotion, a way of anchoring himself to something greater than the circumstances that had once threatened him. His purpose emerged not in what the world offered him, but in what he offered back to it.

I saw this change most clearly in the quiet moments, the ones too ordinary for anyone else to notice. The nights he accepted overtime without hesitation, not because he was eager to work more hours, but because he believed it was the right thing to do. The mornings when exhaustion clung to him but he rose before dawn anyway, his movements steady and unfaltering, guided by something deeper than mere obligation. The countless times he repaired something around the house long after his body asked him to rest, doing it with a patience that spoke of devotion rather than duty.

He never spoke of these acts as sacrifice. He simply lived them.

And in those ordinary acts—the tightening of a bolt, the packing of a lunch pail, the slipping out the door before the rest of us woke — I began to see how purpose takes shape in a man. Not through declarations, but through choices. Not through recognition, but through resolve. His responsibilities did not lighten as the years passed; if anything, they grew heavier. But his spirit toward them changed. Instead of shrinking beneath the load, he expanded within it.

Others depended on him—at home, at work, across the ocean in Italy—and in their dependence, he found a deeper sense of who he was becoming. Duty was no longer simply what he carried. It became the place where his strength was revealed, the place where he understood himself most clearly.

Looking back, I realize this was the season when my father's story crossed an invisible threshold. Sacrifice, once a burden he bore, became the fire that forged his purpose. And in that fire, something inside him began to harden, sharpen, and shine.

Duty was reshaping him from the outside in. Sacrifice was shaping him from the inside out. And together, they were forming the man he would become.

But purpose, once awakened, often comes with a cost—and for my father, that cost was himself.

He did not perform sacrifice in grand gestures. It lived quietly in the fabric of his days, the steady current beneath everything he did. There was no applause for it, no language to define it, no acknowledgment of what it demanded. There was only the persistent surrender of personal wants so that the people he loved could step into a life he once believed was out of reach.

He gave up small pieces of himself long before anyone noticed. Hobbies that once brought him joy faded from his routine, not because he no longer loved them, but because they felt too indulgent for a man carrying the weight he carried. He set aside rest with the thought that he would get to it "later," though later rarely appeared. Dreams he once might have held—vague, tender, fragile things—were quietly postponed into a future he doubted he would ever claim for himself.

Even the simplest desires became negotiable. He would stand in a store, hands grazing a new shirt or tool, then put it back as if wanting something for himself was an error in judgment. His boots were always worn past comfort. His coat, even in bitter winters, remained the same year after year. It wasn't humility. It wasn't self-denial for show. It was conviction—the belief that others were more deserving.

And every choice he made reflected that belief. He worked holidays because overtime meant a little more certainty for the family. While others shared slow mornings and warm gatherings, he walked out into the cold before dawn, convinced that the extra pay mattered more than rest. At home, he didn't fix everything himself—not in the way some fathers did—but he carried the responsibility for ensuring things were taken care of. He relied on his brothers, who came over with tools and know-how, and later on me, the one who made the calls, found the right people, and coordinated what needed fixing. He didn't ask for much; he simply made sure that whatever was broken didn't stay that way for long. It wasn't pride that kept him from hiring help. It was the quiet conviction that our family could handle things together, that solving the problem was part of the duty he carried—even if he wasn't the one turning the wrench.

Even his health became part of what he negotiated away. He endured coughs, swelling, persistent aches with a stubbornness that seemed unbreakable. "I'm fine" became his shield, the phrase he used to protect the family budget as much as to protect us from worry. Only later did I understand the quiet danger in those words—the way they masked pain he believed he had no right to treat.

Sacrifice, for him, was not a dramatic act. It was the daily dying to self that shaped his entire existence.

In the world he came from, this was not unusual. A man's life was measured by what he provided for others, not by what he kept for himself. Comfort was secondary. Desire was negotiable. Duty was absolute. Immigrant fathers, especially, inherit an ethic in which sacrifice becomes less of a choice and more of a calling—a kind of inherited theology passed down silently through generations.

My father lived inside that understanding without ever naming it. He believed that his life existed to build something better for the people he loved, even if it meant setting aside the parts of himself that once longed for more. His sacrifices were not dramatic or heroic. They were steady, persistent, uncelebrated—the kind that accumulate slowly until they become indistinguishable from the man himself.

Looking back now, I realize something essential. My father did not speak the language of self-care. He spoke the language of sacrifice.

Not because he lacked desires or dreams, but because he believed love expressed itself most truthfully in what a man gives up, not in what he keeps.

And yet, even in a life shaped by surrender, there was one place where he allowed himself a quiet kind of joy—his garden. Working the soil behind our home was his small refuge, his proud escape from the factory floor, and his living tie to the land he had left behind in Italy. He planted tomatoes, peppers, herbs, and grapevines with the same reverence his own father once did. And we appreciated that time with him — not because the work was easy, but because it felt like the truest part of who he was. In the garden, his shoulders lowered, his breath softened, and the man who carried so much finally looked at peace.

Even there, though, sacrifice lived beneath the surface. The garden was not indulgence; it was continuity. It was memory. It was hope rooted in earth. It reminded him of where he came from and why he worked so relentlessly to create something better for us.

And in all those quiet, steady dyings—the small, daily surrenders he never named—his purpose was being forged. Sacrifice shaped him in ways neither of us understood then, preparing him for a life where meaning would come not from what he gained, but from what he gave.

The deeper his purpose grew, the more it revealed itself not in grand gestures, but in the quiet, unseen work that held our family together. What looked ordinary from the outside was, in truth, a kind of heroism that rarely announces itself.

My father's sacrifices were rarely dramatic. They were humble and unremarkable to anyone who did not know how much they cost him. He lived his life in invisible efforts—the small acts of perseverance that stitched stability into our days. He patched shoes long past their lifespan, repairing the soles with glue and pressure as if trying to press hope back into worn leather.

He tried to repair whatever broke in the house, even when the work frustrated him, even when calling someone else would have been easier. Some nights, after we were all asleep, he sat alone at the kitchen table with bills spread out in front of him, pencil in hand, balancing budgets with the concentration of a man performing quiet triage.

None of these acts drew attention. There were no words of praise, no applause, no acknowledgment beyond a simple "Thank you" or the silent relief of something working again. He didn't expect recognition. In truth, he might not have known what to do with it. In his world, work was not something to be celebrated. It was something to be continued. You finished a task, and you moved on to the next. You provided, and then you provided again.

As a child, I saw everything and understood very little. I noticed the exhaustion in his face, the way he rubbed his temples after reading a bill, the way he held a repaired shoe with both pride and resignation. But I did not grasp the magnitude of what he was doing. To me, he was simply my father—steady, capable, always rising to meet whatever the day demanded. I did not yet understand that behind each small action was intention, sacrifice, and a steady devotion that expected nothing in return.

I witnessed the effects without seeing the heroism. I saw the repairs, not the cost. The stability, not the strain. The results, not the quiet surrender behind them.

Only later—much later—did I come to understand that some men save their families in ways no one writes stories about. They do not stand on rooftops or battle visible storms. They labor in silence. They give their strength in increments. They hide their fatigue behind steadiness because they believe their families deserve the best parts of them, even when those parts are running thin.

My father was one of those men.

His sacrifices were small in size but vast in impact. And though no one outside our home would have noticed them, those quiet acts were the foundation on which our lives were built. His heroism lived in the spaces most people overlook—in patched shoes, late-night furnace tinkering when the house grew cold, and whispered calculations over kitchen tables. And it was there, in the unnoticed corners of ordinary days, that sacrifice shaped him into something greater than he ever claimed to be.

It was greatness without proclamation—and purpose forged in the quiet fire of responsibility.

The more I look back on those years, the more I see that sacrifice did more than shape his days—it shaped his convictions. What he endured externally began to crystallize internally, forming the moral code by which he lived and by which he quietly expected the rest of us to live as well.

For my father, duty was not merely something he performed. It was the lens through which he understood right and wrong. A man, in his view, kept his word even when it cost him. A father provided first and rested second. A promise—whether spoken aloud or silently made—was sacred. These were not lessons he sat us down to explain. They were truths we learned by watching the way he moved through the world, truths carved into him long before we were born.

Hardship had forged these beliefs. When you grow up in a place where survival depends on integrity, the idea of cutting corners feels like betrayal. When food has been scarce and work uncertain, diligence becomes a moral imperative, not a preference. For him, hard work wasn't simply a virtue. It was a safeguard—a way of keeping instability at bay. It was the discipline that kept fear from gaining ground.

His intolerance for waste came from the same well. Leftovers were never thrown out. Lights were never left on in an empty room. Tools were cleaned, dried, and returned properly because replacing them cost money we did not have. Nothing was taken for granted. Everything held value because everything had once required sacrifice to obtain. Even now, I can see him closing the fridge quickly to preserve the cold, eyeing the thermostat as though every degree was a decision with consequences.

It wasn't stinginess. It was reverence—for resources, for effort, for the thin line between enough and not enough.

There were moments when this moral code felt rigid, even harsh. But it was the framework that allowed him to keep going, the structure that strengthened him when circumstances around him threatened to buckle. It gave him clarity in a world that had once felt unpredictable. It offered stability when life had offered very little of it.

I didn't understand then—but see so clearly now—that his sacrifices did more than sustain our home. They shaped the ethics that ruled it. They taught us not to wait to feel responsibility; they taught us to choose it. We learned that character is built not in grand gestures but in the quiet, consistent honoring of what has been entrusted to you.

And they taught me something else, that I would not grasp until much later in life.

The moral code that guided him wasn't simply inherited. It was forged—hammered into shape by years of toil, scarcity, and resolve—and it became the compass that would direct everything he did next.

From that compass, another part of his story begins to take form, one in which the weight of duty grows heavier and the sacrifices he once embraced begin to demand more than even he expected.

The convictions that shaped my father's life made him steadfast, but they also came with a quiet cost—a cost he rarely acknowledged, even to himself. Duty had become the structure of his days, but beneath that structure lived desires he learned to suppress to keep the family afloat.

There were parts of himself he set aside so early that I'm not sure he ever fully reclaimed them. His own needs slipped to the bottom of every list. His personal dreams were folded away like clothes that no longer fit. Even portions of his personality—the humor, the ease, the spontaneity he must have known as a young man in Italy—were muted by the unrelenting cadence of responsibility. He carried so much for us that there was little space left for the man he might have become had life asked less of him.

Yet despite how deeply he buried those longings, they surfaced at the edges in ways I recognize now with a tenderness that aches.

Sometimes that longing surfaced when he tended the small garden behind our home—his patch of earth in a land that often felt foreign. Working the soil steadied him, grounding him in memories of the countryside he had left behind. Yet even as he knelt among tomato plants and grapevines, there was a quiet yearning in him for something larger, something closer to the expanses he once worked as a boy in Bella. He never spoke of it directly, but the desire lived in the way he paused over the soil, as if listening for echoes of a world he still carried inside him.

Other times it appeared in the shift of his voice when he talked about Italy—the slower rhythms of village life, the communal meals, the long evenings outdoors when work ended with laughter instead of exhaustion. These weren't idle reminiscences or romanticized stories. They were glimpses into a version of himself that felt fuller, more whole, less burdened by the relentless demands of survival. They revealed a man who missed not only the land he left, but the parts of himself that had lived freely upon it.

And there were quieter moments still—moments when he watched another man rest and, for a breath, seemed to envy what it might feel like to stop moving, to let the world carry itself for a while. The longing was never spoken, but it lived in the way his shoulders sagged when he thought no one was looking, in the way his gaze lingered on someone laughing freely, in the way he paused at gardens or open fields as if remembering a version of himself he had left behind.

Now I understand that none of this meant he regretted the life he built. He took immense pride in providing for us, in keeping his promise to give his children a better beginning than the one he received. But pride and sorrow can coexist. Fulfillment does not erase fatigue. A man can accept the weight he carries and still grieve the parts of himself he set down to lift it.

His life became a quiet contradiction—a blend of deep satisfaction and quiet ache. He was proud of the stability he created, yet there were days when the cost of that stability etched itself into his expression. He found joy in seeing us thrive, yet there were traces of loss in the spaces where his own desires once lived. Duty shaped him, sustained him, and gave his life meaning—yet it also narrowed the parts of himself that had once dreamed freely.

A man can give everything and still mourn what he gave up.

And this tension—between who he needed to be and who he longed to be— became one of the defining contours of his journey, shaping him in ways that were both visible and invisible. It deepened the sacrifices he made and carved out the emotional landscape our family lived in, leaving marks that time would reveal slowly, almost tenderly.

By the time I was old enough to understand the shape of my father's sacrifices, their imprint was already stamped onto my life in ways I hadn't yet recognized. His way of moving through the world — the steadiness, the vigilance, the quiet surrender of self for the sake of others—had become the map I followed long before I realized I was tracing his lines.

I inherited his drive almost without noticing it. Hard work felt natural to me, not because anyone demanded it, but because I had watched him build every inch of our life through effort that never paused. Achievement became my version of safety—a way to keep the world steady, to ensure I would never become a burden, to create the kind of security he chased for us year after year. I learned early on that accomplishment wasn't about applause; it was about protection.

I inherited his vigilance as well. Long before I had language for it, I found myself anticipating problems, scanning for shifts in atmosphere, stepping in to carry responsibilities before anyone thought to ask. Some of this was survival in a home shaped by both my father's burdens and my mother's storms. But I learned much of it from watching him—the way he moved through life with a readiness that bordered on instinct. He taught me, without speaking, that preparedness was a form of love.

And I inherited his ethic of provision, the deep-seated belief that caring for others is not a task but a calling. Filling gaps before they widen. Easing burdens before they are named. Offering steadiness even when I felt unsteady myself. In many ways, I lived out the same truth that guided him. Protecting the people you love is sacred work. It is the quiet vow you renew each day, sometimes without even realizing you're making it.

It was only in adulthood—only after carrying my own responsibilities, facing my own uncertainties, and building a life shaped by both effort and fear—that I began to reinterpret his sacrifices with fuller clarity. What I once saw as rigidity, I now recognize as devotion. What I once interpreted as silence, I now understand as self-denial offered in the name of love. What I once mistook for distance was often the exhaustion of a man giving more than he had and refusing to lay any part of that weight on his children.

With time, I began to see the moral arc behind his decisions. He wasn't simply surviving; he was shaping a world for us. He wasn't forfeiting dreams; he was investing them in our future. His life was not defined by what he lost, but by what he gave—and what he gave became the foundation of everything I would later pursue.

His sacrifice built our life. And, in ways I am still discovering, it built my purpose too.

The deeper I looked into my father's life, the clearer it became that his sacrifices were not only acts of duty—they were acts of faith. What he carried on his shoulders each day did not simply weigh him down; somehow, it also lifted him, giving shape to a purpose he rarely spoke of but always lived.

My father never used grand language about calling or mission. He did not frame his choices in theological terms or articulate a philosophy of suffering. But in the quiet repetition of his days, in the constancy of his labor, in the small devotions woven into ordinary moments, he revealed a truth he might not have fully understood himself.

He saw his work as offering, not obligation. Each early morning was a kind of prayer. Each long shift a form of devotion. Each sacrifice a silent way of saying, "This is how I love. This is how I serve."

Duty, for him, was not separate from faith—it was the expression of it.

Prayer became his fuel. Not elaborate or poetic prayers, but the brief, breath-length supplications uttered on the walk to work, or murmured before the bills were opened, or whispered into the quiet of a darkened bedroom. He did not study Scripture academically; he leaned on it. It was a familiar anchor that kept him steady when the world around him felt sharp and shifting. And faith—quiet, unadorned, resilient—stood beside him in the places where his strength alone was not enough.

He lived a kind of theology shaped not by sermons but by survival—a belief that God was found in effort, not ease; in endurance, not escape. For him, holiness lived not in the soft moments, but in the determined ones. He trusted that meaning could be forged through hardship, that purpose was discovered not in what a man received but in what a man gave.

This understanding did not soften his sacrifices; it sanctified them. It gave weight dignity. It gave burden purpose. It allowed him to carry more than most men could, not because he was stronger, but because he believed that nothing given in love was truly lost.

Looking back, I see that sacrifice did not drain his purpose — it defined it. It shaped the man he became. It shaped the home he built.

And in ways neither of us recognized then, it shaped the faith that would one day take root in me as well.

Sacrifice gave my father purpose, but purpose does not make a man invincible. Even the strongest convictions cannot shield a body—or a spirit—from the slow wear of a life spent carrying more than it ever puts down.

Over time, the toll began to reveal itself, not in dramatic moments, but in small, accumulating signs that only hindsight allows me to fully understand. His body bore the first evidence. Aches settled into him and never fully left, becoming familiar companions in his joints and muscles. His knees stiffened in the mornings, requiring a slow, steady rise before they agreed to hold him. His back, shaped by years of repetitive labor and unrelenting strain, carried a curve that told the story long before words ever did. And slowly, almost imperceptibly at first, his waistline began to thicken—not from indulgence, but from the quiet accumulation of fatigue, stress, and a life lived with little time for tending to himself. What some might dismiss as simple weight gain was, in truth, another kind of scar. It was the body's response to years of carrying burdens heavier than any machine part he lifted at the factory.

These were not injuries; they were the physical punctuation marks of a life lived in service of others—signs etched into him by responsibility, endurance, and the sacrifices he made long before anyone noticed the cost.

But the wear did not stop with the body. His spirit began to thin in ways that were quiet, almost invisible. Joy, once present in bursts of laughter or small celebrations, appeared less often. Even happiness seemed to exhaust him. Rest, for him, became something he could not fully enter. The pressure he carried hollowed out his ability to relax, as if any moment of ease might invite risk or unravel the fragile progress he had fought to build.

There were signs—subtle, soft, and largely overlooked—that hinted at the cost he was paying. He began drifting into longer silences. Not the comfortable quiet of a man at peace, but the heavy quiet of someone retreating inward. His eyes sometimes seemed far away, even when he sat right beside us. He moved through routines with mechanical steadiness, masking exhaustion beneath habit. And because this way of living had become normal to him, it became normal to us. Children adapt to the atmosphere they breathe. We saw diligence, not depletion. Consistency, not collapse. We believed his endurance meant he was fine, when in truth it meant he had stopped imagining any other way to live.

It is only now, looking back with the fuller gaze of adulthood, that I understand how much weight he carried beneath the surface—and how steadily that weight eroded parts of him he never named. Purpose forged by sacrifice is powerful, but even iron grows thin when heat is constant.

His body felt it first. His spirit felt it next.

And soon, the cost of a lifetime spent doing what must be done would reveal itself in ways none of us were prepared to see.

And as these strains accumulated—in his body, in his spirit, in the quiet corners of his life—something deeper began to take shape, something I could sense even as a child without fully understanding its contours.

Sacrifice, for my father, was never merely what he did. Over time, it became who he was. It gave him identity — the steady provider, the unshakeable anchor, the man who held the center when everything around him threatened to shift. It gave him meaning—a way to understand his place in a world that had once felt too foreign to claim. And above all, it gave him a way to express love when words did not come easily. Every early morning, every long shift, every quiet surrender of his own desires was an offering laid at the feet of the family he cherished.

But sacrifice does not give without taking.

What it offered in purpose, it claimed back in rest.

What it built in strength, it quietly carved out in softness.

What it anchored in security, it taxed in hidden places no one else could see.

Parts of himself—the dreamer, the boy from Italy with wind in his hair, the man who once believed joy could be simple—were slowly set aside, piece by piece. Not discarded, but buried beneath duty for so long that he no longer reached for them. And all the while, the margin he needed for collapse grew smaller, thinner, and more fragile, even as the world kept asking for more.

This is the paradox of his becoming.

He became the man he was meant to be—solid, dependable, wise in the ways that matter—even as that very becoming required more of him than anyone, including himself, fully realized. His purpose was forged in sacrifice, and that sacrifice shaped him into someone remarkable. But the fire that forged him also heated the metal of his life to the point where it could bend.

There are limits even to the strongest shoulders. The body can carry only so much. The spirit can stretch only so far.

And even the purest purpose, when hammered daily on the anvil of responsibility, leaves its burn marks.

As I look back, I see it clearly now—the gradual shrinking of what he had left to give, the wear hidden beneath familiar patterns, the exhaustion settling deeper even as he kept moving. He would never have spoken of it, never named its cost, and never admitted how close he sometimes stood to collapse.

But the signs were there, quiet yet unmistakable. And they lead us to the next chapter of his story.

SACRED WAYPOINTS

When Burden Turns into Calling

There came a point when the weight my father carried no longer felt like something placed upon him, but something he was meant to lift. Duty stopped being pressure and began becoming purpose, reshaping him quietly from within.

- Where in your life has responsibility shifted from burden to calling?
- Can you name a moment when you stopped resisting a role and began embracing it?

Sit with this truth: Purpose often emerges from the very places we once tried to escape.

The Quiet Cost of Love

My father gave himself away in small, steady pieces—unnoticed sacrifices that stitched stability into our lives. He never called it love, but that is exactly what it was.

- What quiet sacrifices have you made that no one but God sees?
- What parts of yourself have you set aside so others could stand more securely?

Hold this gently: Hidden sacrifice is often the purest form of love.

Identity Shaped by Surrender

Over time, sacrifice didn't just guide what my father did—it shaped who he believed himself to be. He became the man who provided, protected, endured—even when it took more from him than he could name.

- Which identities in your life were formed by necessity before they became choice?
- Are there roles you carry that reveal both your strength and your sorrow?

Reflect on this: Identity formed in sacrifice can reveal purpose—but it can also conceal longing.

The Longings Beneath Duty

Though my father rarely spoke of desire, it lived beneath the surface—in the way he tended the soil, in the softness of his voice when remembering Italy, in the brief glances toward a life where he might have rested.

- What desires in you remain buried beneath what must be done?
- Where does longing still rise, even in a life shaped by responsibility?

Let this sink in: A man can be faithful to his duty and still ache for what he left behind.

The Legacy Sacrifice Leaves in Its Wake

My father's sacrifices did more than sustain us—they shaped me. His vigilance became my vigilance. His drive became my drive. His ethic of provision became the map I followed long before I knew I was tracing his steps.

- What legacies of sacrifice live quietly in you today?
- How have the offerings of those who came before you shaped your becoming?

Listen closely: Some inheritances arrive not through words, but through the weight a parent once carried.

Purpose Forged in Fire

The sacrifices that strengthened my father also thinned him—body, spirit, joy. Purpose gave him meaning, but it also asked for more than anyone realized.

- Where has purpose strengthened you while also stretching you thin?
- What signs of wear do you carry from a life lived faithfully under responsibility?

Remember this: Even iron grows thin when the heat never lets up.

ANCHORS OF THE WORD

Purpose Hidden in Ordinary Work

"Whatever you do, work at it with all your heart, as working for the Lord, not for human masters." (Colossians 3:23 NIV)

My father didn't talk about calling or purpose. He simply rose each day and worked with a steadfastness that spoke louder than words. What looked like burden from the outside was, in truth, the quiet place where he discovered who he was becoming. Scripture reminds us that meaning is not found in the size of the task but in the spirit with which it is offered.

Reflection: Where might God be inviting you to see purpose in work you've labeled only as duty?

The Daily Offering of a Life Given Away

"Therefore, I urge you, brothers and sisters, in view of God's mercy, to offer your bodies as a living sacrifice, holy and pleasing to God— this is your true and proper worship" (Romans 12:1 NIV)

Sacrifice for my father was not dramatic. It lived in the unnoticed corners of his days—the early mornings, the postponed desires, the steady giving of himself for the sake of others. He would never have called it worship, yet Scripture suggests it was exactly that. Holiness sometimes looks like endurance, offered quietly in love.

Reflection: What part of your daily life might God see as worship, even if you have never named it that?

Purpose Forged in Pressure

"This third I will put into the fire; I will refine them like silver and test them like gold. They will call on my name and I will answer them; I will say, 'They are my people,' and they will say, 'The LORD is our God.'" (Zechariah 13:9 NIV)

The pressures that weighed on my father did not just exhaust him; they shaped him. The strain that once bent him became the place where resolve, character, and identity were formed. Refining is rarely gentle, yet it reveals strength that would otherwise remain hidden.

Reflection: What current pressure might be refining something in you rather than defeating you?

Strength Found in Quiet Trust

"...in quietness and trust shall be your strength, ..." (Isaiah 30:15 NIV)

My father rarely spoke of faith, but he lived a version of it that showed itself in perseverance—the kind carried silently, without applause. Scripture reminds us that strength is not always loud or visible; it is often found in the quiet resolve to keep going when no one is watching.

Reflection: Where might God be inviting you to cultivate strength through quiet trust rather than effort?

Love Measured in What One Gives Up

"Greater love has no one than this: to lay down one's life for one's friends." (John 15:13 NIV)

My father laid down his life in increments—hours, dreams, comforts, and parts of himself he quietly surrendered so we could rise. His love was rarely expressed in words, but it was unmistakable in sacrifice. Scripture reframes such surrender not as loss, but as the highest expression of love.

Reflection: What form might sacrificial love be taking in your life right now?

The Harvest of Steady Perseverance

"Let us not become weary in doing good, for at the proper time we will reap a harvest if we do not give up." (Galatians 6:9 NIV)

My father's entire life was built on steady perseverance—showing up, providing, pushing forward even when bone-tired. He rarely saw the harvest of his efforts in the moment, but his faithfulness built the foundation for our lives. Scripture reminds us that unseen work is not forgotten; it is seed planted for a future we may never fully witness.

Reflection: Where are you being asked to remain faithful, even though the harvest feels far away?

LEGACY NOTES

SIX

What the Years Took and What They Gave in Return

"Out of suffering have emerged the strongest souls."

— Kahlil Gibran (1883-1931),
Lebanese-American poet, philosopher, artist and author of The Prophet

---

There comes a point in a man's life when strength no longer announces itself—it simply tries to keep pace with the passing years. By the time my father entered the long middle stretch of his working life, the sacrifices that had once forged his purpose began to show their quiet cost. It didn't happen in a single moment or through any dramatic change. It happened the way weather shapes stone—gradually, imperceptibly, and with a persistence nothing seems able to resist.

Time, for my father, did not strike like a blow. It brushed against him in steady increments, soft enough to overlook, firm enough to leave a mark.

The first signs were subtle, the kind only hindsight allows you to recognize. His steps lost a measure of their quickness, replaced by something more measured, more deliberate. His laughter—once effortless in rare but bright flashes—grew quieter, as though each chuckle had to be rationed. Even his silences shifted. They were no longer the silences of a man gathering strength for the day, but the silences of someone conserving it.

Responsibility had shaped him for so long that he seemed built around it. But decades of carrying what could never be set down began to leave their imprint. Lines deepened across his face, a heaviness settled behind his eyes that no sleep could fully lift, and even his posture started telling truths he kept out of his words.

Factory work, with its repetition and relentlessness, had molded his body in ways no one else could see. The constant lifting, bending, and bracing carved a stiffness into his joints that made cold mornings feel harsher than before. His hands—once quick and precise—bore a slight tremor at the end of a long shift, the kind he tried to hide by rubbing them together as though warming them from the outside could ease the wear growing on the inside.

But the weight he carried inside the home was often heavier than anything the factory demanded. My mother's bipolar struggles—unpredictable, exhausting, sometimes erupting into storms that shook the entire house— became a burden he absorbed with a mix of vigilance and quiet grief. The medications prescribed over the years steadied her at times but never freed her. They only softened the edges of an illness that never truly receded.

As the years passed, her health began to change in ways that were slow at first and then unmistakable. The diagnosis was scleroderma—a progressive autoimmune disease that hardens connective tissue and gradually limits the body's ability to function as it once had. What began as tightness in her skin and stiffness in her hands advanced into something far more invasive, eventually affecting her joints, her strength, and even her ability to swallow. As the disease progressed, my father's role shifted again. Responsibility no longer meant simply providing; it meant guarding, tending, soothing, and advocating. He watched the woman he loved grow smaller inside a body that no longer obeyed her will. He never complained, but the toll marked him—the nights he stayed awake when her breathing was labored, the way he remained within arm's reach of her chair, and the quiet fear that settled behind his eyes even when his expression stayed steady.

Their marriage lasted more than fifty years, and when she passed, the weight that had once felt crushing took on a different form. It became silence. It became absence. It became the ache of a man who had spent his entire life carrying someone—only to find his arms suddenly empty. Loneliness settled into him not as despair, but as a quiet, persistent companion. The assisted-living facility where they spent their later years together felt larger around him, the evenings longer, the air heavier. Responsibility had always given him direction. Now, without her, it also revealed the depth of what he had lost.

Perhaps the most revealing change showed itself in what he stopped expecting. In his younger years, my father moved through life with a forward lean—driven by hope, duty, and the belief that steady effort would widen the future. As he aged, that posture gradually eased. He still planned and provided, but the long horizon receded. His attention fixed more often on what was immediately before him—the next task, the next bill, the next shift, the next obligation that could not be postponed. His focus tightened from building what might come to managing what was required now. His world narrowed, not out of defeat, but out of necessity.

The emotional residue of being the one who must not fail settled deeper into him. It dulled some of the warmth that once rose to the surface. He smiled, but less readily. He spoke, but with fewer words. He carried himself like a man who had learned that ease was something earned in increments far smaller than the labor required to hold everything together.

Time did not hollow him; it refined him, leaving behind a quieter, more concentrated version of himself. But refinement has its cost. As endurance deepened, lightness receded. As devotion matured, spontaneity thinned. The years gave him wisdom, steadiness, and gravity, while quietly taking from him the softness that belongs to those who are not required to carry so much for so long.

Time marked not only his body and spirit, but also the boundaries of who he could afford to be. Before anything could be gained, something had to be relinquished. The losses were never announced and never negotiated. They arrived in small, unremarkable increments, settling into his days until absence felt ordinary, even inevitable.

Of all that responsibility demanded from my father, the most costly losses were not the ones anyone could easily name. They were not recorded on pay stubs or measured in hours worked or shifts missed. What responsibility took from him lived deeper than fatigue. It quietly reshaped the range of his inner life, narrowing what was possible, redefining what was permitted, and determining who he became.

Ease left his life early and never truly returned. Not comfort in the material sense, but softness—the unguarded posture of a man who believes the world will meet him gently. My father moved through life alert, prepared, braced. Even in moments meant for rest, some part of him stayed watchful, scanning for what might go wrong. The habit of vigilance, once necessary, became permanent. Life did not offer him the luxury of lowering his shoulders for long.

Along with ease, certain dreams were quietly surrendered. He never spoke of them, never mourned them aloud, never framed them as losses. But I came to understand that some hopes are not abandoned in moments of decision; they are simply outpaced by obligation. Whatever visions he once carried for himself beyond provision and protection were folded inward and set aside. Not because they didn't matter, but because everything else mattered more. Responsibility did not crush his dreams dramatically. It outlived them.

Space for emotional expression narrowed as well. My father was not unfeeling; he felt deeply. But the language of those feelings grew constrained, filtered through the belief that emotion must never interfere with duty. Worry, fear, sadness, even joy were regulated, managed, contained. Vigilance replaced vulnerability. Presence replaced expression. He showed love by being there, by providing, by fixing what was broken—not by naming what lived inside him. Over time, the inner world that once might have moved freely became disciplined, quieter, more guarded.

Playfulness faded too, almost without notice. I remember a time when he would kick a soccer ball casually with neighbors or friends, laughing in brief bursts, his body loose in a way that felt almost foreign later on. Those moments disappeared, not because he stopped loving the game, but because there was always something else demanding attention. Work schedules tightened. Bodies tired. Responsibility crowded out leisure. Joy did not vanish; it simply became less spontaneous, less physical, less free.

I saw it most clearly during celebrations—birthdays, holidays, and small gatherings meant to mark joy. My father was always there—present, attentive, and generous. He smiled. He participated. But there was a thinness to his joy, as though part of him remained elsewhere, tallying costs, anticipating tomorrow, holding the edges of the moment rather than stepping fully into it. He never withdrew, never dampened the occasion, but neither did he abandon himself to it. Even celebration carried an undertone of restraint.

This subtle distancing was not emotional abandonment. He never left us emotionally. But it was emotional thinning — a narrowing of the bandwidth available for spontaneity, play, and ease. Love remained constant. Presence remained unwavering. But the lighter expressions of self—the unburdened laughter, the relaxed body, the carefree engagement—became rarer as duty hardened into habit.

Responsibility reshaped his identity so thoroughly that certain parts of himself no longer found room to breathe. He became dependable, steadfast, reliable beyond question. But dependability has a cost when it becomes the primary way a man understands his worth. Over time, he learned to carry himself in ways that prioritized stability over softness, endurance over expression, vigilance over vulnerability.

And yet, even in this taking, something else was happening quietly beneath the surface. While responsibility stripped certain freedoms from him, it was also deepening him in ways that become visible only with time.

Yet even as life took from him, it also enlarged him.

For all that time took from my father, it also gave him something rare and enduring. Not gifts that arrive suddenly or shine brightly, but qualities that form only through long obedience to responsibility. What the years returned to him did not erase the losses; they stood beside them, steady and undeniable.

The first gift was wisdom—not the kind learned from books or spoken easily, but the kind shaped by consequence. His understanding of life did not come from theories about how things should work; it came from living with how they actually did. He knew what held and what failed. He understood where effort mattered and where it did not. He could see through false urgency and empty promises because he had lived long enough to watch them collapse. His wisdom was quiet, situational, and deeply practical. It revealed itself not in speeches, but in timing—when to act, when to wait, when to say nothing at all.

People sensed this instinctively. Younger men at the factory began to approach him, not with formal questions, but with small uncertainties they didn't know how to voice. A machine behaving strangely. A supervisor asking too much. A decision that felt off but wasn't obviously wrong. My father listened more than he spoke. When he did answer, his words were measured, never inflated, never dismissive. He didn't offer solutions to impress; he offered perspective to steady. Often, he didn't tell them what to do. He helped them see more clearly, trusting that clarity would lead them where they needed to go.

Alongside wisdom came humility—the kind that does not announce itself or seek recognition. My father never confused endurance with importance. He didn't mistake responsibility for superiority. The weight he carried never made him feel above anyone else. If anything, it made him slower to judge and quicker to understand. He knew how easily circumstances could shape a life, how thin the line was between stability and collapse. That knowledge softened him in ways no sermon ever could.

This humility made him approachable. Neighbors didn't come to him for advice in dramatic ways. They simply showed up. A knock at the door. A pause in the driveway. A quiet question asked while standing side by side rather than face to face. He didn't posture or correct. He listened. Sometimes he spoke. Sometimes he simply stood with them, allowing the moment to settle until its own clarity emerged. His presence carried reassurance—not because he promised solutions, but because he had survived enough to know that most problems could be endured.

Over time, his presence itself became a kind of anchor. He had a way of grounding rooms without trying to. When he entered a space, things slowed slightly. Voices lowered. The emotional temperature adjusted. It wasn't authority in the traditional sense; it was steadiness earned through consistency. People trusted him not because he was charismatic or commanding, but because he was reliable. He showed up. He followed through. He didn't disappear when things grew complicated.

That reliability matured into a quiet authority. My father held no title that demanded deference. He had no formal education that conferred status. Yet within our family—and quietly beyond it—his judgment carried weight. When decisions mattered, when uncertainty lingered, when competing opinions created tension, people looked to him. Not because he insisted on being heard, but because his discernment had been tested and proven. He had lived with the consequences of hard choices long enough to recognize what endured and what did not.

Within our home, this authority took on a particular shape. When family discussions stalled, his voice often settled them. Not through dominance, but through clarity. He had an ability to name what mattered most and let the rest fall away. His sense of proportion—what deserved worry and what did not — was forged through years of carrying far more than his share. He had learned, through necessity, how to separate the essential from the expendable.

And perhaps the most enduring gift the years gave him was a reputation built slowly, patiently, and without strategy. Among coworkers, he became known as the man who could be trusted. Not the loudest. Not the fastest to speak. But the one who would not cut corners, who would not disappear when work grew difficult, who would not compromise what mattered for convenience. Trust accrued around him the way sediment builds in a riverbed—gradually, invisibly, until it became undeniable.

Among friends and neighbors, he became the one people relied on in moments they didn't want to dramatize. Among family, he became the steady reference point—the person whose judgment had been earned through sacrifice rather than opinion. These were not honors he sought. They were byproducts of a life lived under pressure without bitterness.

Looking back now, I see that what the years gave my father did not arrive despite the losses, but because of them. Wisdom emerged because hardship demanded discernment. Humility deepened because suffering revealed how little control any man truly has. Authority formed not through ambition, but through endurance. Presence matured because life required him to remain when retreat would have been easier.

These gains did not erase the cost. They lived alongside it. But together, gifts and losses shaped not only who he became, but the environment we lived within. They influenced how decisions were made, how conflict was navigated, how stability was preserved. They became part of the invisible inheritance passed down to those who watched him live.

The years took much from my father. But they also returned something rare. And that return shaped all of us who stood within the shelter of the life he built.

As the years gave my father a quieter authority and a steadier presence, they also began to change the shape of our family life in ways that were subtle at first, almost imperceptible. Strength, once so clearly defined by what he carried alone, began to express itself differently—not through endurance without assistance, but through the slow acceptance of shared weight.

This was the season when my understanding of him began to widen beyond the narrow lens of childhood. I no longer saw him only as the fixed center around which everything revolved. I began to notice the effort beneath the steadiness, the cost beneath the consistency. What once looked like distance now revealed itself as weariness. What once felt like silence began to sound like restraint. He had not withdrawn from us; he had simply been carrying more than I could see.

With that realization came a quiet shift in roles. It did not arrive with ceremony or acknowledgment. It unfolded in ordinary moments—a request made gently instead of assumed, a pause before a task he once handled without hesitation, a look exchanged that said more than words. I found myself stepping in, not because he asked, but because I sensed it was time.

I began making the calls he once handled himself—to tradesmen, to service companies, to offices where language and systems had grown more complex with time. I sorted through paperwork that had once felt foreign to him, interpreting letters, clarifying options, translating bureaucracy into something manageable. These were not acts of rescue. They were acts of partnership, though neither of us would have named them that way.

Even in the garden—his place of pride and memory—the shift became visible. Where he once bent easily into the soil, he now paused, straightened slowly, and rested his weight before continuing. I worked beside him more deliberately then, taking on the tasks that required strength or flexibility, watching him tend what remained within reach. The garden still grounded him, but it also revealed the passage of time in ways no calendar ever could. Yet even there, his authority remained. He directed with quiet clarity, not as someone losing control, but as someone learning to guide rather than carry.

These moments softened something in me. I began to sit beside him at the table differently. Where once I waited for him to speak, I now listened for what his silence might be holding. I saw the fatigue in his posture, the way his shoulders settled after a long day, the concentration it took simply to remain present. I realized that what I had once interpreted as emotional distance was, in truth, the cost of decades spent being the steady one.

This broader understanding reshaped my view of my mother as well. Her storms, which had once frightened and confused me, began to take on context. I could see more clearly the weight she carried alongside her illness—the fear, the frustration, the loss of control over a body and mind that no longer obeyed her. What once registered as chaos now revealed itself as suffering. My fear gradually gave way to empathy. Not because her episodes diminished, but because my capacity to understand them grew.

In this new awareness, I could see how my father had held both realities at once—his own burdens and hers—without naming either. His endurance had not been stoic indifference; it had been a kind of quiet love, expressed through presence rather than explanation. And as I began to shoulder small parts of what he once carried alone, I understood more fully the cost of that love.

The landscape of our family life was changing, shaped not by crisis, but by time. Authority softened into guidance. Dependence shifted into mutuality. Fear gave way to understanding. The man who had once borne the weight alone now allowed it to be shared, not because he was weak, but because the years had taught him what strength could look like in another season.

And in that sharing, something else emerged—something I could not have anticipated as a child. The years were not shaping only him; they were shaping me. What he had given our family through sacrifice was now returning in another form—through trust, through partnership, through the quiet passing of responsibility from one generation to the next.

What the years gave me in return was beginning to come into focus.

As the years shifted the shape of our family life and I began stepping into spaces my father once filled alone, something else was quietly taking shape within me. Time was not only revealing who he had been; it was teaching me how to see. And in learning how to see him more clearly, I was also learning something essential about myself.

What time gave me through my father was not instruction in the traditional sense. He did not sit me down to explain responsibility, endurance, or sacrifice. He lived them long enough that they became legible. I learned by watching, by standing close, by carrying small pieces of the weight he had shouldered for decades. Over time, clarity replaced assumption. I began to understand not just what responsibility looks like, but what it costs.

I learned that responsibility is never abstract. It has weight. It settles into the body. It shapes posture, pace, and patience. I saw how it sharpened his judgment and steadied his decisions, but also how it narrowed his margins and demanded constant vigilance. Through him, I learned that responsibility is not heroic in the way stories often portray it. It is persistent. It shows up when nothing is celebrated and nothing feels resolved. And once you accept it, it becomes part of how you move through the world.

His perseverance became my internal compass long before I realized I was following it. When uncertainty appeared in my own life, I did not search for inspiration; I defaulted to steadiness. When things felt unstable, my instinct was not to withdraw but to endure. His life taught me that forward motion, even slow and imperfect, is often the most faithful response to fear. I did not inherit his circumstances, but I inherited his orientation toward them.

Time also taught me something quieter, something I would not have understood as a boy.

Strength, I learned, does not announce itself. It does not demand recognition. It does not need to be dramatic. Real strength is consistent. It returns every day. It does what must be done whether it is noticed or not. Watching my father taught me that the loudest displays of strength are often compensations, while the deepest strength moves silently, conserving energy for what matters most.

I inherited from him not possessions, but purpose. There was no material legacy to speak of—no wealth, no accumulation meant to be passed down. What he gave me instead was far more enduring. He gave me a framework for living. A sense that life is not measured by what you secure for yourself, but by what you hold together for others. You do not chase that purpose; you accept it. That meaning is not found in ease, but often forged in obligation embraced willingly.

Perhaps the most significant gift time gave me was a softened vision of him. The father I once saw as immovable, distant, and even severe, slowly revealed himself as something far more complex. The symbol became a man. The myth gave way to humanity. I began to see the fear behind the vigilance, the tenderness beneath the restraint, and the devotion embedded in habits that once felt impersonal.

I reinterpreted his silences. They were not absences; they were containers. I reinterpreted his sighs—not as dissatisfaction, but as release. I reinterpreted his rituals—the careful locking of doors, the methodical handling of money, the repeated checking of details—not as rigidity, but as care expressed through preparation. These were not signs of distance. They were signs of love shaped by responsibility rather than affection.

Over time, I came to understand a truth that only maturity makes visible. Love does not always arrive with warmth. It does not always speak softly or reach out easily. Sometimes love builds. Sometimes it protects. Sometimes it endures quietly so that others do not have to. My father loved us in the only language he fully trusted—presence, provision, consistency.

And in seeing him clearly, I began to see myself more clearly as well. The parts of me that strive, that plan, that anticipate—these were not simply traits. They were inheritances. They were the imprint of a man who showed me, without explanation, how to remain standing when standing is required.

Understanding the man my father was did not diminish him. It deepened him. And it did something else as well. It prepared me for the harder truth that always follows real understanding—the recognition that such strength is never free. To see the gift fully, I would have to reckon with what it cost him.

As my understanding of my father deepened, something else began to surface—not abruptly, but gradually, like a landscape revealing new contours as the light shifts. Time was no longer shaping only how I saw him. It was shaping how he inhabited himself.

The man who had once moved through life with urgency began to move with intention. The edge that necessity had sharpened in him softened, not into weakness, but into perspective. Where frustration had once surfaced quickly, reflection now took its place. Where striving had driven him forward for decades, acceptance began to steady his steps. He no longer seemed to be bracing against life. He was inhabiting it.

I noticed it first in what was missing. The anger that once flickered under pressure no longer appeared. The defensiveness that responsibility had required—the constant readiness to protect, correct, and contain—had eased. In its place was a quieter openness, as though the long fight for stability had finally loosened its grip on his nervous system. He was no longer trying to outrun loss. He was learning how to live alongside it.

He began to speak more often about the past. Not with regret, and not with longing, but with a kind of gentle accounting. Stories surfaced that had never been told before—about Italy, about the early days in Canada, about people and moments I had never known existed in his inner world. It felt as though remembering had become a way of orienting himself, a way of stitching meaning across the years. Looking backward was no longer a retreat; it was a form of integration.

And woven into those reflections, though rarely stated outright, was something else—a quiet satisfaction that settled between his words. He did not speak of achievements in the language others might use. He did not praise success or status. But there were moments, subtle and unmistakable, when I understood that he believed I had made it—not because of what I had accumulated, but because of how I lived. In his way, this mattered more than anything else. He measured a man not by ease or recognition, but by steadiness, responsibility, and honor. And in the way he looked at me, in the way he sometimes paused before speaking, I sensed his approval—restrained, dignified, deeply felt.

His presence changed, too. He moved more slowly now, but there was a richness to his attention that hadn't been there before. He listened without hurry. He lingered in moments he once would have passed through. Even silence felt different—no longer taut or guarded, but spacious, almost companionable. He was still steady, still reserved, but there was a tenderness in him that time had unlocked rather than erased.

There was a moment—ordinary, easily missed—when I realized something fundamental had shifted. We were sitting together, not speaking much, and I sensed that he was no longer driven by fear of what might be lost. He was guided instead by what had already been survived. The vigilance that once ruled him had given way to perspective. He did not need to prove anything anymore. He was no longer holding the world together by force of will. He was allowing it to be held.

This was not the easing of a burden set down. It was the settling of a burden finally comprehended.

With that understanding, something subtle shifted in the inner terrain of his life. Not toward comfort, and certainly not toward relief, but toward acceptance. The years had given him a kind of settled knowing—that his effort had mattered, that what he built had endured, that the values he lived by had not dissolved when he loosened his grip. He no longer measured his life by what remained to be done, but by what had already been faithfully carried.

And it was precisely there, in that quiet reckoning, that the deeper paradox emerged.

As I watched this awareness take root in him, I began to see what I could not have understood earlier. Time had not chosen a single direction with my father. It had been working two paths at once. What it withdrew in one register, it returned in another. Not evenly. Not kindly. But unmistakably.

His body told one story. Movements once effortless now required intention. Familiar tasks slowed, not because he forgot how to do them, but because strength no longer arrived on demand. The confidence that once lived in muscle and habit gave way to a more careful rhythm. He felt the narrowing, even when he did not speak of it. Flesh was asserting its limits, reminding him—and those of us watching—that endurance is finite, even when resolve is not.

Yet at the same time, something else was unfolding.

As physical capacity receded, interior clarity advanced. He had grown less reactive, less hurried to explain or correct. He listened more than he spoke. When he did speak, his words carried a density they had not needed before. He had learned the difference between urgency and importance, between control and stewardship. Time had trained him not to rush toward answers, but to stand comfortably inside questions.

Much had fallen away—illusions, false alarms, the anxious need to stay ahead of what might go wrong. What remained was steadiness. Not the steadiness of vigilance, but the steadiness of perspective. He had survived what once frightened him. And having survived it, he was no longer ruled by it.

Even his hopes had been refined. Some ambitions had dimmed, not through disappointment, but through discernment. The future no longer needed to be seized; it needed to be tended. His attention shifted from what he might still accomplish to what would outlast him. Legacy sharpened, not as aspiration, but as responsibility—a concern for how things would be left, how character speaks when effort can no longer do the talking.

Time had not simply taken from him. It had exchanged strength for depth. Speed for wisdom. Control for meaning.

What life removed from his body, it returned through understanding. What it narrowed in capacity, it widened in clarity. Time did not hollow him out. It clarified him.

He was becoming a man shaped less by striving and more by comprehension, less by effort and more by meaning. The years had refined him into someone quieter, more deliberate, more human—a man who no longer felt compelled to hold everything together because he trusted what had already been built.

And it is here, in this tension between diminishing and deepening, that the chapter turns. Not toward resolution, but toward reverence. Because what time gives in return is never obvious, never balanced, and never without cost.

What endures is not what he could still do, but who he had become.

What time clarified, it did not replace.

Even as the years refined my father into someone quieter and more inward, they never removed the core that had held him steady from the beginning. What diminished around the edges did not hollow out the center. Strength changed form, but it did not disappear. Purpose adjusted its posture, but it did not abandon its place.

There is a temptation, when reflecting on a life shaped by endurance, to either romanticize the struggle or mourn only what was lost. But neither tells the full truth. The more honest story lives in the middle ground, where wear is real, and limitation undeniable, and yet something essential remains intact.

The years thinned his body. They slowed his movements and shortened his reach. But they could not thin his commitment. Even as energy waned, his sense of responsibility did not. He still showed up. Still noticed what needed tending. Still oriented himself toward others before himself, no longer out of urgency or fear, but out of habit shaped into character.

The years taxed his spirit. They introduced a weariness no rest could fully cure. But they did not take his love. Love simply found quieter expressions. It lived in his attention, in his concern, in the way he stayed present even when he spoke less. Affection did not vanish. It matured into constancy.

The years also reshaped his identity. He was no longer the tireless provider, the man whose strength answered every demand. But they did not erase his purpose. Purpose settled deeper, no longer tied to output or performance, but to presence. He remained an anchor, not because he could carry everything, but because he knew what mattered and refused to abandon it.

They quieted him, undeniably. Yet silence did not mean absence. It meant depth. It meant discernment. It meant that when he did speak or act, it came from a place that had been tested and stripped of excess.

I noticed this most clearly in small moments, the ones that don't announce themselves as significant. Watching him sit and listen while others spoke. Seeing him rise more slowly, yet still insist on being there. Not offering solutions immediately, but offering steadiness instead. Even diminished, he remained unmistakably himself.

Time had taken much. But it could not take the way people still oriented themselves around him. It could not take the trust he inspired without demanding it. It could not take the quiet gravity that made others feel held simply by his presence.

And it could not take the love that had always been his truest strength, the love that endured not through force, but through faithfulness.

This is what the years could not take.

And it is here, in what remains, that the chapter finds its emotional landing. Not in loss alone, but in recognition. Because when time has done its work, what survives tells us more about a man than anything that has been worn away.

What remained in my father was not perfection. It was fidelity.

And from that fidelity, the final shape of his life comes into view.

There comes a moment, near the end of any long reckoning, when the accounting must be done honestly—not to tally losses alone, but to see the full shape of what a life has become.

By this point in my father's story, it was no longer possible to separate what the years had taken from what they had given. They were too intertwined, too mutually shaping. Sacrifice had cost him ease, spontaneity, and parts of himself he never reclaimed. Time had thinned his strength and narrowed his physical world. Certain dreams had been laid down quietly, never to be taken up again.

And yet, none of that told the whole truth.

Because what he surrendered did not disappear into absence. It made room. Space opened slowly, almost imperceptibly, for something deeper to take root. What left his hands reshaped his heart. What time removed refined what remained.

His life cannot be understood as a story of hardship alone. Hardship was present, yes—but it was not the point. The point was transformation— the slow, faithful becoming of a man shaped by responsibility, clarified by endurance, and steadied by love that learned to express itself through presence rather than performance.

The years were a burden. They were also a blessing. They demanded much. They returned something quieter, but no less profound. They returned wisdom that could not be taught. They returned authority without ego. They returned a depth of character that made others feel safe simply by standing near him. They returned a man who no longer needed to prove his worth, because his life had already spoken.

When I look back now, I no longer ask whether the years were fair to him. That question feels too small. What matters more is that he met them fully. He carried what they placed on his shoulders. He endured what could not be avoided. And he allowed himself—slowly, reluctantly—to be shaped by what he survived.

This is the accounting that remains. Not a ledger of loss, but a testament of return. Not merely what time took from him, but what it revealed.

The years carved him, yes—but they also disclosed him. They stripped away what could not last and left behind what could.

And in that revelation, I began to see not just the man my father had been, but the man he had become.

That clarity does not end the story. It deepens it.

Because when a life has been lived this fully—when sacrifice has given way to understanding, and endurance to meaning—the next questions are no longer about survival, but about reconciliation. About what must be named. About what still waits beneath the surface, asking to be understood.

What the years took from him shaped what they gave to me.

And what remains to be uncovered lies not in what he carried—but in what he finally began to release.

SACRED WAYPOINTS

When Strength Stops Announcing Itself

In this chapter, my father's strength does not fail—it changes form. What once showed itself through speed, endurance, and output becomes quieter, more deliberate, more inward. Time does not defeat him; it asks him to carry himself differently.

- Where in your life has strength shifted from force to restraint?
- What abilities are fading—and what forms of wisdom might be emerging in their place?

Sit with this truth: Strength that endures longest often learns how to speak softly.

The Weight That Moves Indoors

The heaviest burdens my father carried were not in the factory, but at home—absorbing illness, unpredictability, and grief without release. Responsibility followed him into every room, reshaping love into vigilance and devotion into endurance.

- What responsibilities in your life are invisible to others but heavy to you?
- Who have you been carrying without naming the cost?

Hold this gently: Love expressed through constancy is still love, even when it is weary.

When Responsibility Narrows the Self

Responsibility did not only ask my father to do more; it quietly limited who he could afford to be. Ease, playfulness, and emotional range thinned—not through crisis, but through years of choosing stability over softness.

- What parts of yourself have grown quieter in the name of responsibility?
- Are those parts gone—or simply waiting for permission to breathe again?

Remember this: What is set aside for survival is not always lost forever.

What Time Takes Without Asking

Time does not negotiate. It removes in increments so small they feel normal until absence has a shape. My father's losses were not dramatic; they were cumulative—dreams outpaced, joy rationed, vulnerability disciplined into silence.

- What has time taken from you so gradually that you barely noticed?
- How has absence taught you what once mattered most?

Receive this truth: Loss does not always arrive as tragedy; sometimes it arrives as habit.

The Gifts That Only Endurance Returns

What the years took, they also returned—wisdom shaped by consequence, humility without performance, authority earned through presence. My father became a man others trusted not because he demanded it, but because he endured faithfully.

- Who trusts you today because you chose to remain present and faithful when it would have been easier to step away?
- What qualities are forming in you that no shortcut could produce?

Sit with this truth: Some gifts are given only after much has been carried.

What Remains When Much Is Gone

By the end of this chapter, what stands out is not what my father could still do, but who he had become. Time diminished his body, but it clarified his character. What endured was fidelity—quiet, steady, unmistakable.

- If much was stripped away, what would remain true about you?
- What kind of presence are you becoming as time does its work?

Hold this close: What remains may matter more than anything that was lost.

ANCHORS OF THE WORD 

The Seasons That Shape Us

"There is a time for everything, and a season for every activity under the heavens." (Ecclesiastes 3:1 NIV)

My father's life reveals what Ecclesiastes names so plainly. Time does not judge a life; it orders it. Seasons arrive without asking permission, each one demanding something different from the same man. Strength that once built must eventually yield to wisdom that steadies. The years did not fail him— they simply required a different faithfulness.

Reflection: Where are you resisting a season that is asking you to become something new?

Strength That Grows Inward

"Therefore we do not lose heart. Though outwardly we are wasting away, yet inwardly we are being renewed day by day." (2 Corinthians 4:16 NIV)

The years thinned my father's body, but they clarified his spirit. What diminished externally deepened internally. Scripture reminds us that decline and renewal often occur simultaneously—one visible, the other hidden. The world measures loss; God measures formation.

Reflection: Where do you see outward limitation but inward growth unfolding together in your life?

Bearing Fruit in Old Age

"Planted in the house of the LORD, they will flourish in the courts of our God. They will still bear fruit in old age, they will stay fresh and green." (Psalm 92:13-14 NIV)

Fruitfulness did not leave my father when speed and strength did. It simply changed form. His presence, judgment, and steadiness nourished others long after his physical reach shortened. God's economy does not retire fruitfulness—it redefines it.

Reflection: What kind of fruit is your life producing now, even if it looks different than before?

Carried to the End

"Even to your old age and gray hairs I am he, I am he who will sustain you. I have made you and I will carry you; I will sustain you and I will rescue you." (Isaiah 46:4 NIV)

My father spent most of his life carrying others—family, responsibility, fear, survival. This verse reveals a quieter truth he might never have spoken aloud: There comes a time when the carrier himself must be carried. Strength does not end in abandonment; it ends in surrender.

Reflection: Where might God be inviting you to stop carrying alone?

The Long Obedience

"Blessed is the one who perseveres under trial because, having stood the test, that person will receive the crown of life that the Lord has promised to those who love him." (James 1:12 NIV)

Endurance shaped my father more than talent or opportunity ever could. James names what long obedience produces—not applause, but depth. Not recognition, but character. The crown promised here is not reward for suffering, but the maturity formed through it.

Reflection: What trial in your life is quietly forming something enduring within you?

Purpose Beyond Strength

"Even when I am old and gray, do not forsake me, my God, till I declare your power to the next generation, your mighty acts to all who are to come." (Psalm 71:18 NIV)

By the later years of his life, my father's strength no longer proved itself through doing, but through being. His life became a testimony without words—a proclamation shaped by fidelity rather than force. Purpose did not leave him when strength waned; it matured into legacy.

Reflection: What are you passing on—not through effort, but through who you have become?

LEGACY NOTES

PART III

The Grace To Build What Lasts

SEVEN

Built From the Quiet Pride of Honest Work

"The dignity of work is found not in what it produces, but in who it forms."

— *Pope John Paul II (1920-2005) (adapted)*

Work entered my father's life long before comfort ever did. It arrived before ease, before confidence, before language fully settled on his tongue. After years shaped by sacrifice, endurance, and the quiet accounting of what time had taken and given in return, one truth stood undiminished. Work was never merely how he survived. It was how he stood upright in the world.

What began as necessity slowly became something sacramental—a daily practice through which dignity was restored, identity clarified, and a life made stable enough for others to grow within it. If earlier chapters asked what his labor cost him, this one turns to a different question altogether. What did his honest work create that time itself could not undo?

Before my father could explain himself in words, he explained himself through work. Long before English felt reliable in his mouth, long before he understood the codes and customs of this new country, his body learned where it belonged. It belonged where effort was required. Where hands were needed. Where showing up mattered more than speaking well.

Work became his first language of dignity.

When displacement strips a man of familiarity, pride must be rebuilt from something solid. For my father, that foundation was not confidence or recognition. It was contribution. The factory floor—loud, imperfect, physically demanding—became the place where he reclaimed agency after poverty and migration. It was not romantic. It was not gentle. But it was real. And in a life that had already taught him how fragile security could be, reality mattered more than comfort.

He did not arrive at work expecting fulfillment. He arrived expecting responsibility. And in meeting that expectation day after day, something essential began to take shape inside him. Work was how he claimed space in a country where everything else still felt provisional. It was how he answered the unspoken question every immigrant carries: "Do I belong here?"

His answer was not spoken. It was lived.

Each morning followed a quiet ritual. The preparation was deliberate, almost reverent. Clothes laid out. Boots checked. Lunch packed with care, even when options were limited. These were not habits of vanity; they were acts of self-respect. He did not rush himself into the day. He composed himself for it. To be ready for work was to be ready to be seen—not as a stranger, but as someone who could be counted on.

The factory offered no illusions. It demanded precision, endurance, and attention. It rewarded consistency more than brilliance. My father did not seek advancement or distinction there. His pride did not come from climbing. It came from holding steady—from being the man others relied on when things jammed, slowed, or went wrong. Reliability became his reputation. And in a world that still felt uncertain, being needed became a form of security.

The physical presence of work unmistakably marked him. Callused hands. A back shaped by repetition. A posture formed by long hours of standing, lifting, bracing. These were not signs of degradation to him. They were proof of participation. Evidence that he had entered fully into the life before him. His body told the story before his words ever could. It said, "I am here." "I contribute. I matter."

Work gave him something language had not yet caught up to—a place.

In that sense, the factory was more than a job site. It was a proving ground where dignity was restored incrementally. Not because the work itself was noble, but because he performed it with care. He learned that meaning did not come from the nature of the task, but from the manner in which it was done. He cleaned what needed cleaning. He repaired what could be repaired. He endured what could not be changed. And in doing so, he rebuilt a sense of coherence that poverty and displacement had fractured.

Identity followed contribution, not the other way around.

He did not think of himself as important. He thought of himself as responsible. That distinction mattered. Importance seeks recognition. Responsibility seeks completion. My father oriented himself toward finishing what was in front of him—one shift, one task, one day at a time. Over years, that orientation hardened into character. He became a man whose word aligned with his work, whose effort matched his obligation, and whose sense of self rested on whether he had done what was required of him.

In a new country, where titles were foreign and credentials incomplete, work became how he introduced himself to the world. It was how he earned trust without explanation. How he navigated dignity without entitlement. How he restored order to a life once shaped by scarcity and uncertainty.

Honest work did not make him ambitious. It made him anchored.

And that anchoring mattered far beyond the factory walls. When a man learns to stand firmly in his own effort, he becomes capable of holding space for others. The steadiness my father cultivated at work did not stay there. It followed him home. It shaped how he provided, how he protected, how he endured. Work was not separate from who he was becoming; it was the training ground that formed him.

This is the distinction that matters.

For my father, work was never merely transactional. It was formative. It shaped his posture toward the world and toward himself. It taught him that dignity is not granted; it is practiced. That belonging is not claimed; it is earned through presence and consistency. And that pride, when rooted in reliability rather than status, becomes something durable enough to withstand time.

Honest work was not about ambition. It was about belonging. And from that belonging, everything else he built would eventually rise.

The belonging my father found through work did not seek witnesses. It did not need to be affirmed aloud or reflected back to him by others. Once dignity had taken root through contribution, pride followed—not loudly, not visibly, but steadily, like a quiet certainty that required no defense.

He never spoke about his work in ways that invited admiration. There were no stories shaped for effect, no retellings meant to elevate his effort or dramatize his endurance. When asked about his day, his answers came in a simple mix of English and Italian—just enough to be understood, never more than necessary. *"Bene."* Fine. *"Occupato"*. Busy *"Come sempre"*. Same as always. My mother did not understand English, and he did not try to translate the day into something larger than it was. The work itself did not need narration. It had already done its work on him.

My father did not confuse pride with praise. Praise was external, fleeting, dependent on others noticing. Pride, as he understood it, was internal and settled. It lived in the simple knowledge that he had shown up, done what was required, and left things no worse than he'd found them. He carried that knowledge quietly, the way a man carries something precious he has no intention of displaying.

He seemed to draw a particular satisfaction from effort completed honestly. Not triumph. Not excitement. Something calmer and more enduring. At the end of a long day, when exhaustion pressed in, he did not measure his worth by what had been accomplished beyond his control. He measured it by whether he had given what the day asked of him. That was enough. More than enough.

This was pride as integrity, not status.

He turned away from praise almost instinctively. Compliments made him uncomfortable, not because he lacked confidence, but because they felt unnecessary. When others spoke highly of his work, he deflected or redirected. Anyone would have done the same. It was nothing. He had learned early that attention is unreliable, but effort is not. What mattered was not who noticed, but whether the work had been done properly.

His standards came from within. He did not work harder because someone was watching, nor did he relax when no one was. The presence or absence of recognition made little difference. He approached each task with the same care whether it was visible or hidden, valued or overlooked. That consistency was not performative. It was principled.

He measured a day not by outcome, but by faithfulness. Machines failed. Schedules shifted. Supervisors misjudged. Results did not always reflect effort. None of that unsettled him. He knew what he had given. He knew whether he had cut corners or stood firm. His accounting was internal, and it was honest.

Shortcuts unsettled him deeply. Not because they broke rules, but because they broke trust—first with the work itself, and then with the man doing it. He believed that exaggeration hollowed effort, that corners cut would eventually weaken the whole. He did things the long way, the careful way, even when no one would have known the difference. Especially then.

That discipline shaped everything around him. Tools were cleaned and put away properly. Materials were handled with respect. Time was not wasted, but neither was it rushed. His care extended beyond efficiency into stewardship.

He behaved as though what he touched mattered—not because it was glamorous, but because it had been entrusted to him.

This was pride without comparison.

He did not measure himself against other men. He did not compete for status or recognition. Another man's success did not threaten him, nor did another man's failure elevate him. His sense of worth was anchored elsewhere. He asked only whether he had met his own obligation—whether he had honored the work, the people who depended on it, and the standards he carried inside himself.

There was a deep freedom in that posture. Without the need to impress, he moved through the world unburdened by performance. Without the need for applause, he remained steady regardless of outcome. His pride did not inflate him; it grounded him. It allowed him to stand firmly without standing above anyone else.

At home, this pride expressed itself quietly. He did not announce his fatigue or list his sacrifices. He did not seek sympathy for what he carried. Instead, pride lived in provision made without resentment, in repairs done without complaint, in presence maintained even when energy was thin. It showed up in the way he kept his commitments, the way he honored his word, and the way he continued to do what was his to do long after novelty had worn away.

Self-respect, for my father, was not something granted by others. It was something maintained through consistency.

He knew who he was because he knew what he had given. And that knowledge did not require affirmation. It simply rested within him, quiet and unshakeable.

He carried pride the way he carried everything else—quietly, responsibly, without display. And in a world that increasingly confuses visibility with value, that kind of pride remains one of the rarest forms of strength.

Over time, the meaning of my father's work revealed itself not in what it accumulated, but in what it stabilized. The true measure of his labor was not found in pay stubs or promotions, but in the quiet architecture it erected around our lives—structures so steady they were easy to overlook, and so durable they outlasted circumstances that might have undone lesser foundations.

What his work built first was stability. Not comfort. Not excess. Stability.

In a world that had proven volatile early and often—shaped by poverty, migration, illness, and uncertainty—stability was not a given. It had to be constructed deliberately, day by day, through choices that favored reliability over relief and consistency over ease. My father understood this instinctively. He did not try to eliminate risk; he tried to contain it. His labor became the primary tool through which chaos was held at bay.

Bills were paid on time. Always. Even when it required sacrifice, even when it meant postponing something for himself, even when the margin was thin. The lights stayed on. The heat came when winter arrived. There were no dramatic conversations about money because he believed those conversations belonged to adults, not children. We did not grow up wondering whether essentials would disappear. That certainty—quiet, unspoken, dependable— was one of the greatest gifts his work provided.

Food was always present. It was not elaborate or indulgent, but it was steady. Meals appeared with regularity, shaped by routine rather than abundance. Hunger did not remain in our home, even when money was scarce. There was a calm in knowing that nourishment would come, that the table would be set, that the day would hold at least this much. My father understood that predictability feeds more than the body. It steadies the nervous system. It tells children, without explanation, that tomorrow will arrive with what it needs.

This was the deeper shelter his work created. Not walls alone, but assurance.

I came to understand this shelter more clearly as a boy in the 1970s, when I was growing up and going to school in our little town of Guelph. Like everywhere else, the town buzzed with talk of *The Godfather*. Mario Puzo's story had captured the imagination of a generation, and the Mafia was everywhere—quoted, glamorized, mythologized. My friends made the connection quickly. I was Italian. Jokes followed. Comments. A kind of borrowed notoriety that I didn't know how to receive.

I felt uncertain—not sure whether I was supposed to feel pride, embarrassment, or something in between. We lived in a town full of immigrants, each family carrying its own version of history, but this particular story seemed louder than the rest. When I brought it home and mentioned it to my father, expecting perhaps a shrug or a smile, his response was immediate and firm. He shut it down. No discussion. No explanation.

At the time, I didn't understand why.

Looking back now, I do understand something I couldn't then.

What was being celebrated on the screen—the stories wrapped in the language of family, loyalty, and honor—was everything my father was quietly working against in real life. The glamorization of shortcuts. The confusion of power with dignity. The idea that respect could be seized rather than earned, taken through fear rather than built through effort.

Those stories dressed up violence as virtue. They masked crime with tradition and cruelty with code. They suggested that a man's worth could be proven by domination, intimidation, or bloodline rather than by sacrifice, responsibility, and restraint.

For my father, this was never entertainment. It was never cultural identity. And it was never harmless. It was an affront—not to his heritage, but to the honest life he was building.

He had come from a world where survival demanded integrity because there were no shortcuts that didn't come with consequences. He understood, at a level deeper than words, that anything taken rather than earned eventually takes something from you in return. He knew that real authority was not loud, not feared, not imposed. It was quiet. It was steady. It was proven day after day by showing up, providing, and enduring without spectacle.

The life he was building stood in direct opposition to the mythology on those screens.

He was teaching us—without speeches, without lectures—that family was not a shield for wrongdoing. It was a responsibility. That honor was not claimed by force. It was accumulated through restraint. We did not demand that respect. Others gave it when life made it unavoidable.

And I absorbed that distinction long before I could articulate it. I learned that there was a difference between loyalty and complicity. Between strength and menace. Between belonging to something and hiding behind it. My father's life made those lines clear—not through argument, but through example.

He chose the slower road. The harder road. The honest road. And in doing so, he showed me that a man does not need to dominate the world to be powerful within it.

His answer to chaos was never dominance or spectacle. It was order. Consistency. Showing up. The dignity he was constructing did not come from fear or reputation, but from reliability. From doing the work no one applauded so his children would not confuse notoriety with honor.

That moment, though I could not name it then, was part of the shelter his work provided. It drew a moral boundary without words. It said, "This is not who we are." "This is not how a man builds a life."

In a life where so much could not be controlled—illness that worsened, moods that shifted without warning, systems that felt foreign and unforgiving— work became the one variable he could influence reliably. He could show up. He could complete what was asked of him. He could bring order to at least one corner of a world that often resisted it. And in doing so, he created a predictability that extended far beyond the factory gates.

Our home was shaped by reliability rather than abundance. There were fewer surprises, but also fewer shocks. We lived within limits, but those limits were clear. And clarity itself is a form of safety. Children flourish not only where there is joy, but where there is consistency—where the ground beneath them does not shift unexpectedly. My father's labor provided that ground.

Emotional safety grew quietly out of that consistency.

He did not create safety through reassurance or explanation. He created it through presence. Through routine. Through the dependable repetition of effort that told us, day after day, that someone was holding the center. Even when storms came, internal or external, there was a sense that they would be weathered, not indulged. That they would pass through a structure strong enough to absorb them.

Work became his way of protecting what he loved. Not by force, but by faithfulness.

Each shift completed was an act of love, whether he named it that way or not. Each paycheck earned was not simply income; it was insulation against fear. Each routine honored was another beam added to the shelter he was building around us. His effort said what his words rarely did.

"You are held. You will not fall through the cracks. Tomorrow will arrive, and it will be met."

What his work built could not be repossessed. It could not be downsized by market forces or erased by illness. Even when circumstances tightened, even when his body weakened, the structures his labor had erected remained. Stability persisted. Predictability endured. The emotional climate of the home—shaped by steadiness rather than volatility—continued to hold.

This is the quiet miracle of honest work.

It creates things that do not appear on balance sheets. It builds environments where people can grow, where fear does not have the final word, where the future feels inhabitable rather than threatening. My father did not eliminate hardship from our lives. But he contained it. He refused to let it define the whole.

His labor was not merely productive. It was protective. And in that protection, something sacred took shape—something that would endure long after the work itself was done.

What he built was not wealth. It was shelter. And that shelter could not be taken.

What my father built through work did not stop at shelter. Over time, it became structure—a moral framework that ordered how life was lived, how choices were made, and how responsibility was understood. His labor shaped not only outcomes, but ethics. It taught us how to stand in the world with coherence.

The rules were never posted. They were never announced as principles. They were embedded in practice, reinforced through repetition, and revealed most clearly when something went wrong.

- **Finish what you start.**
  This was not spoken as a maxim, but lived as expectation. A task left undone lingered like an unresolved chord. Whether it was work at the factory, a repair at home, or a commitment made casually, incompletion unsettled my father. Not because he was compulsive, but because he believed unfinished work displaced responsibility onto someone else. To begin something was to accept the obligation to see it through. Anything less felt like a quiet form of dishonesty.

- **Do not leave others to clean up your mess.**
  My father had little patience for excuses, especially the kind that tried to make inconvenience someone else's problem. If something broke, it was addressed. If a mistake was made, it was corrected. If effort fell short, it was redoubled—not explained away. He did not raise his voice often, but there was a particular firmness when someone avoided accountability. Responsibility, in his view, did not end when circumstances became uncomfortable.

- **Earn what you take responsibility for.**

  He instinctively understood the difference between entitlement and stewardship. Nothing was assumed. Nothing was owed. What you carried, you earned the right to carry through effort and reliability. This belief shaped how he approached work, money, and even authority. He did not trust shortcuts because shortcuts bypassed formation. They promised results without requiring character. And character, to him, mattered more than outcome.

- **Be accountable even when unseen.**

  This might have been the deepest ethic his work instilled. My father did not work for recognition. He worked for alignment—between what he promised, what he did, and who he believed himself to be. He behaved the same when no one was watching as he did when others depended on him. That consistency created a kind of moral gravity. It made him trustworthy without explanation. It made his presence stabilizing without being controlling.

I saw this ethic expressed in the way he treated tools. Nothing was abused. Nothing was left carelessly. Tools were cleaned, returned, stored properly— not because they were expensive, but because they represented effort. Someone had worked to make them. Someone else might need them next. Respect for tools was respect for labor itself.

Time was treated with the same care. He did not waste it, but neither did he rush through it. He arrived early. He stayed until the work was done. He did not inflate hours or dramatize effort. You honored time, like trust, by how faithfully you showed up inside it.

Commitments were handled similarly. Once given, they were fixed points. He did not make many promises, but the ones he made were durable. He understood that reliability is cumulative—built slowly through repeated follow-through, and destroyed quickly by casual neglect. To disappoint someone unnecessarily was, to him, a moral failure rather than a logistical one.

Mistakes, when they happened, were handled without defense.

This might have been one of his most formative lessons. He did not argue to preserve ego. He corrected to preserve integrity. If he misjudged something, he adjusted. If he fell short, he absorbed the cost quietly. Excuses were unnecessary when responsibility was already accepted. This posture taught us that accountability is not humiliation. It is alignment restored.

What is striking in hindsight is how little instruction accompanied all of this.

He did not lecture. He did not sermonize. He did not outline values or insist we adopt them consciously. He lived them long enough that they became atmospheric. They entered the household the way habits do—through repetition, not explanation. Over time, they formed the background against which decisions were made.

This is how moral inheritance actually works. Not through speeches, but through presence. Not through rules, but through rhythm. Not through enforcement, but through example.

We learned what mattered by watching what he refused to compromise. We learned how to behave by observing how he corrected himself. We learned the weight of responsibility by seeing how seriously he carried even small obligations.

Work ethic, in this sense, was not about productivity. It was about coherence. About living in a way where effort, word, and character were aligned. About building a life that did not require constant justification because it rested on consistency.

His work did not simply support life. It structured it.

It gave shape to days and meaning to effort. It created an internal order that made decisions clearer and boundaries firmer. It taught us that integrity is not situational—it is practiced everywhere, especially where no one is applauding.

And those values did not remain confined to him.

They passed into us quietly—shaping how we approached responsibility, how we understood accountability, and how we measured ourselves when no one else was keeping score. Long after specific tasks were forgotten, the moral architecture his work built remained intact.

This was the deeper legacy of honest labor. Not what it produced, but what it formed. And from that formation, something lasting took root—something that would continue shaping lives long after the work itself was finished.

When work has given a man his first language of dignity, he can simply set it down when the years say it is time. Even after the shifts ended and the routines loosened, my father carried work within him—not as obligation, but as orientation. It had shaped his posture toward life for so long that stillness felt unfamiliar, almost suspect.

And yet, there was pride in how that chapter ended.

He retired earlier than most. Not abruptly, not dramatically, and not as an act of withdrawal—but because he could. The bills were paid. The obligations met. The long arc of provision had held. For a man who measured worth by responsibility fulfilled, this mattered deeply. Early retirement was not an escape from work; it was evidence that the work had done what it was meant to do.

He never spoke of it boastfully. But there was a quiet satisfaction in knowing he had finished his part with integrity intact. He had not been pushed out. He had not been undone by the years. He stepped away because he had earned the right to do so—because the structure he had built could now stand without his constant reinforcement.

Still, retirement did not arrive as relief. It arrived as disorientation.

The days opened, wide and unstructured, and he did not know how to inhabit them at first. Time, once parceled into shifts and responsibilities, now waited without instruction. There were no bells, no supervisors, no problems that required his steady attention. What others might have welcomed as freedom felt to him like a question he was not prepared to answer.

"Who am I when I am no longer needed in the same way?"

He did not ask this aloud. He lived it quietly. Mornings still came early, even when there was nowhere specific to go. He lingered over small tasks, stretching them gently, as though effort itself were a form of reassurance. He watched the world continue without his participation and felt both gratitude and unease—relieved that the burden had passed, unsettled that it had passed him by.

Rest, for him, was never neutral. It carried a faint edge of guilt.

Sitting too long felt undeserved. Pauses needed justification. Even leisure had to resemble usefulness to feel legitimate. He tended the garden longer than necessary. He straightened things that were already straight. He found reasons to be in motion, not because anyone demanded it, but because motion had long been his proof of worth.

Work lingered in his stillness.

It showed up in the way he scanned rooms, noticing what needed adjusting. In the way he listened for problems before they were named. In the reflex to step forward when something felt unfinished or uncertain. Even without a factory floor beneath his feet, he remained oriented toward contribution. Usefulness had become second nature—not ambition, but instinct.

This was both his anchor and his limitation.

Work had given him dignity when everything else felt provisional. It had restored order when life felt fragile. It had taught him how to stand upright in a world that did not always offer welcome. And because it had done all of that, releasing it fully required something more than permission. It required grace.

There was an ache in no longer being necessary in the same way.

Not an ache of resentment, but of displacement. The skills he had honed over decades were now largely invisible, unrequested. The steadiness he brought so naturally had fewer places to land. The world, which had once relied on his reliability, now moved with a different rhythm. He stood at its edge, not excluded, but no longer essential.

And yet, he did not cling.

He did not demand relevance or insist on being consulted. He adjusted slowly, imperfectly, with the same humility that had marked his working life. He learned—haltingly—that usefulness could take different forms. That presence could replace productivity. That simply being available, attentive, and grounded was still a contribution, even if it did not resemble labor as he had known it.

But the transition was not seamless.

There were moments when he seemed unmoored, unsure where to place his energy. Moments when he drifted, not aimlessly, but cautiously, as though waiting for instruction that would not come. Work had once organized his days from the outside. Now he had to learn how to organize himself from within.

This is the quiet cost of a life shaped by honest labor.

When work becomes a source of dignity, stepping away from it is not merely a change in schedule. It is a reorientation of identity. The hands that once knew exactly what to do must learn how to rest without self-reproach. The mind that once measured worth through contribution must learn a different scale.

My father carried this tension without complaint.

He held his retirement the way he held everything else—without drama, without entitlement, with a sober gratitude that it had been possible at all. He knew what it represented. The years of showing up had not only sustained us; they had sustained him long enough to choose his ending with honor.

Work had anchored him. Now he had to trust that what it had built within him would hold, even without constant exertion. This is where the deeper grace enters.

Not the grace of escape, but the grace of release. Not forgetting the work, but allowing its fruits to remain without continual proof. Letting dignity rest where it has already been earned.

For a man whose life had been shaped by doing what must be done, learning how to be without doing became its own final discipline—one that demanded a courage equal to any labor he had ever performed.

I did not learn about work from advice my father gave. I learned it by proximity. By watching how he entered his days. By observing what he honored without speaking. By noticing what he refused to compromise even when no one was watching.

Work, in our home, was never framed as a path to self-expression. It was stewardship—of opportunity, of responsibility, of whatever had been placed in our care. We did not ask what work would give us. We asked what it required of us. We did not search for meaning in a job; we brought meaning to it through faithfulness.

This understanding took root early, before I had language for it.

I absorbed the holiness of showing up—not as an idea, but as an atmosphere. Mornings mattered. Commitments mattered. What you agreed to do mattered. The day did not belong to you until you had honored what it asked. Work was not glorified, but it was respected. And respect, I learned, was a form of reverence.

I saw how consistency carried more weight than intensity.

My father did not surge forward and collapse. He did not perform and then disappear. He returned. Again and again. His strength lived in repetition, not display. Over time, I came to understand that this kind of steadiness shapes outcomes long before anyone notices it shaping character.

Consistency, I learned, is a moral force. It stabilizes systems. It earns trust. It creates environments where others can relax because someone else is paying attention.

Watching him build his life this way quietly formed my own relationship to effort. I did not grow up believing work should make me famous or fulfilled in obvious ways. I grew up believing work should make things hold. That it should leave fewer problems behind than it finds. That it should be done well even when no one is looking.

Achievement, as I came to understand it, was not about validation. It was about contribution.

I learned to measure success not by applause, but by usefulness. Not by how visible my effort was, but by whether it eased the weight on others. This shaped my ambition in ways I did not fully appreciate until much later. I did not chase work that made me feel important. I gravitated toward work that felt necessary.

My pride—such as it was—formed along the same lines. It was never loud. Never comparative. Never satisfied by winning alone. Pride, as modeled by my father, lived quietly in the knowledge that I had done what was mine to do. That I had met the obligation placed before me. That I had not cut corners, exaggerated my role, or abandoned my post when things became difficult.

This reframed how I understood dignity. Dignity did not come from being seen. It came from being reliable. It did not require recognition. It required alignment between word and effort.

I learned that work carries a moral weight independent of outcome. That even when results are modest, faithfulness is not. That even when the world does not notice, character is still being formed. This truth has followed me into every season of my own life—shaping how I prepare, how I decide, how I endure.

My father never told me to work hard. He showed me how to work faithfully.

And in doing so, he handed me something far more enduring than instruction. He gave me an internal compass—a way of orienting myself when choices multiply and clarity thins. When I am unsure what to pursue, I ask whether the work will allow me to be present, dependable, and useful. Whether it will ask something real of me. Whether it will require integrity rather than performance.

This inheritance has guided me more often than ambition ever could. I learned that work does not need to announce me. It needs to anchor me. It does not need to elevate me above others. It needs to hold others steady. It does not need to make me visible. It needs to make me faithful.

Watching my father build his life one honest day at a time taught me that grace does not always arrive as relief. Sometimes it arrives as constancy—the quiet ability to keep showing up without resentment, without spectacle, without needing the world to notice.

That lesson has shaped the man I became. And it continues to shape the work I choose to do—not as a search for identity, but as an expression of it. Grace rarely announces itself in the places we expect. It does not always arrive through insight or revelation. Often, it hides in repetition—in the faithful return to tasks that appear unremarkable, even forgettable. This is where my father lived most of his life. Not in moments that demanded interpretation, but in days that required consistency.

He never spoke of his work in spiritual terms. He did not frame it as calling or vocation. And yet, looking back, I can see that his labor functioned as a form of prayer—enacted not with words, but with the body. Each morning he rose, each task he completed, each responsibility he met without complaint became a quiet offering. Not because he intended it to be holy, but because he performed it with attention, restraint, and fidelity.

There is a kind of grace that lives inside monotony. The factory floor did not inspire reflection. The routines were repetitive, the outcomes predictable. One shift looked much like the next. But this was precisely where faithfulness took root. When nothing feels meaningful on its own, meaning must be carried by the manner in which a thing is done. My father did not romanticize repetition. He accepted it. And in accepting it, he transformed it.

He showed up again. And again. And again.

Not waiting for motivation. Not requiring recognition. Not seeking transcendence. His faithfulness did not depend on variety or reward. It depended on commitment. And commitment, practiced daily, becomes a spiritual discipline whether or not it is named as such.

There was grace in the way he handled tools—cleaned, returned, cared for as though neglect would be a kind of dishonesty. Grace in the way he measured time—not wasted, not rushed, but respected. Grace in the way he corrected mistakes—quietly, without defensiveness, as if error was not a threat to dignity but part of honest effort. These were not moral gestures performed for effect. They were habits formed over decades, shaped by a belief he might never have articulated but clearly lived: "What is entrusted to you deserves care."

His work did not require language because it carried its own integrity.

Faith, for him, was not primarily expressed through speech. It lived in alignment—between what he believed and how he behaved, between obligation and follow-through, between effort and outcome. He did not separate the sacred from the practical. He did not reserve reverence for church alone. It appeared in the ordinary fidelity of doing what was required, especially when no one was watching.

This is the holiness most people miss. Not the holiness of moments, but the holiness of continuity. Not the holiness of feeling, but the holiness of faithfulness. In his life, grace did not interrupt the ordinary. It inhabited it.

I think now of how rarely he complained, not because the work was easy, but because complaining felt like a misuse of breath better spent completing what remained undone. I think of how little he dramatized his fatigue, how he allowed tiredness to exist without giving it authority. These were not acts of suppression. They were acts of discipline—the kind that refuses to let passing discomfort redefine purpose.

He did not preach grace. He practiced it. Daily. In silence. Through endurance that did not ask to be admired. Through repetition that did not demand relief. Through devotion that required no audience.

What made his work sacramental was not its nature, but its consistency. He did not treat responsibility as something to escape once survival was secured. He treated it as something to be honored—a trust to be carried with care. Even when his body slowed, even when recognition faded, even when usefulness changed shape, the posture of faithfulness remained.

This is the grace that forms a life. Not sudden. Not spectacular. But cumulative. Layered. Earned through return. And passed on not through instruction, but through example.

In the end, his work did not make him visible. It made him faithful. And in that faithfulness, grace did its quiet work—shaping a man, steadying a family, and leaving behind a legacy that could never be measured by output alone.

When the hands that once built and carried finally grow still, what remains becomes unmistakably clear. Noise falls away. Output no longer distracts. What endures is not effort, but effect—not motion, but meaning.

In my father's later years, there was less to point to in the visible sense. Fewer hours worked. Fewer problems solved by force of will. The physical acts that had once defined his days receded quietly, almost respectfully, as though time itself understood what it was asking him to release. And yet, nothing essential collapsed. The life he had built did not unravel when his labor slowed. It held.

That, I came to understand, was the truest evidence of his work.

Trust endured. People still leaned toward him—not necessarily for solutions, but for grounding. His judgment remained a reference point. His presence still steadied rooms. Even without the strength to do what he once had, he carried the authority of someone whose life had proven dependable. Trust does not require activity to survive; it requires consistency over time. And consistency, once established, becomes its own inheritance.

Stability endured as well. Not the kind measured by income or productivity, but the deeper stability of a life ordered by responsibility. The rhythms he had set—the habits of preparation, the respect for limits, the insistence on follow-through—continued to shape the atmosphere around him. Even in stillness, his influence remained active. The structure he built did not depend on his constant reinforcement. It had been constructed to last.

Moral clarity endured. Long after his working years ended, the values forged through honest labor remained intact. "Finish what you start. Do not leave things undone. Be accountable even when no one is watching." These principles did not weaken with age. If anything, they stood out more clearly once effort no longer filled the frame. When the work stops, character speaks louder.

And perhaps most profoundly, the sense that his life had held endured. Not perfectly. Not without cost. But sufficiently. The home he helped create did not fracture under pressure. The family he carried did not scatter for lack of grounding. The values he lived by did not dissolve when circumstances changed. His life had done what it was meant to do. It held.

There came a moment—subtle, unannounced—when I realized that his work had not ended. It had simply changed hands.

I recognized it in myself first not through intention, but through instinct. In the way I prepare before acting. In the discomfort I feel leaving something unfinished. In the quiet satisfaction of having done what was required even when no one notices. His labor had not merely supported me; it had shaped me. The invisible structure he built became the framework through which I moved in the world.

What he constructed through decades of honest work now lived beyond him. Not as memory alone. As pattern. As posture. As inheritance.

The shelter he built was never meant to be temporary. It was designed to outlast the hands that assembled it. And in that sense, his work succeeded in the deepest way possible. It did not collapse when he stepped back. It continued to function—holding, guiding, steadying—long after production ceased.

This is what lasts when the hands grow still. Not the output. Not the accolades. But the trust others feel when standing near what you built. The stability that remains when pressure returns. The moral clarity that does not need reinforcement. A life that held—and continues to hold—because it was constructed with care.

The truest measure of my father's work is not what he produced. It is what endured. That endurance now prepares the ground for what comes next—not merely a reckoning with what was built, but with what must be understood, reconciled, and carried forward in a new way.

There is a particular grace reserved for those who build without spectacle. It does not announce itself in the moment or clamor for recognition. It waits. It endures. And only later—when the noise has faded and the hands have finally come to rest—does its full shape emerge.

This was the grace my father lived inside.

Work, for him, was never merely effort expended or income earned. It was grace received and grace given. Grace received in the dignity it restored to a life once stripped by poverty and displacement. Grace given in the steadiness it extended to everyone who stood in the shelter of what he built. His labor was not transactional; it was relational. It connected him to the world, to his family, to himself, and—whether he would have named it this way or not—to God.

Pride, in his hands, was redeemed from ego into dignity. He did not take pride in being seen. He took pride in being faithful. In showing up. In finishing what was his to finish. In carrying responsibility without complaint and without comparison. His pride was quiet because it was secure. It did not need applause to survive. It rested on the simple truth that he had done what was asked of him, and done it honestly.

A life like that is not built quickly. It is assembled slowly, day after day, through choices that rarely feel significant in isolation. It is built through repetition rather than revelation. Through constancy rather than intensity. Through faithfulness when no one is watching. My father's life did not arc toward drama or distinction. It settled into something far rarer—a coherence that held.

This is the grace of honest work. It does not promise ease. It does not eliminate cost. But it creates something that time or circumstance cannot undo. It forms a way of being in the world—one grounded in responsibility, integrity, and care—that outlasts the seasons of productivity that first gave it shape.

And now, standing at the edge of what he built, the question turns quietly toward me—and toward anyone who inherits such a legacy. What does it mean to receive not wealth, but a way of being? Not accumulation, but orientation? Not answers, but a posture toward life forged through effort and fidelity?

What remains to be reconciled between work and worth, between dignity and rest, between the grace of building and the grace of letting go?

Those questions do not undo what has been built. They deepen it.

My father did not build loudly—but what he built still stands.

SACRED WAYPOINTS

Work as Belonging

In this chapter, my father doesn't simply work to earn a living—he works to earn a place. Before language felt steady, before confidence arrived, contribution became his way of saying, "I am here. I matter."

- Where in your life are you trying to "belong" through performance rather than presence?
- What part of you is still trying to prove you deserve your place?

Sit with this truth: Sometimes the first form of dignity is simply showing up.

The Ritual That Restores Dignity

Each morning carried a quiet order—boots checked, lunch packed, clothes laid out with care. It wasn't vanity. It was self-respect practiced in small, faithful motions.

- What daily practice helps you stand upright on hard days?
- Where could you treat your ordinary routines as holy instead of hurried?

Ask God for steadiness: Teach me to honor what I repeat.

Pride Without Applause

My father carried pride the way he carried everything else—without spectacle. He didn't need admiration. He needed alignment. "I did what was mine to do."

- Where have you confused praise with worth?
- What would it look like to live from self-respect instead of validation?

Hold this gently: Integrity is a quieter form of confidence.

The Boundary Between Honor and Notoriety

When *The Godfather* made 'Italian' feel like a story to wear, my father shut it down—not out of shame, but out of protection. He refused to let glamor rewrite the kind of life he was building. One that was honest, earned, clean.

- Where do you feel pressured to borrow an identity that isn't yours?
- What values are you quietly defending in your home, even if no one applauds you?

Sit with this truth: Honor is built slowly—and it must be guarded.

The Shelter Honest Work Builds

His labor didn't just provide income—it built a structure: bills paid, food present, tomorrow dependable. In a volatile world, his consistency became safety.

- What "shelter" are you building for the people you love?
- Where is faithfulness creating stability that cannot be measured?

Ask God for clarity: "Lord, show me what my steady efforts are really building."

Grace Hidden in the Ordinary

My father didn't preach devotion. He practiced it—in repetition, in unseen accountability, in the care of doing things the right way when no one was watching.

- Where is God inviting you into faithfulness, not spectacle?
- What ordinary task could become an offering if you did it with love?

Hold this gently: Grace often arrives disguised as constancy.

When the Hands Grow Still

As time slowed him, what endured wasn't output—it was trust, stability, moral clarity. His work outlived his working.

What do you want to remain when your own hands grow still?

What part of your legacy is already being formed in the way you live today?

Sit with this truth: The truest measure of a life is not what it produced—but what endured.

ANCHORS OF THE WORD 

Work as Vocation, Not Performance

"Whatever you do, work at it with all your heart, as working for the Lord, not for human masters." (Colossians 3:23 NIV)

My father never spoke of work as calling or ministry, yet he lived this verse with quiet precision. His labor was not shaped by applause or advancement, but by faithfulness to what was placed before him. Scripture reframes work not as transaction, but as offering. When effort is given without spectacle, it becomes devotion enacted through the body. His work did not seek recognition; it sought alignment.

Reflection: Where have you allowed your work to become performance instead of offering?

Building That Holds

"Unless the LORD builds the house, the builders labor in vain. Unless the LORD watches over the city, the guards stand watch in vain. In vain you rise early and stay up late, toiling for food to eat— for he grants sleep to those he loves." (Psalm 127:1-2 NIV)

What my father built did not collapse when his hands grew still. That is how I know his labor was not vain. Stability endured. Trust remained. The house—literal and unseen—held. Scripture reminds us that lasting work is not measured by scale or speed, but by whether it stands when the builder steps away. His faithfulness cooperated with grace in ways no balance sheet could capture.

Reflection: What are you building that would still stand if you stepped back?

Reputation Without Display

"A good name is more desirable than great riches; to be esteemed is better than silver or gold." (Proverbs 22:1 NIV)

My father never managed his image. He simply lived within his values long enough for trust to accumulate around him. Scripture distinguishes reputation from recognition. One is earned slowly through coherence; the other is borrowed and easily lost. His good name did not come from visibility, but from consistency—an integrity that required no explanation.

Reflection: Are you pursuing being known, or being trustworthy?

Faithfulness in the Ordinary

"Whoever can be trusted with very little can also be trusted with much, and whoever is dishonest with very little will also be dishonest with much." (Luke 16:10 NIV)

My father's life unfolded almost entirely in the realm Scripture calls "the little." Repetition. Routine. Responsibility that rarely felt remarkable. Yet this is precisely where faithfulness is tested and formed. The gospel does not elevate spectacle; it sanctifies consistency. Grace took root not through moments, but through return.

Reflection: What "small" responsibility is shaping your character right now?

Integrity Without Witness

"Be careful not to practice your righteousness in front of others to be seen by them. If you do, you will have no reward from your Father in heaven." (Matthew 6:1 NIV)

My father worked the same way whether anyone noticed or not. Scripture warns against righteousness that depends on an audience, because visibility distorts intention. His labor remained inwardly anchored. He did not need witnesses to remain faithful. His integrity was complete even when unseen.

Reflection: How does your effort change when no one is watching?

A Quiet Life That Builds Respect

"… and to make it your ambition to lead a quiet life: You should mind your own business and work with your hands, just as we told you," (1 Thessalonians 4:11 NIV)

This verse could have been written over my father's life. Quiet work. Honest hands. A dignity that required no explanation. Scripture affirms that a life ordered this way earns respect not by assertion, but by coherence. His presence steadied others because it was grounded, not performative.

Reflection: Where might a quieter faithfulness bring greater peace than striving?

Stewardship Before Success

"The LORD God took the man and put him in the Garden of Eden
to work it and take care of it." (Genesis 2:15 NIV)

Before achievement enters the story, stewardship does. My father treated
work not as conquest, but as care. Tools mattered. Time mattered. Finishing
mattered. Scripture roots dignity not in domination, but in tending what has
been entrusted. His labor reflected this original posture—guarding what he
was given, and leaving it better than he found it.

Reflection: What has been entrusted to you that needs tending rather than
proving?

Learning to Rest Without Fear

"… for anyone who enters God's rest also rests from their works, just
as God did from his." (Hebrews 4:10 NIV)

When work has been a man's first language of dignity, rest can feel like risk.
Retirement asked my father to trust what had already been built—to believe
that faithfulness does not evaporate when effort slows. Scripture frames rest
not as idleness, but as confidence that the work is sufficient. Letting go
required grace equal to any labor.

Reflection: What would it mean to trust that your worth does not require
constant effort?

What Is Passed Without Words

"Impress them on your children. Talk about them when you sit at home and when you walk along the road, when you lie down and when you get up." (Deuteronomy 6:7 NIV)

My father taught without instruction. His values transferred through proximity, not lecture. Scripture reminds us that formation happens through repetition and presence. What is lived consistently is absorbed deeply. His work ethic became a moral inheritance long before I knew its name.

Reflection: What are you teaching others simply by how you live?

What Endures

"Therefore everyone who hears these words of mine and puts them into practice is like a wise man who built his house on the rock." (Matthew 7:24 NIV)

Storms came. Illness came. Time came. And still, what he built held. Scripture does not promise that faithful lives avoid storms—only that they endure them. The final testimony of my father's work is not what he produced, but what remained standing when effort ceased.

Reflection: When the storms come, what in your life will still be standing?

LEGACY NOTES

EIGHT

What His Life Conveyed Long Before Words Could Say

"Preach the Gospel at all times. When necessary, use words."

— Attributed to St. Francis of Assisi (1181-1226)

Before I ever understood what my father believed, I learned how he stood. Before he explained anything about life, responsibility, or faith, he showed me—quietly, repeatedly, without commentary—what it looked like to inhabit a day with integrity. His lessons did not arrive in sentences. They arrived in posture. In tone. In the way he entered a room, met a problem, or carried silence without needing to fill it. Long before I could name values, I was living inside them.

My father was not a man of instruction. He did not gather us for talks or offer guidance shaped for memory. He did not narrate his principles or frame his choices as lessons. And yet, looking back now, it is clear that nothing formative was missing. What he chose instead—whether consciously or by instinct—was far more enduring. He lived his values so consistently that explanation would have been redundant. Character, in our home, was not taught. It was absorbed.

If the previous chapter asked what his honest work built, this one turns toward a quieter architecture. It asks what his way of being conveyed before words ever entered the conversation. What was passed from father to son not through advice, but through proximity. What took root simply by being near him, watching him move through ordinary days with a steadiness that never sought attention.

I did not learn who he was by what he claimed. I learned it by what he refused to do. He did not exaggerate himself. He did not defend his choices. He did not dramatize hardship or translate effort into entitlement. He carried himself with a restraint that felt unremarkable at the time and revelatory in hindsight. Nothing about him pressed outward. Everything about him held inward.

Formation, I would come to understand much later, happens long before comprehension. Children are shaped not by what adults say they value, but by what they embody when no one is watching. We absorb tone before theology. We learn posture before principle. And what is modeled consistently becomes internalized so deeply that it feels instinctive rather than inherited.

This is how my father taught.

I watched him prepare for the day without complaint. The same careful movements. The same unhurried attention to what needed to be done. There was no visible resistance to the hours ahead, no ritual of dread or self-pity. He did not announce resolve; he practiced it. Morning after morning, he entered his responsibilities as though they were not burdens to escape, but obligations to honor.

I watched how he handled frustration—most often without explosion. When things went wrong, and they often did, he rarely reached for volume or blame. His restraint was not passivity; it was containment. He absorbed pressure without immediately transferring it to the room. He allowed difficulty to remain his to carry rather than something to discharge onto others. At the time, I did not know this was unusual. I thought it was simply how adults behaved.

But he was not perfect. There were moments when frustration did surface—briefly, unevenly—not as anger, but as strain. It showed up when expectations collided with limits, when what he wanted to give his family exceeded what circumstances allowed. These were not outbursts born of temper; they were leaks from a man who carried a standard shaped by memory. He had known scarcity as a child in Italy, and the desire to provide more than he had once received pressed constantly against him. When that desire felt thwarted, frustration sometimes escaped—loud, but not cruel, and visible.

Even then, the lesson remained intact. His frustration did not seek a target. It did not humiliate or wound. It passed through him rather than lodging itself in others. In those moments, I did not learn that strength means the absence of strain. I learned that responsibility can stretch a man to his edges without breaking his character. His expectations of himself were high—sometimes higher than circumstances could meet—but even when he faltered, the center held.

Looking back, I can see that those moments made the lesson more honest, not less. They revealed that restraint is not the same as ease, and composure is not the same as indifference. They showed me that love can carry pressure without disguising it, and a man can struggle without surrendering the values that guide him.

And I noticed how rarely he justified himself. He did not explain why he worked the way he did, or why certain lines could not be crossed. He did not defend his decisions or invite agreement. His life stood on its own coherence. What he did aligned with who he was, and that alignment removed the need for commentary.

These were not dramatic moments. They were quiet repetitions, layered day upon day, shaping something beneath the surface. Values entered my life atmospherically—through rhythm rather than rule, through example rather than explanation. I learned what mattered not because it was named, but because it was consistently present. I learned what was unacceptable not through correction, but through absence.

Only much later did I recognize what had been happening all along. My father was teaching by inhabiting his values so fully that they required no explanation. His life itself was the lesson—steady, restrained, coherent. And long before I could articulate what I had learned from him, I was already living it.

Silence was one of my father's primary moral languages, though I did not recognize it as such at the time. In a world that often equates silence with absence, withdrawal, or emotional neglect, his quiet carried a different weight. It was not the silence of someone who had nothing to say. It was the silence of someone choosing carefully when speech would help—and when it would not.

He instinctively understood something that I would come to appreciate only much later: Words can escalate what action is meant to contain. When tension rose in our home, when circumstances pressed in, when emotions threatened to spill past their edges, he often responded not by speaking more, but by speaking less. His restraint was not confusion. It was judgment. He sensed when words would inflame rather than heal, dramatize rather than steady.

There were moments when silence functioned as protection. Not avoidance, not denial, but shielding. He absorbed the emotional turbulence of a situation rather than amplifying it. When my mother's illness surged, when stress sharpened the air, when fear hovered close to the surface, he did not narrate the danger aloud. He did not name worst-case scenarios or voice anxieties that could not yet be resolved. His quiet held the line between what was happening and what did not need to be said in front of children. Silence, in those moments, was not emptiness. It was a barrier against chaos.

I remember how arguments could lose momentum in his presence—not because he dominated them, but because he refused to feed them. Where others might have responded with justification or defense, he stayed measured. Where volume might have invited counter-volume, his stillness interrupted the cycle. He did not need to win exchanges. He needed to keep the room from tipping into something harder to recover from. Silence became a way of lowering the temperature without announcing that he was doing so.

This was dignity at work.

He did not believe every feeling required articulation. He did not assume that emotional honesty demanded immediate expression. Some things, he seemed to understand, grow more dangerous when rushed into language. Silence allowed time for clarity to emerge, for emotion to settle into something more manageable. It created space where reaction could soften into response.

Importantly, his silence was never cold. It did not create uncertainty or distance. It did not leave us guessing whether we were loved or safe. Quite the opposite. His quiet carried a steadiness that reassured rather than confused. Even when he said little, his presence communicated attentiveness. He was there. He was watching. He was holding the situation, even if he was not explaining it.

In this way, silence became a form of trust.

He trusted that action would speak louder than commentary. That showing up mattered more than narrating effort. That consistency over time would communicate values more reliably than explanation in a moment. He did not feel compelled to justify himself or defend his choices verbally. The integrity of his life did that work for him.

There were situations where words would have made things worse—where explanation would have sounded like excuse, where commentary would have turned pain into spectacle. In those moments, his silence preserved proportion. It kept problems from expanding beyond their proper size. It allowed difficulty to remain contained rather than contagious.

But his silence was not absolute. There were rare moments when it cracked— not into chaos, but into something sharp enough to mark me.

I clearly remember one of those moments. I was young, newly driving, still careless in ways only youth can afford to be. I damaged the car. It was not catastrophic, but it was real. Metal bent. Something precious diminished.

When I told him, his reaction startled me. His voice rose. His face tightened. Emotion broke through in a way I had almost never seen.

At the time, I felt only the sting of it—fear, embarrassment, the sudden awareness that I had crossed an invisible line. But looking back now, I understand what was happening beneath the surface. Cars were not replaceable conveniences in our world. They were acquired through patience, sacrifice, and years of steady labor. Nothing came easily. Nothing was assumed. To damage something hard-won was not merely an inconvenience; it was a reminder of how fragile progress could be.

His eruption was not about anger in the way people often mean it. It was about responsibility. About care. About the moral weight of things earned slowly and held together deliberately. In that moment, I learned—more clearly than through any lecture—that what costs effort must be treated with respect. That carelessness is never neutral when resources are scarce. That provision carries with it an obligation to protect what has been provided.

And just as quickly as it appeared, the emotion subsided. He did not linger in it. He did not rehearse it. He did not turn it into a story about himself. The point had been made, and he returned to his customary restraint. Even his anger was disciplined—arriving only when necessary, leaving once it had done its work.

As a child, I sometimes wished for more words. I wanted reassurance phrased clearly, emotions named explicitly, intentions spelled out. I mistook his quiet for emotional distance because I did not yet understand how much care it took to remain measured under pressure. Only later did I see that his silence was not the absence of feeling, but the discipline of feeling governed.

He felt deeply. That was never in question. What distinguished him was his refusal to let feeling become the loudest voice in the room. Silence was how he honored responsibility—to himself, to his family, to the moment. It was how he prevented his inner strain from becoming someone else's burden.

He did not use silence to disappear. He used it to steady the room.

And in doing so, he taught me something profound without ever naming it—that maturity is not measured by how much we express, but by how carefully we choose what truly needs to be expressed. That restraint itself can be an act of love. That sometimes the most responsible thing a man can do is to hold his words until they can serve, rather than satisfy.

Silence, in my father's life, was never empty. It was intentional. It was protective. And it was formative—shaping the emotional architecture of our home in ways words alone never could.

Love, in my father's hands, did not arrive wrapped in tenderness. It did not lean toward sentiment or announce itself through affection. It did not soften its voice to make itself easier to receive. And yet, it was everywhere—so constant, so reliable, that it was almost invisible while it was happening.

He loved through presence. Not the expressive presence that fills a room with warmth, but the steadfast presence that refuses to leave when circumstances become heavy. He was there in the mornings before the house woke. There in the evenings when fatigue settled into his bones. There during illness, during uncertainty, during stretches when chaos threatened to spill beyond its bounds. His love did not ask how it felt to stay. It stayed because staying was required.

Provision was one of its clearest forms. He understood love first as responsibility fulfilled. Bills paid. Food present. Shelter intact. These were not gestures meant to impress; they were obligations taken seriously. To provide was not, for him, a role he performed. It was a vow he lived inside. Even when resources were thin, even when worry pressed close, he did not waver. He absorbed pressure so others would not have to carry it. That absorption was not dramatic. It was sacrificial.

Consistency was another language of his love. He returned each day to the same obligations without resentment. He did not renegotiate his commitment when things became difficult. He did not withdraw when appreciation was absent. He showed up because showing up mattered more than being acknowledged. Over time, that consistency created a sense of safety that did not rely on reassurance. It told us, without words, that what mattered would continue to be held.

Protection, too, was love's expression in his life.

He guarded the boundaries of the home quietly. He managed risk. He anticipated problems before they arrived. He paid attention when others relaxed. This vigilance was not driven by fear; it was driven by care. He understood how easily stability could be lost because he had lived without it. His watchfulness was not about control—it was about containment. He took responsibility for what could go wrong so others might live without constant alertness.

During illness, this love revealed its depth.

When my mother's struggles intensified—emotionally and physically—he did not retreat. He adjusted. He became more watchful, more deliberate, more present. He learned new rhythms of care without complaint. He stayed through confusion, through exhaustion, through moments that asked more than seemed reasonable. There was nothing tender in the conventional sense about this devotion. It was not poetic. It was not gentle. But it was faithful.

He did not love with softness. He loved with endurance.

Sacrifice, for him, was never theatrical. He did not narrate what he gave up. He did not frame his choices as losses. He simply oriented his life toward what needed to be done and allowed desire to recede when it interfered. There was no bitterness in this, only a quiet acceptance that love often requires subtraction. To love was to remain even when comfort invited retreat.

There were countless moments when leaving—emotionally, mentally, or physically—would have been easier. Moments when detachment would have reduced pain. Moments when distance might have preserved energy. He did not take those exits. He stayed engaged, alert, responsible. That staying shaped the emotional climate of our home more than affection ever could have.

As a child, I did not always recognize this as love. I noticed what was absent more easily than what was present. There were fewer hugs than I might have wanted. Fewer verbal affirmations. Fewer moments of overt reassurance. I mistook restraint for distance, seriousness for severity. I did not yet understand that some men express love not by reaching outward, but by holding inward—by containing themselves so others can feel safe.

Only later did I see the pattern clearly.

He loved us by refusing to make his strain our burden. By staying steady when fear would have justified withdrawal. By choosing responsibility over relief again and again. His love did not seek to soothe emotion; it sought to preserve structure. It did not aim to make us feel better in the moment; it aimed to ensure that life would hold over time.

Endurance, I came to understand, was his devotion.

It was not flashy. It did not sparkle. It did not announce itself. But it was relentless in its fidelity. He did not leave. He did not abandon. He did not grow careless with what had been entrusted to him. Even when weariness pressed close, even when recognition faded, even when the effort felt asymmetrical, he remained.

He loved without softness—but never without faithfulness.

That distinction matters. Because softness can come and go with mood, energy, and circumstance. Faithfulness remains when all of those are depleted. Faithfulness stays when tenderness is exhausted. Faithfulness continues when affection would falter. My father's love was built on that kind of durability. It did not rely on feeling. It relied on commitment.

And that love shaped me more deeply than I could have known.

It taught me that love does not always sound like reassurance. That it does not always look like warmth. That sometimes love shows up as vigilance, as consistency, as a man standing between chaos and the people he is responsible for. It taught me that devotion can be quiet and still be absolute.

He did not love loudly. He loved dependably.

And in a world that often confuses affection with commitment, his life stands as a different kind of witness. One that insists love can be practical without being cold, restrained without being absent, and unspectacular without being small.

His love held. And because it held, everything else was able to remain standing. Standards entered my life the same way his love did—without announcement, without explanation, without negotiation. There were no lists, no lectures, no corrective speeches designed to shape my behavior. Instead, there was orientation. A steady alignment toward what was solid, restrained, and real. I learned what mattered not because he told me, but because he lived in a way that quietly refused alternatives.

He taught standards by what he rejected.

Exaggeration made him uneasy. Not because it was dramatic, but because it distorted proportion. When stories grew larger than necessary, when details were inflated for effect, something in him stiffened. He rarely corrected the speaker outright. He simply disengaged. The energy left his posture. His attention shifted elsewhere. The message was unmistakable: Truth does not need decoration. Effort does not require embellishment. To overstate is to cheapen what might otherwise have been sufficient.

Performance unsettled him even more.

Anything that smelled of self-display—of effort angled toward attention rather than completion—felt suspect. He did not admire cleverness when it sought applause. He did not trust confidence that needed to be witnessed. He understood instinctively that performance consumes energy without producing substance. The work that mattered, in his view, was rarely visible while it was being done. And when something required spectacle to justify itself, he assumed it lacked depth.

I absorbed this before I could articulate it.

I learned to be wary of dramatizing my own effort. To distrust the urge to narrate hardship for validation. To feel discomfort when praise arrived too easily. Not because success was wrong, but because attention was unreliable. What mattered was alignment—between what I said, what I did, and what I was willing to carry without being seen.

Abandonment of responsibility was the one thing he could not abide.

Once something was agreed to, it became fixed. Circumstances could complicate it. Fatigue could strain it. But the commitment itself did not dissolve simply because it became inconvenient. He did not romanticize perseverance; he normalized it. To casually walk away from what you had taken on was, in his view, a breach of character rather than a change of plans.

He did not scold when others failed this standard.

He simply did not trust them again.

That quiet withdrawal was far more instructive than correction would have been. It taught me that reliability is cumulative and fragile. That trust, once eroded, does not return easily. And that responsibility, once accepted, becomes part of who you are. You do not renegotiate it when conditions shift.

Perhaps the most formative standard he transmitted was this: Do not make yourself the center.

He recoiled from self-importance with an instinctive clarity. Not ambition, not leadership, not competence—but ego. The kind that bends conversations toward oneself. The kind that frames every situation as a referendum on personal worth. He had little patience for it, not because it offended him personally, but because it disrupted order. When a man makes himself the center, everything else becomes distorted—effort turns performative, responsibility becomes conditional, and truth becomes negotiable.

My father stood outside that gravity.

He did not insert himself unnecessarily. He did not dominate rooms or conversations. He did not need to be seen as decisive or impressive. His authority came from steadiness, not assertion. When he spoke, it was because something needed to be said—not because silence made him uncomfortable.

This taught me something subtle and enduring.

That influence does not require volume. That respect does not require insistence. That leadership, when it is real, rarely advertises itself. I learned to value substance over presence, contribution over charisma, completion over credit.

He respected effort more than appearance.

Work done quietly, imperfectly, faithfully—this earned his regard. Flashy results achieved through shortcuts did not. He could tell the difference immediately. And he oriented himself toward the former without comment. Tools mattered because they had been used. Time mattered because it had been honored. Promises mattered because they had been kept.

When mistakes occurred, he did not rush to protect image. He corrected the mistakes.

There was no defensiveness in this, no posturing. Error was not a threat to dignity; avoidance of responsibility was. That distinction shaped how I learned to handle my own failures. Not by explanation. Not by justification. But by alignment restored through action.

What strikes me now is how little enforcement accompanied all of this.

He did not hover. He did not police behavior. He did not threaten consequences. Instead, he trusted that orientation—once internalized—would govern choice more effectively than rules ever could. And he was right. The standards he lived inside became the standards I carried, often without realizing where they had come from.

Alongside that trust lived something quieter and more personal—my fear of letting him down. Not a fear born of punishment or anger, but of disappointment—of failing to live up to a steadiness he never demanded but always embodied. His expectations were rarely spoken, yet they were unmistakable. Because he carried himself with such coherence, the thought of falling short did not feel like breaking a rule; it felt like breaking alignment.

I did not worry about being caught. I worried about being unworthy of the trust he extended so freely. His restraint placed the burden of choice where it belonged—inside me. And that internal reckoning proved far more formative than any external correction ever could.

I learned what was unacceptable not because he named it, but because it had no place in his life.

Dishonesty did not survive proximity to him. Neither did laziness masked as cleverness. Neither did self-pity disguised as depth. These things simply failed to take root because the environment did not support them. His presence was clarifying. It revealed what held weight and what did not.

This is how standards truly transmit. Not through enforcement, but through atmosphere. Not through correction, but through coherence. Not through rules, but through example sustained long enough to be absorbed.

He did not give me commandments. He gave me a compass. An orientation toward truth without spectacle. Toward responsibility without drama. Toward effort without self-congratulation. Toward fidelity without performance.

And once that orientation settles into a person, it does not need constant reinforcement. It begins to govern instinct. It shapes reaction. It informs choice long before deliberation begins.

He did not teach me how to behave; he showed me how to stand. I did not learn emotional regulation from techniques or instruction. I learned it the way most children do—by borrowing the nervous system of the adults around me. And the system I borrowed most consistently was my father's.

He did not eliminate fear from our lives. There was too much uncertainty for that—illness, money, immigration, moods that shifted without warning. But he did not dramatize fear either. He absorbed it. Held it. Worked around it. Fear existed in our home, but it was not given the authority to run the room. And because it wasn't amplified, it never became overwhelming.

When pressure arrived—and it arrived often—his body told the story before his words ever did. He slowed rather than sped up. His voice lowered rather than rose. His movements became deliberate, not frantic. Even when I could sense tension in him, it rarely spilled outward. I watched him remain grounded in moments when escalation would have been understandable, even justified. That steadiness was not accidental. It was chosen. And choice, repeated over time, becomes pattern.

As a child, I did not name this as regulation. I simply felt its effects. Rooms felt safer when he entered them. Conversations settled. Chaos narrowed. There was a physical sensation of containment that followed him, as though his presence created boundaries fear could not easily cross. I did not yet know how much work that kind of containment required. I only knew that when he was near, things felt more manageable.

He managed emotion the way he managed work—without theatrics, without denial, without surrender. He did not pretend everything was fine. But he also refused to let emotion dictate direction. Fear was acknowledged internally and addressed practically. Worry became planning. Anxiety became preparation. Uncertainty became attention. He transformed emotion into action not to escape it, but to give it a proper place.

This taught me something long before I could articulate it. Feelings are real, but they are not always in charge.

I watched him navigate crises without panic. Illness worsened. Systems failed. Plans unraveled. And still, he remained oriented toward what could be done next rather than what could be feared endlessly. His steadiness did not come from optimism. It came from practice. From having lived long enough to know that fear, when allowed to swell unchecked, solves nothing. But fear, when held firmly and quietly, can be survived.

When those crises arrived, something else happened as well. I grew up faster than expected. I am not sure whether it was because my father needed help, or because I felt—without being asked—that I should provide it. As the eldest, I sensed an internal shift—a movement toward responsibility that did not come with ceremony or instruction. It simply arrived, as necessity often does, and settled into place. I began paying closer attention. Anticipating needs. Holding myself more carefully. Not because anyone demanded it, but because the moment required it.

My father did not delegate this responsibility to me. He did not announce it or burden me with it. But his way of standing inside pressure created space for me to step forward. I learned, in real time, that maturity is not assigned. It is assumed when stability matters more than comfort. Watching him remain composed when things were fragile taught me that fear does not excuse abdication. It invites participation.

Over time, I noticed how his presence lowered the emotional temperature of the room. Not because he suppressed others, but because he modeled restraint so convincingly that escalation felt unnecessary. When someone else grew agitated, he did not match their intensity. He countered it with calm. When emotions threatened to spill over, he became more grounded, not less. Calm, I learned, is not passive. It is active resistance to chaos.

I did not realize then that my own nervous system was being shaped in those moments. I thought I was simply watching my father be himself. Only later did I recognize how deeply his regulation had become my inheritance.

As I grew older, I found myself responding to pressure in ways that surprised me—but not always cleanly, and not always immediately. There were moments when chaos met me first as panic, when the weight of a situation surged faster than composure could arrive. I felt the internal pressure keenly, and at times it spilled outward before I could gather it. Panic, for me, was not a collapse so much as a venting—a momentary release before order could be restored.

And yet, even then, something steadier followed.

Once the initial surge passed, I could find my footing. When uncertainty lingered, I focused. When fear pressed in, I did not need it to disappear before I could move forward. I could stand inside it without being consumed. Calm did not arrive as perfection; it arrived as recovery. As the ability to return—to regulate, to respond, to choose the next right step after the noise had cleared.

That capacity did not originate in me. It was borrowed, absorbed, and slowly made my own through years of proximity—and through the quiet responsibility I learned to carry before I knew its name.

I came to understand that regulation is not the absence of reaction. It is the willingness to regain control after reaction has had its say. My father was steadier than I have ever been, but even my partial inheritance of that steadiness has shaped how I move through difficulty. I do not always meet chaos with silence or composure. But I have learned not to stay there. I have learned how to return to center.

In that sense, what he passed on was not an impossible standard, but a direction. Not perfection, but recovery. Not the elimination of fear, but the confidence that fear does not get the final word.

I learned that fear does not require expression to be acknowledged. It requires containment to be managed. I learned that calm is not the absence of emotion, but the mastery of it over time. I learned that steadiness under pressure is not a personality trait—it is a relational gift, passed from one nervous system to another, imperfectly but enduringly.

Before I knew how to manage fear, I learned how to stand inside it.

And even now, when I falter, that lesson continues to hold—quiet, embodied, and unspoken. It is—one of the most faithful inheritances of all.

My father did not speak the language of faith easily. He did not reach for religious vocabulary, nor did he frame his life in theological terms. Belief, for him, was not discussed or defended. It was something to be carried. Something to be lived quietly, without commentary or display.

If faith existed in his life—and I believe now that it did—it existed first as posture.

It showed up in how he accepted obligation without protest. In the way he honored what had been entrusted to him, whether or not it was fair, and whether or not it was chosen. He did not ask whether responsibility aligned with his preferences. He asked whether it was his. And once that was settled, he bore it.

There was reverence in that.

He treated responsibility as something almost sacred—not because it elevated him, but because it placed a claim upon him. He behaved as though duty itself deserved respect. As though turning away from what was required would fracture something internal, something more consequential than comfort or ease. This was not moral rigidity. It was fidelity.

His faith, such as it was, lived in obedience long before it lived in explanation.

I saw it in how he returned to the same obligations day after day without resentment. In how he resisted shortcuts, not merely as practical risks, but as violations of trust. In how he refused to dramatize his suffering, even when suffering would have justified attention. He did not make his pain a currency. He did not ask it to speak on his behalf.

There is a kind of belief embedded in that restraint.

He behaved as though life itself were something to be stewarded carefully— not conquered, not negotiated, but tended. Tools were respected. Time was honored. Commitments were kept. None of this was framed as virtue. It was simply how things were done. And yet, looking back, I can see the spiritual logic beneath it. He lived as though what he touched mattered. As though effort carried moral weight. As though fidelity, practiced quietly, was its own form of reverence.

Prayer, in his life, was not spoken aloud. It was enacted.

It lived in the daily return to tasks he did not choose but accepted. In the consistency that refused to abandon what had been started. In the discipline of doing what was required without needing to feel inspired. His devotion did not depend on mood or clarity. It depended on commitment. And commitment, repeated often enough, becomes something very close to worship.

He did not talk about God often. But he lived as though something larger than himself was always watching—not in judgment, but in trust. As though faithfulness itself was the response being asked of him. This was not fear-based obedience. It was grounded responsibility. The kind that does not ask for reward, only coherence.

Suffering, when it came, was handled the same way.

He did not spiritualize it. He did not narrate it. He did not explain it into meaning. He bore it. Quietly. Without embellishment. Without complaint. This was not denial. It was restraint—the belief that suffering does not need amplification to be endured. That pain does not require performance to be legitimate. That dignity can be preserved even when answers are absent.

At the time, I did not recognize this as faith. I thought faith looked like words. Like certainty. Like proclamation.

Only later did I understand that what I had witnessed was a form of belief more ancient and more demanding. A belief expressed not through conviction, but through constancy. Not through explanation, but through endurance. Not through clarity, but through trust lived one day at a time.

He believed with his life long before he ever needed words. That is why his faith endured. It did not rely on language to survive. It was carried in action, in restraint, in the faithful honoring of what had been entrusted to him.

When words were insufficient—or unnecessary—his life bore the weight of witness.

This was holiness without articulation. Not loud. Not performative. But faithful. And it formed something in me long before I knew belief could live that way.

There is a kind of understanding that does not arrive on time. It comes late—after the urgency has passed, after the questions that once demanded answers have quieted, after the man you were trying to understand no longer needs to explain himself. It arrives not as revelation, but as recognition. And when it does, it carries weight.

My understanding of my father came this way.

As a child, I experienced him from the inside of need. I measured his presence by warmth, his love by words, his nearness by emotional availability. I wanted reassurance made explicit, care translated into language I could recognize. In that framework, his restraint felt like distance. His silence felt like withholding. His vigilance felt like tension rather than protection.

I did not yet know how to read him. That literacy came later—only after life had required of me some of the same things it had required of him.

It came after I had carried responsibility long enough to feel how it narrows your margins. After I had learned how easily fear can masquerade as urgency. After I had discovered how much discipline it takes not to transfer pressure to those you love simply because you are tired of holding it yourself. Only then did the shape of his choices begin to make sense.

I began to see that what I had interpreted as emotional distance was, in fact, emotional containment.

He was not absent. He was absorbing. He was not disengaged. He was regulating. He was not withholding affection. He was guarding stability. His silence was not emptiness—it was labor.

And, memories rearranged themselves. I remembered moments when he stood quietly at the edge of chaos and realized that his stillness had kept things from tipping. I recalled evenings when his few words had prevented situations from becoming larger than they needed to be. I thought of decisions he made without explanation—choices that frustrated me at the time, but now revealed themselves as acts of foresight rather than control.

What I once experienced as tension, I now recognize as vigilance born of love.

There was a particular season—unremarkable on the surface—when this recognition settled fully into me. I was no longer young. I had begun to shoulder responsibility that could not be set down easily. I knew what it meant to lie awake rehearsing contingencies, to carry concern quietly so others could rest, to choose restraint not because it was easy, but because it was necessary.

And in that season, I saw him. Not as a symbol. Not as a standard. But as a man who had been doing this long before I understood what it cost.

I realized then how much of himself he had withheld—not because he lacked feeling, but because he had too much of it to release carelessly. How often he had chosen steadiness over self-expression. How frequently he had taken the harder path of containment rather than the easier relief of discharge.

His restraint had not been coldness. It had been courage. The recognition carried grief with it.

Grief for the version of myself who could not receive his love in the language it was offered. Grief for the questions I asked too early, before I had the capacity to hear the answers. Grief for the ways children often misinterpret the very protections that make their lives possible.

But it also carried gratitude—deep, steady, clarifying. Gratitude for the way he held the line when letting go would have been simpler. For the way he bore weight invisibly so others would not have to. For the consistency that never announced itself, but never failed either.

I came to understand that love does not always arrive with softness. Sometimes it arrives with structure. Sometimes it looks like reliability. Sometimes it takes the form of a man who refuses to let his internal strain become someone else's inheritance.

His love had been preventative. It stopped chaos before it started. It contained fear before it spread. It created an environment where others could grow without knowing what had been absorbed on their behalf.

What I once experienced as distance, I now recognize as devotion. Devotion not to comfort, but to outcome. Not to expression, but to protection. Not to being understood, but to being faithful.

That recognition did not diminish the longing of childhood. But it did transform it. It allowed me to honor the love I received in the form it was given, rather than the form I once demanded.

And in doing so, it gave me something rare. Not just clarity about him—but mercy for myself.

Because I, too, have misunderstood. I, too, have held back when others wanted more. I, too, have chosen restraint over expression and been misread because of it. Understanding my father taught me that being unseen does not mean being absent, and that love sometimes does its deepest work where it remains unnamed.

Some lessons cannot be taught early. They require lived context. They require time to ripen.

My understanding of my father did not come when I wanted it. It came when I was finally able to receive it. And when it arrived, it did not feel like discovery. It felt like recognition of something that had been there all along.

There are inheritances no one asks for. They arrive quietly, without ceremony or consent, already woven into the way you move through the world. You do not sign for them. You do not examine them in advance. You simply discover, over time, that they are already yours.

This was how my father's life passed into mine. Not through instruction. Not through expectation stated aloud. But through posture—absorbed so early and so consistently that it felt less like inheritance and more like instinct.

Long before I recognized it, his way of being had taken up residence in me.

I see it now in the way I prepare before acting. In the reflex to steady a room rather than animate it. In the discomfort I feel leaving something unresolved, even when walking away would be easier. I recognize him in my attention to details others overlook, in my hesitation to dramatize difficulty, in the quiet resolve to finish what I begin regardless of recognition.

These are not habits I consciously adopted. They are behaviors I woke up one day to find already formed.

Inheritance, I have learned, does not always announce itself as gift. Sometimes it arrives as weight. A seriousness that enters the room before you do. A sense of responsibility that feels older than your own years. An internal expectation to hold things together even when no one has asked you to.

There were moments when I resented this. When I wondered why ease came more naturally to others, why rest felt like it had to be justified, why stepping back stirred discomfort rather than relief. I did not yet know that these reactions were not personality quirks, but echoes. Traces of a man who had lived so long in the posture of responsibility that it had become contagious.

His vigilance had shaped my alertness. His restraint had trained my caution. His endurance had normalized carrying more than my share without complaint.

This inheritance was both burden and gift.

The burden was the weight of seriousness. The quiet expectation to be dependable. The instinct to step forward when things feel unstable. The internal pressure to be useful even when usefulness is not required. These traits can narrow a life if they are not held with care. They can make joy feel indulgent and rest feel provisional.

But the gift was deeper.

Because along with the weight came capacity. The ability to remain grounded under pressure. The reflex to orient toward what can be done rather than what can be feared. The steadiness that allows others to exhale because someone else is paying attention. These qualities are not flashy. They do not draw applause. But they build environments where people can function, grow, and recover.

I did not choose this inheritance. But I recognize its worth.

I see how it shapes my decisions long before I analyze them. How it guides my responses when uncertainty rises. How it positions me toward responsibility not as obligation imposed, but as trust received. I carry forward his imprint not because I am trying to imitate him, but because he formed the lens through which I understand what it means to be faithful to what has been placed in my care.

There is humility in acknowledging this. Because it means admitting that much of who I am was formed before I had language or agency to decide otherwise. It means recognizing that autonomy is often overstated, and that we are shaped as much by proximity as by choice. It means honoring the quiet ways love, restraint, and endurance travel across generations without asking permission.

This inheritance does not demand replication. It demands stewardship.

To carry it faithfully does not mean to live as he lived in every detail. It means to honor the posture beneath the pattern—to recognize when restraint is necessary and when it has outlived its purpose; when responsibility must be carried forward and when it must be shared; when vigilance protects and when it constricts.

What he passed to me was not a script. It was a stance.

A way of standing inside the world that privileges steadiness over spectacle, responsibility over recognition, faithfulness over ease. That stance now lives in me whether I acknowledge it or not. And in acknowledging it, I gain the freedom to carry it consciously rather than unconsciously—to let it guide without letting it rule.

This is the paradox of unchosen inheritance. It binds you and it equips you. It limits you and it strengthens you. It asks to be honored, not blindly repeated. I did not choose what was passed to me. But I choose, now, how to carry it.

Faithfully.

There is a difference between what is taught and what is caught.

Words can instruct, clarify, persuade. But lives—lived steadily, consistently, without contradiction—do something far more enduring. They form.

My father rarely explained himself. He did not translate his values into language or package his beliefs into lessons. He lived them long enough, quietly enough, that they entered the air around him. And in that atmosphere, I was shaped before I was aware of being formed.

What he lived became contagious.

Not because it was imposed, but because it was coherent. Because his way of moving through the world aligned effort with responsibility, restraint with care, presence with love. Over time, those alignments took root in me—not as rules I followed, but as reflexes I trusted. His legacy did not remain behind him as memory. It moved forward through me as motion.

This is the weight of what is caught rather than taught. It carries no syllabus. It offers no exemption. It settles into the body before it reaches the mind.

And because it arrives without permission, it eventually demands discernment. What was absorbed must, at some point, be examined. Not to reject it, but to understand it fully—to decide what must be kept, what must be refined, and what must finally be laid down with gratitude rather than guilt.

Formation is powerful. But freedom requires reckoning.

There comes a moment when inheritance must be held up to the light—not to diminish its value, but to ensure it serves life rather than constrains it. The very patterns that once protected and steadied can, if left unexamined, become burdens carried longer than necessary. What was once adaptive can become limiting. What once preserved can begin to cost.

This does not negate the gift. It honors it. Because only what is truly seen can be carried wisely. And only what is carried wisely can be passed on without distortion.

My father gave me more than instruction. He gave me a way of standing in the world.

Now the work turns quieter still. Not toward building for survival, not toward forming through proximity, but toward understanding the ground beneath all of it—the foundation his life laid not just for me, but for everyone who stood within the reach of his steadiness.

What supported his endurance? What allowed such constancy to take root? What held him when no one else could?

Those questions lead not backward, but deeper. Because before a life can form others, it must itself be anchored. And beneath everything my father lived—beneath the work, the restraint, the silence, the love expressed without tenderness—there was something more fundamental still.

There was a ground he stood on long before I ever noticed the steadiness it produced. A set of convictions so deeply embedded that they no longer needed articulation. A moral and spiritual footing that bore the weight of responsibility without collapsing under it. What he built on the surface endured because what lay beneath it held.

That foundation shaped how he carried strain, how he endured without bitterness, how he remained oriented when no one was watching. It was not visible in any single action, but it was present in all of them—quiet, load-bearing, and rarely named.

Only now do I see that everything he passed on rested there first. And it is to that unseen ground—what supported him before he supported us—that the story must now turn.

He taught me who to become long before he ever explained himself.

SACRED WAYPOINTS

The Lessons That Enter Before Language

Before I could name values, I lived inside them. My father didn't teach with speeches—he taught with posture, tone, and repetition. His coherence formed me long before I understood what was happening.

- Where have you been shaped more by what was modeled than by what was said?
- What 'tone of life' are you passing on in ways you don't even notice?

Sit with this truth: Formation begins before comprehension.

Restraint That Holds the Room

Most days, my father handled frustration without explosion—not because pressure wasn't real, but because he refused to make it contagious. And when frustration did surface, it wasn't cruelty; it was the strain of a man carrying standards shaped by childhood scarcity and a fierce desire to provide more than he'd ever had himself.

- When you feel pressure rise, do you discharge it—or contain it with care?

- What standard are you trying to live up to that no one else can even see?

Pray simply: "Lord, teach me the strength of measured response."

When Carelessness Meets Cost

When I damaged the car as a young driver, my father's emotion erupted in a way that startled me. Not because he was angry by nature, but because hard-won things carried moral weight in our home. What is earned slowly must be treated with reverence.

- Where are you being invited to treat what you have with more care?
- What do you dismiss as "just a thing" that is actually someone's sacrifice?

Sit with this truth: Stewardship is love expressed through attention.

Silence as Protection

There were situations where words would have made things worse—where explanation would have sounded like excuse, where commentary would have turned pain into spectacle. My father's silence preserved proportion. It kept problems from growing past their proper size.

- Where are you using words to manage anxiety rather than serve truth?
- What would become calmer if you stopped narrating it and simply acted wisely?

Ask God for restraint: "Lord, help me speak only what builds."

Love Without Tenderness, Never Without Fidelity

My father's love did not arrive as softness. It arrived as presence, provision, vigilance, and staying. He held the line so others could live with less fear. The warmth I wanted was not always there—but the faithfulness was.

- Who has loved you more through constancy than through affection?
- Where are you being called to love in ways that don't feel 'expressive' but are deeply faithful?

Sit with this truth: Fidelity is a form of tenderness.

The Standards That Govern from Within

My father did not enforce rules; he created orientation. Don't exaggerate. Don't perform. Don't abandon what you agreed to. Don't make yourself the center. And I carried those standards with a quiet fear of letting him down—not fear of punishment, but fear of disappointing a steadiness I deeply respected.

- What standard inside you is really an inheritance?
- Where are you living for approval when you were meant to live from integrity?

Pray for freedom: "Lord, refine my standards without chaining my heart."

Calm That Becomes Contagious

My father's regulation shaped my nervous system. I learned how to stand inside fear. And yet I'm not perfect—sometimes chaos meets me first as panic, a venting of pressure before calm returns and solutions appear. Still, the deeper inheritance remains: the ability to come back to center.

- When you react first, how quickly do you return to what is wise?
- Where do you need recovery, not perfection?

Sit with this truth: Calm is not a trait—it is a practice of returning.

What Was Passed Without Permission

Some legacies arrive unchosen—seriousness, vigilance, responsibility that feels older than your years. They can be weight and gift at the same time. The work is discernment: what must be kept, what must be refined, and what must be gently laid down.

- What part of your inheritance strengthens you—and what part constricts you?
- What do you carry automatically that needs to be carried consciously?

Ask God for discernment: "Lord, show me what to steward and what to release."

ANCHORS OF THE WORD

The God Who Sees What Is Quiet

"But the LORD said to Samuel, 'Do not consider his appearance or his height, for I have rejected him. The LORD does not look at the things people look at. People look at the outward appearance, but the LORD looks at the heart.'" (1 Samuel 16:7 NIV)

My father's life trained my eyes to look past what is loud and impressive. His character was not something you could admire from a distance; it had to be lived near to be understood. The most enduring things about him were not visible in public moments, but in private ones—how he entered a day, how he carried pressure, how he refused to make himself the center. God's measure is not spectacle. It is substance.

Reflection: Where have you mistaken visibility for value in your own life?

The Quiet Power of Integrity

"The righteous lead blameless lives; blessed are their children after them." (Proverbs 20:7 NIV)

My father rarely gave instruction, but his integrity instructed anyway. His consistency became a kind of shelter—moral, emotional, and spiritual—one

I lived inside long before I could name it. The blessing wasn't a speech or a lesson. It was an environment shaped by steadiness.

Reflection: What kind of 'atmosphere' are you building for the people who live near you?

Restraint as Strength

"My dear brothers and sisters, take note of this: Everyone should be quick to listen, slow to speak and slow to become angry." (James 1:19 NIV)

My father's silence was not absence; it was discipline. He understood that words can multiply what action is trying to contain. Even when frustration surfaced—and it did—his emotion was not cruel or targeted. It was pressure leaking from high expectations he carried for himself. Then restraint returned, as if even his anger knew it could not stay.

Reflection: When you feel pressure rising, do you reach for volume—or for steadiness?

Wisdom That Uses Few Words

"The one who has knowledge uses words with restraint, and whoever has understanding is even-tempered." (Proverbs 17:27 NIV)

I used to want more explanation. I thought love would sound like reassurance. Over time I learned that my father's quiet was often protection—keeping chaos from spreading, keeping pain from becoming spectacle, keeping problems their proper size. His silence did not mean he felt less. It meant he governed what he felt with care.

Reflection: Where might your restraint be a form of love—not avoidance?

Love Without Tenderness, Love with Fidelity

"And over all these virtues put on love, which binds them all together in perfect unity." (Colossians 3:14 NIV)

My father's love did not arrive as softness. It arrived as staying. As showing up. As providing without resentment. As being the anchor when storms threatened to overtake the room. His devotion was not sentimental—but it held everything together.

Reflection: What does love look like in your life when it is not expressed in words?

Character in the Small Things

"Whoever can be trusted with very little can also be trusted with much, and whoever is dishonest with very little will also be dishonest with much." (Luke 16:10 NIV)

My father passed down standards without policing them—don't exaggerate, don't perform, don't abandon what you agreed to, don't make yourself the center. I learned what mattered by what he quietly rejected. That created a fear in me—not of punishment, but of letting him down. His trust made integrity feel personal.

Reflection: What 'small faithfulness' is revealing who you are becoming?

Calm That Is Practiced, Not Pretended

"Do not be anxious about anything, but in every situation, by prayer and petition, with thanksgiving, present your requests to God. And the peace of God, which transcends all understanding, will guard your hearts and your minds in Christ Jesus." (Philippians 4:6-7 NIV)

My father did not eliminate fear; he refused to feed it. His steadiness shaped my nervous system—calm became contagious. And yet I learned I am not perfect. Sometimes panic came first, a release of internal pressure before composure returned. Still, the inheritance remained: the ability to come back to center and move toward what can be done next.

Reflection: When anxiety spikes, what helps you return—not to control, but to clarity?

The Weight of What Is Caught, Not Taught

"Therefore, since we are surrounded by such a great cloud of witnesses, let us throw off everything that hinders and the sin that so easily entangles. And let us run with perseverance the race marked out for us," (Hebrews 12:1 NIV)

Some inheritances arrive without consent. You wake up one day to find—postures, instincts, and reflexes already formed. My father's way of living moved into me before I could name it. The question now is stewardship: what must be kept, what must be refined, and what must be gently laid down so it does not become a burden disguised as legacy.

Reflection: What patterns have you inherited that you need to examine with honesty and grace?

The Foundation Beneath the Life

"May the favor of the Lord our God rest on us; establish the work of our hands for us—yes, establish the work of our hands." (Psalm 90:17 NIV)

Before a life can form others, it must be anchored. Beneath my father's work, restraint, silence, and love expressed without tenderness, there was a deeper ground that held him steady. A foundation. And it is there—beneath us all—that the next chapter begins.

Reflection: What foundation is establishing your life when no one is watching?

LEGACY NOTES

NINE

The Foundation He Laid Beneath Us All

"The foundation of every state is the education of its youth."

— Plato (428 BCE-348 BCE), Greek philosopher

Only later did I understand what Plato was pointing toward. Not lessons or doctrine, but the deeper work beneath them all—the shaping of what a person stands on long before weight is applied. Education, in this sense, is not what is taught. It is what holds when teaching is no longer available.

That is where my father lived.

He was a physically strong man. Broad-shouldered. Capable. A body shaped by labor rather than display. His hands were large—thick-palmed, steady, marked by years of use. Hands that lifted without flourish, repaired without hesitation, and rested only when the work allowed it. They carried the quiet authority of someone accustomed to bearing weight.

His strength showed in how he lifted, how he stood, how he moved through space with an economy that suggested confidence without aggression. Nothing about his presence reached outward to impress. It settled inward, grounded and assured. As a child, it was easy to assume that this visible strength explained the steadiness he carried—that his composure came from muscle and endurance alone, from a body that knew how to work and how to hold.

Only later did I understand that the body was not the source of his steadiness, but its expression.

Those hands could carry load, yes—but they could also restrain. They could repair rather than discard. They could hold tension without needing to release it immediately. They reflected a strength that was not reactive, not performative, but contained. A strength shaped by something deeper than muscle memory.

Physical power can lift. It can protect. It can endure strain for a time. But it cannot, by itself, explain restraint. It cannot explain silence chosen over reaction, or responsibility carried without complaint, or a man who does not need reassurance when effort goes unseen. Muscle bears weight; foundation determines whether a man remains upright under it.

At the time, I mistook what I could see for what mattered most. I assumed the steadiness lived in his shoulders, his back, his hands. I did not yet know to ask what those hands were standing on.

Only later did I recognize that his strength did not originate in the body alone. It was anchored. Integrated. Supported by something unseen that allowed his physical presence to remain calm, measured, and reliable even when life demanded more than strength could reasonably supply.

His hands told the story first. But they were not the whole story.

Physical strength alone does not explain a life that does not buckle.

He never announced what grounded him. He never explained the source of his resolve or named the principles that governed his choices. There were no speeches about belief, no declarations made in advance of hardship. And yet, through years that demanded far more than strength of body could supply— years marked by illness, uncertainty, responsibility, and quiet strain—he remained upright in a way that felt deeper than temperament and sturdier than muscle.

Something beneath him did not shift. Foundations are like that.

They are rarely discussed because they are meant to be stood on, not admired.

I grew up watching a man whose physical presence communicated solidity before he ever spoke. When he entered a room, things seemed to settle. Not because he dominated, but because his posture suggested readiness. He did not fidget. He did not hurry unnecessarily. He carried himself as someone accustomed to bearing weight, both literal and unseen. Even in stillness, there was a sense of strength held in reserve.

At the time, I thought this was simply who he was—a strong man, built for endurance. Only later did I begin to understand that I was witnessing not just physical capability, but formation. The body reflected something deeper. His strength was not merely muscular; it was integrated. It was the outward expression of an inner footing that had been tested long before I knew to ask what held him.

Because steadiness, I came to see, is rarely accidental.

Physical strength can lift. It can protect. It can endure strain. But it cannot, on its own, explain restraint. It cannot explain silence chosen over reaction, or responsibility carried without complaint, or a life that does not seek reassurance when effort goes unseen. Muscle can bear weight for a time. But it is foundation that prevents collapse.

As I grew older, I began to assume—quietly, instinctively—that my father's strength must be the source of everything else. His steadiness. His authority. His ability to endure without complaint. I watched the way his body moved through the world, the confidence of it, the certainty with which he occupied space, and I concluded that this was the foundation. Muscle. Capacity. Physical resilience. If I could build that, I reasoned, perhaps I could build what he carried so effortlessly.

So, I tried to mirror it.

I pushed my body toward strength as though it were an inheritance I could claim deliberately. I lifted. I hardened. I learned how to carry myself so that presence alone might signal something unspoken. Part of this came from admiration, but part of it came from necessity. On the playground, my devotion to study marked me as different. Academic effort—something I pursued not for praise, but out of respect for what my father had never been given the chance to pursue—made me visible in ways I did not always want to be. Strength, I learned early, could serve as armor.

I did not resent the teasing. I understood, even then, that my education was a privilege his sacrifice had earned. My father had left school in fifth grade, not because he lacked ability, but because his family needed him in the fields. He had not been afforded the luxury of study. So, I studied seriously—not as rebellion, but as continuation. But seriousness, especially in children, often draws challenge. And when it did, I believed that physical strength was the language that would restore balance.

For a long time, I thought I was honoring him by becoming strong in the ways he appeared strong.

But as my own responsibilities grew, the limits of that understanding became clear. I encountered pressures that demanded more than stamina—decisions without clean outcomes, obligations that offered no recognition, seasons where effort felt asymmetrical to reward. In those moments, I discovered how quickly footing can erode when affirmation is absent. Muscle helps you carry weight, but it does not tell you where to stand when the ground begins to shift.

My father did not seem to need that affirmation.

He did not look to others to confirm his strength or justify his endurance. He did not seek permission to hold the line when things became difficult. Even when nothing improved—when circumstances tightened rather than eased— he remained oriented toward responsibility rather than relief. His strength did not flare outward in frustration. It held inward. Contained. Deliberate.

That kind of endurance does not come from the body alone. It implies anchoring.

Foundations reveal themselves only under weight—not when effort is visible, but when it is hidden; not when strength is applauded, but when it is simply required. Looking back, I can see how often my father lived under burdens no one noticed. The weight of provision carried year after year. The weight of my mother's illness borne without spectacle. The weight of vigilance maintained so others could feel safe. His body carried some of this, yes—but far more was borne beneath the surface, where muscle yields to grounding.

And still, there was no collapse. The absence of collapse was itself evidence of support.

Something held him when nothing improved. Something steadied him when physical strength alone would have been insufficient. His hands could lift and endure, but it was the ground beneath his life that allowed him to remain composed, restrained, and reliable across decades.

He did not seek reassurance. He did not require validation. He did not need permission to keep standing. He behaved as though the ground beneath him was trustworthy—even when the path ahead was not.

This, I came to understand, was the foundation he never named.

His physical strength gave shape to his presence, but his unseen footing gave it authority. He did not perform strength; he embodied it. And because it was anchored, it did not need to announce itself. He did not have to prove he could carry weight. He simply did.

This is why he could remain silent without disappearing. Why he could absorb pressure without transferring it. Why he could protect without posturing.

If what you stand on is solid, you do not need to demonstrate it. If the ground holds, you do not need to insist that you are strong.

Only later did I recognize how rare this combination is—physical strength paired with inner anchoring, capability joined to restraint. Many men have strength without foundation, and it spills outward. Others have conviction without capacity, and it collapses under strain. My father carried both quietly, without naming either.

What he never explained allowed him to remain upright.

And now, standing where I stand—with the clarity that comes only after weight has been applied to my own life—I can see that before a man can form others, something must first have formed him. Before steadiness can be transmitted, it must be anchored. Before strength can endure, it must rest on something deeper than muscle.

That unseen ground—quiet, assumed, rarely examined—was the true source of his strength.

If strength explained how my father carried weight, it did not explain why he carried it the way he did. Beneath the physical anchoring, beneath the restraint and endurance, there was something more exacting still—a moral ground that did not shift with circumstance, mood, or advantage.

He did not speak of ethics as concepts. He did not debate values or frame his decisions in moral language. And yet, his life revealed a coherence so consistent that it could only have rested on internal rules that were already settled. Right and wrong, for him, were not negotiated emotionally. They were not adjusted based on fatigue, pressure, or outcome. They existed prior to preference.

Responsibility preceded comfort. Duty came before desire. Care outweighed self-expression.

These were not ideals he aspired to in moments of clarity. They were assumptions he lived inside, even when clarity was absent.

What struck me, looking back, was how little energy he spent justifying himself. He did not explain why he did what he did, nor did he ask to be understood. When something fell to him—an obligation, a consequence, a burden—he absorbed it without commentary. There was no appeal to fairness. No rehearsal of mitigating factors. No effort to outsource discomfort to those around him. He bore what was his to bear, quietly and fully.

This was not stoicism for its own sake. It was structure.

He seemed to understand that once you begin negotiating responsibility with feeling, responsibility dissolves. If obligation must first pass through preference, it becomes optional. If duty must feel right to be honored, it will eventually be abandoned. My father did not live that way. What was required was done because it was required. Feeling followed later—if it followed at all.

This is why moral shortcuts unsettled him so deeply. Not because he was rigid, but because shortcuts violated order. They promised relief without resolution. They offered escape without repair. Whether it was cutting corners at work, explaining away a failure, or shifting blame to preserve comfort, he recoiled instinctively. These maneuvers did not merely break rules; they weakened foundations. They transferred weight rather than carrying it.

I saw this most clearly in how he handled mistakes—his own and others'. When he erred, he corrected. Not defensively. Not publicly. Simply and fully. He did not require acknowledgment for owning error, nor did he dramatize accountability as virtue. Correction was not a moral performance; it was maintenance. You fixed what you damaged. You restored alignment. And then you moved forward.

When others avoided consequences, he did not rage. He withdrew trust.

That, more than anything, revealed the seriousness of his moral ground. Trust, for him, was structural. It supported cooperation, safety, and continuity. When it cracked, the system weakened. He did not shame those who broke it; he simply refused to build on unstable footing again.

This ethic shaped the environment of our home without ever being announced. There was a sense that choices mattered even when no one was watching. That consequences were not punishments imposed from above, but realities borne from within. This was not fear-based morality. It was responsibility-based living. You did what was yours to do because failing to do so distorted the whole.

Only much later—after I had entered professional worlds shaped by incentives, optics, and negotiated accountability—did I recognize how unusual this was. I encountered systems where rules bent easily under pressure, where outcomes justified means, where responsibility could be redistributed with the right explanation. And I felt, often without knowing why, a quiet resistance rise in me.

It was not moral superiority. It was dissonance.

Something in me resisted solutions that required ethical amnesia. I struggled with choices that asked me to separate success from integrity, or performance from consequence. I found myself more troubled by how something was achieved than by whether it worked. At the time, I did not frame this as inheritance. I thought it was simply my disposition.

Now I know better.

I carried into those spaces not a set of rules, but a foundation. A belief—absorbed long before it was conscious—that care must come before self-expression, that obligation must outrank preference, that responsibility cannot be delegated simply because it is inconvenient. These convictions did not make life easier. In many cases, they made it heavier. But they also made it coherent.

My father understood something that took me decades to articulate. A life that avoids consequence may feel lighter in the moment, but it becomes unstable over time. Weight deferred does not disappear; it shifts. And what is shifted eventually collapses somewhere else—onto someone else.

He refused to be that someone.

So, he bore consequences quietly. Paid what was owed. Stayed when leaving would have been easier. Accepted limits without complaint. Not because he lacked imagination, but because he understood order. The order that allows families to function. The order that allows trust to accumulate. The order that allows dignity to endure even when circumstances erode comfort.

His morality was not loud. It did not seek to persuade or perform. It did not require agreement or applause.

It was structural. It held him upright when nothing else improved. It gave weight to his restraint. It gave authority to his silence.

And it explains something I could not see as a child but recognize clearly now. His steadiness was not merely personal virtue. It was load-bearing ethics. A moral ground strong enough to support others without announcing itself.

That ground shaped him long before it shaped me.

And only now—standing on that same ground myself, often without realizing when I first stepped onto it—do I see that what steadied my father was more than discipline or resolve. The footing he never named, but never abandoned, was not only moral. It was spiritual.

Because faith, in my father's life, never arrived as vocabulary. It did not announce itself through claims or declarations. It did not ask to be named, defended, or admired. It lived instead as posture—quiet, enduring, and assumed—like the ground beneath his feet. He did not speak often about God, belief, or meaning. And yet, looking back, it is impossible to separate how he lived from what he trusted.

He did not articulate his faith. He stood on it.

I came to understand this not through moments of clarity, but through years of observation. Through the way he accepted without bitterness what could not be changed. Through the way he carried burdens that were never his idea and rarely his choice. Through the way he bore responsibility as something almost sacred—not tragic, not unfair, but entrusted.

There was reverence in that acceptance.

And yet, faith was not absent from his life in visible ways. It simply arrived without commentary. Every Sunday, without debate or explanation, we went to Mass. It was not framed as obligation or lesson. There were no conversations afterward about doctrine or belief. No insistence that we understand what we were doing or why it mattered. We went because that was what was done. Faith, like work, entered our lives through repetition rather than instruction.

Looking back, I see how quietly formative that was. The ritual itself mattered less than the return. The steadiness of it. The way one hour was set apart not for productivity, but for orientation. He did not speak of God often, but he placed us weekly in a space where attention was drawn beyond ourselves— where silence, posture, and restraint carried meaning. Without saying so, he conveyed that life rested on something larger than effort alone.

Faith, for him, did not need to be explained to be practiced.

When circumstances tightened rather than eased, he did not ask why aloud. He did not interpret suffering as punishment or failure. He did not search for explanations that would make pain feel productive. He absorbed what came and oriented himself toward what remained required. His response to hardship was not despair, nor was it denial. It was obedience—to reality, to responsibility, to whatever had been placed before him.

This is a form of faith that rarely draws attention. It does not rely on certainty. It does not demand resolution. It does not insist on understanding before commitment. It simply continues.

I watched him live inside limits without resenting them. Illness altered plans. Fatigue narrowed margins. Some dreams never found daylight. And still, he did not dramatize loss or rehearse grievance. He did not frame his life as something taken from him. He framed it—if he framed it at all—as something given to be carried. That posture did not erase sorrow, but it kept sorrow from becoming sovereign.

His suffering was never performative. He did not make it visible to claim sympathy. He did not narrate it to extract meaning. He did not ask it to justify his choices or soften expectations. Pain existed, but it did not get to reorganize the moral center of his life. He treated suffering as something to be endured with dignity rather than explained into significance.

That restraint, I now see, was deeply spiritual. Because faith, at its most elemental, is not about answers. It is about trusting without explanation. It is about remaining faithful when meaning is unclear and outcomes are withheld. My father lived this kind of faith instinctively. He behaved as though life itself were worthy of care even when it did not reward him for that care. As though responsibility mattered regardless of recognition. As though something larger than circumstance was quietly watching—not to judge, but to be honored through fidelity.

Prayer, in his life, did not sound like words. It sounded like return.

The weekly return to Mass. The daily return to obligation. The return to work when fatigue pressed close. The return to steadiness when fear would have justified retreat.

Each return was an act of trust. Not trust that things would improve, but trust that faithfulness itself mattered. That showing up had value even when no one noticed. That carrying what was given was enough.

I did not recognize this as faith when I was young. I thought faith was something spoken. Something confident. Something visible in proclamation. What my father lived did not fit that template. It was quieter, heavier, and far less certain. It did not seek reassurance from belief; it enacted belief through responsibility.

Only later—after I had encountered versions of faith that were louder but less durable—did I begin to see what he had embodied all along.

His life suggested a belief that did not need to be proven. A reverence that did not require language. A trust that did not depend on outcomes. He behaved as though obligation itself was sacred. As though the care of what had been entrusted to him—family, work, time, effort—was a form of devotion.

And because he did not dramatize it, it endured.

He did not divide life into sacred and ordinary, or reserve reverence for moments that announced themselves as meaningful. He treated the ordinary with care precisely because it was ordinary. Tools were respected. Time was honored. Promises were kept. Nothing about this was explained as spiritual, yet all of it carried spiritual weight.

This was belief embedded in behavior. Faith that did not seek admiration. Reverence that did not need language. Prayer enacted not through request, but through return.

My father stood on faith long before he ever spoke of it. And perhaps that is why it held. Because what is carried quietly is often carried longest. And what held him did not remain contained within him.

His foundation radiated outward.

What he carried within himself—steadily, silently, without explanation— became the ground the rest of us stood on. Long before I had words for stability or containment, I lived inside their effects. Our family did not feel anchored because circumstances were kind. It felt anchored because someone was holding the center.

That someone was my father. His grounding created an emotional architecture that shaped daily life in subtle but decisive ways. There was space to breathe in our home—not because tension was absent, but because it was managed. Fear entered, but it did not overtake. Conflict surfaced, but it did not spiral. Uncertainty pressed in, but it did not dismantle the structure holding us together.

Others could rest because he remained alert. He watched for cracks before they widened. He noticed shifts in mood, rhythm, and pressure long before they became visible problems. This vigilance was not anxious or controlling; it was preventative. He understood instinctively that you do not declare stability—you maintain it. And maintenance, by its nature, is quiet work.

When crises came, they came hard—but they did not take over.

Illness intensified. Resources tightened. Emotional weather shifted unpredictably. Yet decisions were made without panic in most cases. Conversations stayed contained. There was rarely a sense that the situation might tip into something unmanageable. Even when outcomes were uncertain, the posture remained steady. The question was never "Will this break us?" but "What needs to be done next?"

That orientation mattered.

However, worry, though rarely spoken, did live in our home. It moved quietly beneath the surface, shaped by illness, by finances, by the fragility my father knew too well from earlier years. But it was not allowed to roam freely. He took it upon himself to carry it—absorbing uncertainty so it would not become the organizing force of our days. Concern existed, but it was contained. Anxiety was present, but it did not rule.

This created emotional containment—not by suppressing feeling, but by giving it boundaries. Fear could be acknowledged without being amplified. Worry could be felt without being handed authority. There was room for unease, but not for chaos. And because of that containment, children were allowed to remain children longer than circumstances might otherwise have permitted. The weight did not disappear; it was redistributed. Much of it settled onto his shoulders.

Moral clarity emerged from the same ground.

Right and wrong did not shift with mood. Decisions were not negotiated emotionally or revisited endlessly once made. There was an internal coherence to how things were handled—an unspoken sense that some lines simply did not move. Not because they were enforced loudly, but because they were rooted deeply. That clarity reduced confusion. It removed the need for constant explanation. We did not have to guess where the ground was. We could feel it beneath us.

Predictability under strain became one of the family's greatest securities.

Not predictability of outcomes, but of response. We could anticipate how my father would meet difficulty, calmly and deliberately, without spectacle. Even when worry hovered, his posture did not fracture. That consistency created trust. And trust, repeated over time, becomes confidence—the quiet assurance *that* this will hold.

I remember moments when decisions felt final—not rigid, but settled. Once something was determined, it did not wobble under second-guessing or emotional revisiting. That steadiness was reassuring. It meant energy could move forward rather than inward. It allowed us to live rather than brace.

His grounding did not eliminate hardship. It contained it.

That containment shaped the atmosphere of our home more than comfort ever could. Ours was not a quiet household. It was loud—full of voices, opinions, laughter, frustration, debate. The volume came from passion, not anger. From engagement, not volatility. Life was lived out loud around the table, in the kitchen, across rooms. Emotion was present. Energy moved freely.

But within that liveliness, there was structure.

There was less drama, but more durability. Less emotional sprawl, but more endurance. Less reassurance spoken aloud, but more reassurance built into the rhythms of daily life. Feelings could rise without overtaking the room. Disagreement could exist without destabilizing the center. The noise never tipped into chaos, because something steadier held beneath it.

The shelter my father provided was not silent. It was secure.

It did not mute expression; it contained it. It allowed passion without panic, intensity without fracture. And because that containment was so consistent, it was easy to overlook. Like all strong foundations, it did its work quietly, beneath the surface, becoming visible only when we stepped beyond it and realized how much it had been holding all along.

Only then did we understand what kind of shelter it was—not one that quieted life, but one that made life possible without fear of collapse.

Only later did I recognize how much effort it takes to create that kind of stability—and how rare it is. Many homes are governed by whichever emotion arrives strongest. Ours was governed by something steadier. Someone had decided, long before I was aware of it, that chaos would not be allowed to reorganize the family's center.

That decision lived inside my father.

But it did not stop there. Some of that vigilance traveled forward.

I absorbed more than I realized—the alertness, the seriousness, the instinct to anticipate what might go wrong before it arrived. What had protected us also shaped me. I learned early to read rooms, to sense strain, to prepare internally even when nothing had been said aloud. This was not damage; it was inheritance. But like all inheritances, it carried both strength and weight.

His inner ground became our outer shelter. And in time, parts of that ground became mine.

It was not built through speeches or plans, but through posture—through his refusal to abandon responsibility when things grew heavy, through his insistence on staying oriented toward what mattered even when no one noticed. The family rested not because everything was safe, but because someone was standing watch.

And that watchfulness did not exhaust him. Because it was anchored. What he stood on held him. And because it held him, it held us.

This is how foundations work. They are rarely admired. Rarely thanked. They do not announce themselves while they are doing their job. They simply carry what rests upon them. And when they are sound, life moves forward without constant fear of collapse.

We lived inside that soundness.

At the time, it felt like normalcy. Like the natural order of things. Only much later did I understand that what felt ordinary was, in fact, the result of something extraordinary—a man who had learned how to stand on something deeper than circumstance, and who allowed the rest of us to stand there too.

But foundations pay a price for that stability.

To be the ground is to accept a particular kind of invisibility. What holds is assumed. What supports is stepped on without thought. Strength becomes background. Reliability becomes expectation. The measure of success is not recognition, but the simple fact that nothing falls apart.

Foundations are not thanked while they hold. They are trusted without question. And because their work happens beneath the surface, they are rarely noticed until strain begins to show.

He did not stand at the center of the structure. He stood beneath it. Holding weight so others could move freely above him. Decisions rested on him. Worry collected there. Responsibility settled and stayed. And because he did not dramatize the load, it was easy to forget how much he carried—or to mistake endurance for ease.

And it is there—beneath the soundness we relied upon—that the cost of being the ground begins to emerge.

Strength, when it is reliable, is often taken for granted.

No one asks who supports the one who never falters. No one checks the strain on the structure that never cracks. When a man becomes the ground, the assumption follows that he requires no ground himself. That he will simply continue to hold, because he always has.

My father rarely invited support. Not because he did not need it, but because his identity had been shaped around being the one who provided it. To admit fatigue felt, perhaps, like a breach of role. To ask for relief would have required language he had never cultivated. So, he absorbed instead. Quietly. Habitually. Without protest.

Looking back now, I can see moments that passed unnoticed at the time—small signals of exhaustion that did not announce themselves as such. The slower movements at the end of long days. The way his silence deepened not from distance, but from depletion. The narrowing of his world as responsibility crowded out everything nonessential. None of it came with complaint. None of it asked for acknowledgment.

He carried solitude inside responsibility.

There is a loneliness particular to being load-bearing. It is not the loneliness of isolation, but the loneliness of asymmetry—of giving more support than one receives, of being essential without being accompanied. Others rest because you remain alert. Others speak freely because you are containing what might otherwise overflow. Others move forward because you are standing still, absorbing force.

And the cost of that posture is cumulative.

I can see now how often my father stood alone in decisions that affected us all. How rarely he unburdened himself aloud. How he took worry upon himself as part of leadership, believing—perhaps rightly—that some anxieties should not be passed down. He did not want us to inherit fear. So, he inherited it instead.

Some of that worry did leak into the house, as worry always does. It moved through tone, through pacing, through vigilance. It became part of the emotional weather we lived inside. And over time, some of it passed into me—not through instruction, but through proximity. I learned to scan. To anticipate. To carry concern quietly, believing this was part of loving well.

This is one of the costs of being the ground. The weight does not disappear. It transfers.

What my father absorbed allowed others to feel safe, but it also meant he rarely felt held in the same way. Strength, when it becomes structural, is not often reciprocated. It is relied upon. And reliance, over time, can be isolating.

There is also the question of what happens when the ground itself begins to weaken.

Foundations are not designed to announce their limits. They hold until they cannot. And when wear finally shows, it often surprises everyone—especially those who assumed strength was infinite. I think now of moments when my father's body began to falter, when illness narrowed his capacity, when the physical strength that once made carrying easier no longer compensated for the weight. Even then, he adjusted instead of withdrawing. He redistributed effort internally. He found new ways to hold.

But the holding never stopped.

What strikes me most now is not how much he carried, but how little he asked in return. There was no ledger. No quiet resentment. No sense that sacrifice entitled him to obedience or praise. He did not convert endurance into authority. He simply continued to be reliable.

That kind of strength leaves no trace while it is happening.

Only later—when you begin to carry weight yourself—do you recognize what it costs to remain unseen while holding everything together. Only then do you realize that foundations, too, need ground. That even the strongest structures are shaped by what supports them. And that no one stands alone as long as they appear to.

To be the ground is to absorb force without recognition. It is to be trusted without being tended.

It is to hold life together while remaining largely upheld. This is not a complaint. It is a truth.

And now, standing where I stand, I can honor both the gift and the cost of that posture—recognizing not only what his steadiness gave us, but what it required of him to remain so long, so quietly, beneath us all.

There are moments in adulthood when the narrative you've been telling yourself quietly rearranges. Not because something new has happened, but because something old finally becomes visible.

For years, I believed my steadiness was earned. That my ability to remain composed under pressure, to shoulder responsibility without spectacle, to stay oriented when circumstances tightened, was simply temperament, or discipline, or resolve. I mistook inheritance for identity. I assumed the ground beneath me had always been there because I had built it.

Only later did I realize I had been standing on something that predated me.

I began to see it in retrospect, by tracing moments backward. Times when I did not collapse even though I was stretched thin. Decisions I made calmly when panic would have been reasonable. Seasons when fear pressed close, but never reorganized the center of my life. At the time, I called this competence. Now I recognize it as support.

I had been held.

There were situations that asked more of me than I knew how to give. Responsibilities that arrived before confidence did. Moments when the margin between holding and breaking felt impossibly narrow. And yet, something steadier than my own strength kept me upright. I did not always know what to do—but I knew how to stand while figuring it out.

That posture was not invented. It was remembered.

I began to notice how often my responses echoed his. The instinct to slow down rather than speed up under pressure. The refusal to dramatize difficulty. The tendency to absorb strain inwardly rather than discharge it outwardly. Even my silences—measured, deliberate—felt familiar. They carried the same weight his had once carried in rooms I had not yet known how to read.

I had not learned these things consciously. They had arrived by proximity.

Foundations transmit downward quietly. They do not announce themselves as inheritance. They simply make collapse less likely. You grow up assuming the ground is firm because it always has been. You step forward believing steadiness is normal—until you encounter situations where it is not.

That is when the realization sharpens.

I began to see how much of my life I had navigated on borrowed footing. How many early decisions had been steadied by a confidence I had not yet earned. How often I had moved through uncertainty with an internal sense of containment that did not originate with me. My strength, I came to understand, had been scaffolded.

My father had been carrying me long after he stopped lifting me.

Gratitude, when it arrived, was not emotional at first. It was structural. A recognition that my life had been shaped by something stable enough to disappear beneath notice. That the absence of collapse had not been accidental. That the quietness of my father's strength had not diminished its reach—it had extended it.

I was standing on him long before I knew it.

And this realization did not make me smaller. It clarified me. It placed my own effort in its proper context. I did not have to diminish what I had built to honor what had held me. I could see now that strength is often cumulative—layered across generations, transmitted through posture rather than permission.

The foundation beneath my life was not only something he stood on. It was something he passed on by remaining upright.

There is humility in this recognition. And freedom. Because once you see that you were supported before you understood support, you no longer need to pretend self-sufficiency. You can honor the ground without being trapped by it. You can carry forward what steadied you while examining what must now be shared, softened, or re-balanced.

Inheritance, when seen clearly, does not demand replication. It invites stewardship.

I began to ask quieter questions. Not whether I was strong enough—but what I was standing on. Not how much I could carry—but whether I was still grounded while carrying it. Not whether I could endure—but whether endurance alone was still what the moment required.

These were questions my father never needed to ask aloud. He answered them with his life. Now they were mine to hold—consciously. I was standing on him long before I knew it. And seeing that truth did not weaken my footing. It revealed it.

But recognition is not the end of inheritance.

To see what held you is not the same as knowing how to stand on it wisely. Foundations that are never examined can become unyielding. What once stabilized can, over time, begin to limit. Strength carried forward without reflection can harden into posture rather than purpose—faithfulness preserved without flexibility, endurance mistaken for completeness.

This is the question that arrives next—not abruptly, but inevitably. Because every foundation eventually asks to be understood, not merely relied upon.

My father's way of standing in the world saved much. It steadied others. It created shelter. It made endurance possible when collapse would have been easier. But no foundation is meant to be duplicated without discernment. What was necessary in one life may become excessive in another. What protected one generation may quietly constrain the next if it is carried unchanged.

Strength, I have learned, does not consist only of holding. It consists of knowing what must still be held, and what—having done its work—may finally be held differently.

This is not a turning away from what formed me. It is a turning toward understanding it fully. Because inheritance, once recognized, invites a deeper responsibility—not imitation, but discernment.

There are elements of my father's grounding that must be honored without hesitation—his fidelity, his refusal to abandon responsibility, his restraint under pressure, his willingness to carry what was given without complaint. These are load-bearing virtues. They deserve reverence.

But there are also elements that require gentler handling. The vigilance that never rests. The seriousness that rarely softens. The posture of being the ground, always, even when others could help carry weight.

These, too, were formed by necessity. They made sense in a life shaped by scarcity, migration, illness, and unrelenting responsibility. But necessity does not always translate cleanly across generations. What was survival can become over-functioning. What was steadiness can become self-erasure. What was devotion can quietly crowd out rest.

Understanding the foundation does not mean dismantling it. It means asking what it was built for—and whether its purpose has shifted. This is where discernment begins. Not with rejection, but with gratitude refined by clarity. Not with imitation, but with stewardship. To honor a foundation is not to freeze it in place. It is to understand its role, its limits, and its cost—and then decide how it will serve life now.

The question that remains is not whether my father's strength was sufficient. It was. The question is how that strength must now evolve.

What does it mean to remain faithful without remaining rigid?

What does it look like to carry responsibility without carrying it alone?

What happens when endurance is no longer the highest virtue required?

These are not questions of critique. They are questions of maturity. Because eventually, every son who has been supported must decide how he will stand—not by replacing the ground beneath him, but by learning how to live upon it without being consumed by it.

Understanding the foundation invites discernment, not imitation. And discernment, once begun, changes the nature of what comes next. It does not ask whether the foundation was strong enough—it already was. It asks how that strength is meant to be carried forward now.

Which parts must be honored intact, and which must be allowed to soften.

Where endurance must give way to rest.

Where responsibility must learn to be shared.

Where what was borne faithfully for decades may finally be held differently.

Not abandoned. But released into its next, truer form. This is the threshold the story now crosses.

Because my father's foundation was never dramatic. It did not announce itself or ask to be admired. It did not rely on explanation or seek reinforcement. I did not notice it while it was doing its work. Like all true foundations, it remained out of sight—quiet, assumed, dependable.

It held.

It held through years when strength was required daily and recognition rarely arrived. It held when obligation outweighed ease, when illness narrowed options, when worry pressed in without permission. It held not because it was rigid, but because it was anchored. Not because it resisted weight, but because it knew how to bear it.

What he stood on did not make him louder. It made him steadier. And because it held him, it held the rest of us.

Only now, with the distance of time and the clarity that comes from carrying weight myself, do I see how rare that kind of grounding truly is. Many lives are built on effort alone. Others on identity, ambition, or will. But effort exhausts, identity fractures, and will eventually fails. My father stood on something quieter and stronger—a way of inhabiting responsibility that did not require constant proof.

What he built endured because what he stood on never shifted. That ground still holds.

It holds in the habits I did not consciously choose but now recognize as inheritance. It holds in the reflex to steady rather than escalate, to absorb rather than discharge, to remain present when leaving would be easier. It holds even when I question it—perhaps especially then—because questioning does not erase what has already been laid.

Foundations do not disappear when building stops. They remain—supporting, shaping, waiting. And yet, there comes a moment when the work changes. When builders must rest. When endurance must make room for tenderness. When strength must learn a different expression.

The ground that once made building possible now asks something else of those who stand on it. Not more effort. Not more proving. But understanding. Integration. Release.

What happens when the hands that carried so much finally loosen their grip?

What remains when strength is no longer required to be visible?

What kind of courage does it take to stop building—and simply be?

The chapters that follow turn toward those questions. Toward rest after endurance. Toward reconciliation after vigilance. Toward love that no longer needs strength to justify itself. Because before my father supported us, something deeper held him. And now, standing on what he stood on, the work turns quieter still.

He was the ground beneath us long before we learned how to stand.

SACRED WAYPOINTS

The Worry He Carried First

Concern lived in our home, but my father carried it as leadership—absorbing what he could so we could keep living. Some of that vigilance also passed into me.

- What worries are you carrying that no one sees?
- What weight have you inherited that now needs gentler handling?

Sit with this truth: Love sometimes looks like containment.

A Loud House Held by Quiet Structure

Our home wasn't quiet—we were passionate. But the noise didn't become chaos because something steadier held beneath it.

- Where is your family's energy missing a center?
- What boundary would keep passion from becoming panic?

Ask for wisdom: Help me build a home where emotion can rise without ruling.

The Loneliness of Being Load-Bearing

To be the ground is to be assumed. Strength becomes background. The measure of success is the absence of collapse.

- Who holds the one who holds everything?
- Where do you need support but feel unable to ask?

Sit with this truth: To be the ground is to absorb force without recognition.

Standing on Him Without Knowing It

I thought my steadiness was mine—until life applied weight and I recognized his posture in my own.

- Where have you survived because you were supported before you understood support?
- What part of your resilience is borrowed, not self-made?

Offer gratitude: "Thank You, Lord, for the ground that held me before I learned to stand."

Discernment, Not Imitation

Not everything inherited must be carried unchanged. What protected one generation can quietly constrain the next.

- What parts of your foundation must be honored intact?
- What parts must be softened so you can live, not just endure?

Sit with this truth: Strength includes knowing what to hold—and what to release well.

The Ground That Still Holds

My father's foundation didn't announce itself. It held. And because it held him, it held us.

- What is still holding your life, even though you've never named it?
- What would change if you stopped proving and started trusting the ground?

Pray simply: "Lord, let what held me become what heals me."

ANCHORS OF THE WORD 

The Ground That Holds

"When the storm has swept by, the wicked are gone, but the righteous stand firm forever." (Proverbs 10:25 NIV)

My father did not avoid storms; he stood through them. What endured was not circumstance, but footing. When pressure came, he did not relocate his values or renegotiate responsibility. He remained upright because something beneath him did not move. Stability, I learned, is revealed not in calm but in resistance to collapse.

Reflection: What remains steady in you when pressure rises and outcomes are uncertain?

Built Below the Surface

"They are like a man building a house, who dug down deep and laid the foundation on rock. When a flood came, the torrent struck that house but could not shake it, because it was well built." (Luke 6:48 NIV)

Foundations are not visible because they are not meant to be admired. They are meant to be trusted. My father never explained what grounded him, but his life bore the unmistakable marks of someone who had dug deep long before weight arrived. What held was not impulse, strength, or optimism—it was preparation beneath sight.

Reflection: Where have you done unseen work that now carries more than you realize?

Moral Ground Without Theater

"He has shown you, O mortal, what is good. And what does the LORD require of you? To act justly and to love mercy and to walk humbly with your God." (Micah 6:8 NIV)

My father did not speak of ethics; he walked inside them. Justice showed up as responsibility accepted without excuse. Mercy appeared as care without self-display. Humility lived in restraint rather than retreat. His morality did not persuade—it supported. It was structural, not rhetorical.

Reflection: Where does your integrity quietly support others without recognition?

The Strength That Is Assumed

"Everyone who hears these words of mine and puts them into practice is like a wise man who built his house on the rock." (Matthew 7:24 NIV)

The truest measure of wisdom is not explanation, but endurance. My father's foundation was assumed because it held. No one asked what supported him because nothing ever fell apart. Only later did I see how much weight had been absorbed below the surface so others could move freely above it.

Reflection: What part of your life is trusted simply because it has never failed?

Quiet Security

"The fruit of righteousness will be peace; the effect of righteousness will be quietness and confidence forever." (Isaiah 32:17 NIV)

Our home was not silent—it was alive, loud with passion and presence. Yet beneath the noise was containment. Worry existed, but it was bounded. Fear appeared, but it was not given authority. That quiet confidence did not come from ease; it came from someone holding the center.

Reflection: Where has your faith created quiet security for others without being named?

The One Who Holds the Holder

"Unless the LORD builds the house, the builders labor in vain. Unless the LORD watches over the city, the guards stand watch in vain." (Psalm 127:1 NIV)

To be the ground is to carry weight unseen. But no foundation stands alone. Only later did I recognize that even my father—strong, steady, uncomplaining — was himself held by something deeper. His endurance was not self-generated. It rested on trust, return, and reverence lived rather than spoken.

Reflection: Who—or what—holds you when you are holding everything else?

Strength That Learns to Release

"The end of a matter is better than its beginning, and patience is better than pride." (Ecclesiastes 7:8 NIV)

Foundations are meant to be relied upon—but also examined. What once protected can, if unrefined, begin to constrain. Strength that never rests can harden into posture rather than purpose. Honor does not require imitation; it requires discernment.

Reflection: What part of your strength is ready to be carried differently now?

LEGACY NOTES

The Courage To Love Without Words

TEN

Presence That Endured When Words Fell Short

I came to understand this opening quote—slowly, and only with time:—that love is not only something you feel, but something you do, and something you say. Not as a rebuke to my father's life, but as an expansion of it. He lived the first truth with unwavering fidelity. Love, for him, was something you did. You showed up. You stayed. You carried weight without complaint. You endured. And for many years, I believed that was the whole of love—not because he defined it that way, but because it was the only version I had ever known.

He was always there. And yet, there were moments when I needed him to arrive differently.

This is not a story about absence. My father did not disappear. He did not retreat when things became heavy. He did not abandon responsibility when it pressed hardest. His presence was consistent to the point of being structural. It stabilized our family. It made life predictable enough to live inside. When things threatened to fracture, he held the center. When fear pressed in, he contained it. When chaos loomed, he stood firm. His love was faithful, durable, and real.

But endurance, I would come to learn, is not the same as intimacy.

There were moments—quiet, unremarkable ones—when I felt a distance I could not name. Not because he was unkind. Not because he was inattentive. But because the language of love in our home was primarily practical, and my need was becoming relational. I did not yet know how to articulate this tension. I only knew that something in me was reaching for connection, while the love being offered was protection.

Protection is powerful. It keeps families intact. It creates safety. It allows children to grow without constantly scanning for threat. But protection does not always translate into understanding. And safety does not automatically produce closeness. You can be held securely and still feel unseen. You can be loved deeply and still long to be known.

My father's silence had always served a purpose. It steadied rooms. It lowered temperatures. It kept problems from becoming performances. In many ways, it was an act of care. But as I grew older, that same silence began to register differently. What once felt like strength began, at times, to feel like distance— not because it was intended as such, but because my needs were changing and his language did not.

There were things I wanted to hear. Not explanations. Not assurances. Just recognition.

I wanted my inner life acknowledged—not managed, not protected, but met. I wanted moments when presence leaned forward instead of standing guard. When silence gave way to naming. When love risked articulation, even if imperfectly. These were not demands I could have voiced at the time. They emerged slowly, often only in hindsight, as a quiet ache rather than a clear request.

What complicated this longing was the knowledge—felt even then—that my father was giving everything he knew how to give. His love was not withholding; it was faithful to the form it had learned. And yet, fidelity to one form of love does not guarantee that all needs are met. This is one of the hardest truths to accept without turning it into blame.

What holds a family together is not always what heals it. Presence can stabilize without connecting. Love can be faithful and still feel distant. Silence can protect—and still withhold.

None of this negates what my father gave. It simply acknowledges that love, when confined to endurance alone, can leave parts of the heart untouched. There are wounds that do not come from harm, but from omission. From what was never said because no one knew how to say it. From what was never offered because it had never been modeled.

As a child, I interpreted this distance as normal. As an adult, I began to recognize it as relational. And that recognition brought with it a new kind of grief—not sharp, not dramatic, but persistent. The grief of knowing that something essential was missing, even though nothing obvious was wrong.

My father's presence did not fail. But it did not always translate.

This is the dilemma at the heart of this part of the story. How do you honor a love that endured while naming the places where it fell short? How do you speak honestly about longing without turning faithfulness into fault? How do you hold gratitude and grief in the same hand without letting either slip?

The words of bell hooks do not diminish my father's love. They complete the conversation around it. Love is something you do,—yes. And love is also something you say. Not because words are superior to action, but because human hearts are shaped by both. Doing sustains. Saying connects.

My father sustained us. And still, there were moments when I needed him to connect.

This chapter begins there—not in accusation, but in truth. In the space between what was given and what was needed. In the quiet recognition that courage does not only look like carrying weight. Sometimes, it looks like learning to speak.

His strength did not fail us, but it did not always interpret itself in ways we could feel as closeness.

There is a kind of love that builds walls strong enough to keep the storm out and still leaves the rooms inside dim. My father's endurance did the work it knew how to do. It preserved structure, kept life upright, and ensured that nothing essential collapsed. Because of that, it was easy—especially for a child—to assume that what was missing did not matter, or that wanting more would somehow diminish the magnitude of what had already been given.

I did not question his love so much as I questioned my place inside it.

Silent strength has limits, though they are rarely visible at first. It excels at protection and containment, absorbing pressure without spectacle and keeping the system intact. What it does not always do is translate care into reassurance or steadiness into emotional clarity. A family can remain standing while its members are left unsure of where they stand with one another.

This was the boundary I did not yet know how to name.

There were moments when I struggled quietly—confusion I could not yet articulate, fear that had no language, disappointment I felt guilty for feeling at all. I did not know how to bring these things to him, not because he was unkind or unavailable, but because his strength had taught me a particular grammar of survival. You carried what you could, you did not burden others unnecessarily, you solved what was solvable and endured what was not. That grammar had saved much, but it had also narrowed the space where vulnerability could comfortably breathe.

I did not feel forbidden to speak; I felt unprepared.

His silence, so often a gift, sometimes became a mirror in which I could not find myself reflected. When I was unsure, he remained steady. When I was overwhelmed, he stayed composed. When I needed reassurance that could be named, he offered presence that did not explain itself. To him, this was care—holding the line and keeping things from unraveling. To me, at times, it felt like distance, not because he had stepped away, but because he had not stepped toward.

This is the subtle difference between being supported and being understood. Support says, "You will be fine." Understanding says, " I see where you are."

My father was exceptional at the first. The second did not come as naturally, not because he lacked feeling, but because his way of loving had been forged under conditions where feeling could not afford too much voice. His life had taught him that stability mattered more than articulation, that reassurance was proven through consistency rather than spoken into existence. He trusted that if he stayed, worked, and held responsibility without flinching, the message would be received.

Often it was. Sometimes it was not.

There were situations where his silence felt like steadiness to him and like opacity to me. Not abandonment—never that—but a sense that something solid was present without being interpretable. I could feel that care existed, but I could not always tell what it meant about me. Did he understand what I was carrying? Did he worry? Did he approve? His strength answered the question of survival, but it did not always answer the question of connection.

And yet, I hesitated to want more.

How do you ask for emotional clarity from a man who has given you safety at great personal cost? How do you name a longing without making it sound like accusation? I learned early to translate need into self-sufficiency, to read presence as enough even when something in me remained unresolved. I mistook restraint for maturity without realizing it was also adaptation.

Silent love preserves order, but it does not always invite conversation.

This is not a criticism so much as an observation shaped by gratitude and grief held together. My father's strength was necessary and life-giving. Without it much would have fractured. But when strength becomes the primary language of love, it can crowd out other dialects. Endurance can become so respected that tenderness feels unnecessary, and protection can become so complete that connection is assumed rather than pursued.

What went unspoken was not indifference; it was complexity.

He did not lack care, but he lacked a map for expressing it differently. His love spoke fluently in action and restraint, less so in attunement and naming. He assumed that staying was the message, holding was the answer, and governed silence would be read correctly.

And often, it was.

I can count on one hand the number of times I remember hearing the words 'I love you' spoken aloud in our home. Not because love was absent—it was not—but because it was rarely verbalized. Those words were not withheld out of coldness or distance; they simply were not part of the language he trusted most. Love, in his world, proved itself through reliability, sacrifice, and endurance. To say it felt unnecessary when he believed he was already living it.

Sometimes that was enough. Sometimes it was not.

The absence of spoken affection did not register as deprivation when I was young; it registered as normal. I learned to read meaning in consistency rather than in language, to interpret care through presence rather than expression. And yet, as I grew older, there were moments when I felt a quiet uncertainty— not about whether he loved me, but about whether he saw me fully. Whether what I was carrying internally had a place to land. Whether reassurance needed to be earned through steadiness rather than received through words.

That tension—the space between what was given and what was needed— became one of the quiet shaping forces of my inner life. It taught me resilience, but it also taught me how easily strength can be mistaken for sufficiency, and how love can be faithful without being fully felt. I learned how to endure without asking, how to assume that silence meant care, and how to translate absence of language into proof of character.

Strength can hold a family together, and still leave emotional questions unanswered.

Those questions did not undo what my father built. They did not diminish the magnitude of what he carried or the sacrifices he made. But they remained—patient, unresolved—asking not whether his love was real, but whether presence alone could finish the work endurance had begun.

Silence was my father's native language, and he spoke it with discipline and care, but it was a language that required fluency from those around him—a fluency children do not yet possess. He assumed that restraint would be read as devotion, that consistency would be understood as affection, that the absence of withdrawal would communicate belonging. What he did not account for was how much interpretation that required, or how easily silence, when met by an unformed inner world, could be filled with meanings he never intended.

As a child, I did not lack safety, but I often lacked translation. I could feel that something steady surrounded me, yet I could not always locate myself within it. When fear surfaced, when uncertainty pressed inward, when shame or confusion arrived without clear shape, I did not know how to bring those experiences into the open without disrupting the order he worked so hard to maintain. His silence felt composed, intentional, even generous—but it also felt closed, as though entering it required permission I did not know how to ask for.

There were moments when I wanted reassurance not because I doubted his love, but because I needed to hear it find me personally, spoken into the particular contours of who I was becoming. I wanted language that would meet me where I stood, words that would not simply imply care through endurance, but would name it directly, unmistakably, without requiring me to infer or decode. Yet asking for that felt risky, not because he would refuse, but because I did not know how to invite it without sounding needy, weak, or disruptive to the steadiness he embodied.

In the absence of words, other things sometimes took their place. Fear learned to speak quietly to itself. Shame rehearsed questions no one else could hear. I filled gaps with assumptions—about expectations, about worth, about what had to be proven in order to be secure. Silence, which to him meant trust and dignity, occasionally registered in me as distance, not because he had withdrawn, but because I lacked the tools to interpret what his presence was already offering.

Children, I have come to understand, do not naturally translate restraint into reassurance. They do not intuit that what is unspoken is still true. They tend to experience love as conditional when it is not named, not because it is withheld, but because they do not yet know how to separate behavior from belonging. Silence assumes an emotional literacy that develops later, often only after one has learned how easily meaning can be lost when it is left implicit.

In those moments, words would have not weakened his strength or diminished his authority. They would have clarified it. They would have made visible what was already present but indistinct. A sentence spoken aloud could have relieved a thousand quiet calculations. A simple naming—"I see you," "I'm proud of you, you are enough here"—would not have replaced the love he lived, but it might have anchored it more securely in my inner world, giving shape to what I otherwise had to hold abstractly.

It took many years for me to realize that what was missing was not affection, but language. He did not withhold love; he withheld articulation, not out of neglect, but out of instinct. He trusted action more than expression, believing that words were fragile and deeds endured. And in many ways, he was right. That belief shaped him—and it shaped me. I absorbed, almost without noticing, the idea that love is proven through provision, care is measured by what you carry, and the greater the responsibility you shoulder, the clearer your devotion must be.

I see that inheritance in my own life now. I express love most fluently through providing—through protecting margins, anticipating needs, building stability. There is a part of me that still believes that if I can give more, hold more, secure more, then I am loving well. It is not a belief I chose consciously; it arrived the same way his silence did—through repetition, through example, through years of watching love enacted rather than spoken.

At the same time, I notice the counterweight. Perhaps because I heard the words so rarely growing up—so rarely that I can count the memories on one hand—I find myself saying them often now. I tell my wife I love her easily, repeatedly, sometimes with an almost reflexive urgency, as though naming it aloud ensures that she cannot miss it. I do not know whether this is balance or compensation, whether it is simply maturity or a quiet overcorrection, but I recognize the pattern for what it is—a desire to make explicit what once had to be inferred.

His silence preserved his dignity. It protected the structure of our home. It prevented volatility and excess. And it taught me how to endure, how to provide, how to stand. But words preserve understanding, especially across generations, especially in moments when fear and self-doubt are eager to explain silence on their own terms. I learned later—long after the moments when I needed it most—that the silence I once struggled to interpret had never been empty. It had simply been untranslated. And part of my work now, as a husband and uncle, is learning how to carry forward the strength of what he gave while giving language to what I once had to discover on my own.

There were many seasons when I felt my father's love without ever hearing it named, and that distinction mattered more than I understood at the time. I did not doubt that he cared; what unsettled me was the quiet question of whether I was meeting the conditions that made that care secure. His love lived in what he carried, in what he provided, in what he refused to abandon. But because it rarely arrived with language, it often required interpretation—and interpretation is a heavy burden for a child who is still learning how to read the world.

At the same time, my childhood was not devoid of warmth or joy. I remember happy, ordinary days that felt uncomplicated in the moment—piling into the car as a family, stopping to pick up a bucket of chicken from KFC, driving to the local park, and spreading out on the grass while my brother and I ran off to play. In those moments, I watched the strain lift from my father's face, if only briefly. His shoulders softened, his voice lightened, and sometimes a simple smile or laugh escaped him, unguarded and genuine. That was his presence at its most visible—not explanatory, not verbalized, but real. I felt loved there, in the ease of his laughter and in the way the world seemed to pause for him when responsibility loosened its grip.

Still, when love is unnamed, the mind inevitably begins to supply its own explanations. Children are especially skilled at this, and especially unforgiving with themselves. Silence does not remain empty for long; it fills with questions, then assumptions, then quiet conclusions that feel reasonable in the absence of clarification. When affection is not withdrawn but neither spoken, a child can begin to wonder whether love must be maintained through performance, through obedience, or through being easy to carry and careful not to become a problem.

I felt loved, but I did not always feel assured.

That difference became clear only years later. Feeling loved is experiential; it lives in moments, gestures, shared routines like those afternoons at the park. Feeling assured is cumulative; it settles into the body as a kind of certainty that does not rise and fall with mood or misstep. Assurance tells a child not only that love exists, but that it remains intact, even when disappointment enters the room. Without words, that assurance was harder to access.

When my father was disappointed, his restraint deepened rather than broke. He did not scold or withdraw dramatically, nor did he explain himself. He simply grew quieter and, more contained. And because his silence already carried so much weight, it was difficult for me to distinguish between disappointment and distance. I could feel the shift, but I lacked the language to interpret it accurately, so I did what many children do and assumed the shift must somehow be about me.

Silence invites projection, and the most vulnerable voice in the room is often the one that fills it.

I learned early how to read subtle changes in tone, posture, and pacing. I noticed when the room felt heavier, when my father's attention narrowed, when his quiet turned inward. That sensitivity sharpened my awareness, but it also sharpened my self-scrutiny. Without reassurance to anchor interpretation, I began to equate restraint with judgment, quiet with evaluation, seriousness with disapproval. I did not articulate these thoughts aloud; they lived privately, shaping how carefully I moved through the emotional terrain of our home.

Responsibility followed naturally. If love was expressed through provision and steadiness, then my task—unspoken but deeply internalized—was to be worthy of what was being carried on my behalf. I worked hard, behaved carefully, anticipated expectations rather than testing boundaries, and took pride in being low maintenance, in not adding strain, in making myself easy to hold. None of this was demanded explicitly; it arose from inference rather than instruction, and inference, unlike affirmation, rarely settles the nervous system.

I did not feel unloved; I felt uncertain about how secure that love was when I faltered.

Children often interpret restraint as conditionality because they lack the perspective to separate a parent's internal discipline from relational judgment. My father's restraint was about himself—about not discharging pressure outward, about keeping order, about remaining grounded—but from my vantage point it could look like evaluation, like quiet assessment, like love that remained present yet unreadable.

Over time, this ambiguity taught me self-reliance, but it also taught me self-surveillance. I learned to monitor my impact, to notice when I might be disappointing, to correct course before disappointment could deepen. Those skills later served me well in leadership and responsibility, but they were born in a context where reassurance was implied rather than spoken, and implication always leaves room for doubt.

I did not need more protection, I needed translation.

Words would not have weakened my father's strength; they would have clarified it. They would have placed boundaries around silence so it did not have to carry everything on its own. They would have told me explicitly that disappointment did not threaten love, restraint was not withdrawal, and steadiness did not require perfection from those being held.

Instead, I learned to carry responsibility early and quietly. I learned to let affirmation come from achievement rather than attachment, and to feel secure when I was useful, dependable, and aligned. These lessons did not damage me, but they did shape me. They taught me how to be strong, and they also taught me how easily doubt can creep in when strength wavers.

Only much later did I understand that the love I questioned had never been absent; it had simply never been named. And without names, children invent meanings that feel safer than hope. Self-blame feels controllable—if love depends on me doing better, then at least I know what to do.

This is the quiet cost of unnamed love. It does not negate devotion, but it complicates security.

My father's love was faithful, constant, and real, visible in laughter at the park and in the steadiness that carried us home. But because it was rarely spoken, it left space—space that responsibility rushed in to fill, space that vigilance occupied, space that a child's imagination worked hard to manage. What was not said did not disappear; it simply took a different shape.

And it took years, distance, and maturity to see this clearly—: I carried not a lack of love, but an excess of interpretation. Silence had asked me to guess, and I did the best guessing I could with the tools I had. Love was felt, unmistakably so, but it was not named—and what is not named often becomes heavier than it needs to be, especially for those still learning how to hold it.

Strength was never announced as an expectation in our home, but it was modeled so consistently that it became an assumption I absorbed without question. I did not remember being told to be strong; I learned it by watching what survived. My father endured. He carried weight without complaint. He absorbed pressure without discharging it. And in doing so, he taught me— quietly and thoroughly—that strength was the safest way to belong.

I learned early that restraint was admirable, composure was respected, and needing less made you easier to carry. Care was given generously through provision and presence, but it was not negotiated through emotion. So, I adapted. I mirrored what worked. I learned to regulate inward rather than reach outward, to steady myself rather than seek steadiness from someone else. Strength became not just a trait, but a strategy.

Over time, strength turned into currency. It was how worth was measured— not explicitly, but experientially. The less I needed, the more I felt aligned. The more I managed quietly, the more secure I believed myself to be. I did not arrive at this conclusion through instruction; I arrived there by recognizing patterns. In our family, endurance moved life forward. Expression did not. So, I invested in endurance.

An unspoken rule formed beneath this pattern, subtle but powerful—don't need too much. Don't ask for what cannot be easily given. Don't introduce volatility into a system that is already working hard to remain intact. My father never articulated this as principle or policy, but his restraint—repeated quietly over years—taught it all the same. Care, I learned, was not withdrawn when I needed something; it was preserved when I did not add strain.

I remember a small moment that carried more weight than it appeared to at the time. We were shopping for back-to-school items, a practical errand with a clear purpose. My brother spotted something on a shelf—something he liked, not something he needed. Without thinking, I blurted out that he should get it anyway, a reflexive generosity that felt harmless in the moment. My father overheard. He didn't raise his voice or scold. He simply said, clearly and firmly, "If you don't need it, put it back."

The lesson landed immediately. Not harshly, but decisively. There were limits to what could be provided. Limits that were not negotiable, not because love was scarce, but because order mattered. Provision had boundaries. Love did not. I understand that distinction now. I did not then. What I absorbed was simpler and more enduring—wanting was not enough, and asking for more than necessary risked misalignment.

As a result, I became self-reliant early—not in dramatic ways, but in quiet ones. I learned how to sit with discomfort without naming it, how to absorb disappointment without asking for reassurance, how to carry uncertainty without seeking relief. These skills would later be praised as maturity, competence, leadership. But they were first learned as survival. They were ways to stay inside the limits of what could be given without threatening the structure that held us.

Children model what survives, not necessarily what is healthiest. I watched endurance keep our family upright, and I internalized endurance as the safest posture. Expression felt riskier by comparison. It required language, vulnerability, and the possibility of misunderstanding. Strength, by contrast, asked for nothing and promised stability in return. So, I chose strength.

Over time, this translated into emotional self-containment. I learned how to hold feelings rather than share them, how to minimize needs before they were visible, and how to solve internally what might have been eased relationally. I did not experience this as deprivation. It felt like responsibility. Like competence. Like becoming the kind of person who could be trusted with weight.

But there is a cost to learning strength without expression. Emotional weight does not disappear when it is carried quietly; it accumulates. Without language, feelings have nowhere to go but inward. They settle into posture, habit, and expectation. I did not know how to ask for care because I had learned—slowly, instinctively—that care was something I received by being strong enough not to ask.

This inheritance of silence did not make me cold. It made me capable, and cautious. It taught me to read rooms, to manage impact, to stay composed even when I was uncertain or afraid. It also taught me to underestimate my own need for reassurance, connection, and naming. I carried emotional weight fluently, but I did not yet know how to set it down.

Looking back, I can see how faithfully I mirrored my father—not only in his steadiness, but in his self-containment. I learned to endure quietly because that was the form love had taken around me. It was not imposed. It was transmitted. And like all inheritances absorbed without language, it shaped me before I ever had the chance to examine it.

This is the quiet paradox of silent strength. It passes down stability, but it also passes down pressure. It teaches children how to hold, but not always how to be held. It forms people who can endure almost anything—and who sometimes struggle to believe they are allowed to need more.

When love is expressed only through endurance, children learn to endure quietly too.

With time, the question shifted. It no longer asked what I lacked, but what my father had been given to work with. And that change altered everything.

Compassion does not arrive by excusing harm or minimizing absence; it arrives by widening the frame. By seeing a life not only through its effects, but through its conditions. When I began to look at my father this way—not as the center of my unmet needs, but as a man shaped by forces long before I arrived—his silence took on a different meaning. It was no longer simply what I experienced. It was what he inherited.

My father loved with the tools he had.

Those tools were forged in scarcity, in migration, in early responsibility, in a world where survival required restraint and emotion was something managed privately or not at all. He did not grow up in an environment that rewarded articulation or emotional naming. He grew up in one that demanded usefulness, reliability, and endurance. Feelings were real, but they were secondary. What mattered was whether the work got done, whether the family was fed, whether tomorrow could be trusted to arrive.

Emotional language is not innate. It is taught, modeled, practiced in safety. And my father did not grow up in a context where such practice was possible, much less encouraged. What he learned instead was how to show care through action, how to love by staying, how to protect by absorbing pressure. Silence, for him, was not avoidance; it was discipline. It was how to keep going without falling apart.

Once I saw this, blame began to loosen its grip.

His restraint was not a rejection of connection, but a form of stewardship. He was guarding what he knew how to guard. He was offering what he had learned to offer. To ask him for emotional fluency would have been to ask him for a language he had never been taught to speak. And yet, even without that language, he communicated devotion in ways that were consistent, costly, and real.

This realization did not erase the ache of what was missing. But it relocated it. The grief no longer sat between us as accusation. It rested alongside gratitude, complex and unresolved, but honest. I could mourn what I did not receive without diminishing what I did. I could acknowledge the limits without turning them into indictments.

I came to understand that he did not choose silence freely. It had been handed to him, reinforced by necessity, and validated by survival. In that sense, it was inheritance rather than intention. And inheritance, when unexamined, repeats itself not out of malice, but out of familiarity.

There is compassion in recognizing this.

It allows space for grief without demanding fault. It honors devotion without pretending completeness. It acknowledges that love can be deeply present and still constrained by history, culture, and circumstance. My father did not fail to love me. He loved me faithfully within the contours of what he knew.

Holding this truth required maturity. It asked me to resist the simplicity of blame and the comfort of resolution. It required me to hold two realities at once: that his love sustained me, and his silence shaped me in ways that were sometimes heavy. Neither truth cancels the other. Together, they tell a fuller story.

Understanding limitation does not erase love. It dignifies it.

It recognizes the cost of devotion expressed under constraint. It honors the courage it takes to give what you can when what is asked of you exceeds what you were ever shown. And it allows the next generation to carry forward what was given without being bound to repeat what was never meant to be permanent.

This is where compassion becomes generative rather than excusing. It does not ask us to pretend the silence did not matter. It invites us to see why it existed, and to decide—consciously, gently—what we will do with that understanding now.

In seeing my father more clearly, I began to see myself more clearly too. The strength I carried, the restraint I defaulted to, the hesitation around naming need—all of it made sense in light of what had been modeled. What once felt like personal deficiency began to look like lineage.

And lineage, once recognized, can be honored without being reenacted.

This did not require confrontation. It required compassion. A compassion that neither softened the truth nor hardened into resentment. A compassion that could hold grief and gratitude in the same hand without needing to resolve them.

My father gave me what he had. And what he had was shaped by a life that asked him to survive before it ever asked him to speak.

Knowing this does not change the past. But it changes how I carry it forward.

Clarity carries responsibility, and once you recognize what shaped you, you are no longer free to repeat it unconsciously. There comes a quiet moment when inheritance turns into choice—when the patterns that once felt inevitable present themselves not as destiny, but as material. This is where fidelity is tested, not by whether we preserve what we were given unchanged, but by whether we allow it to grow. Loving more fully than you were loved is not an indictment of the past; it is stewardship of it.

For me, that stewardship began with language.

I had learned how to stay, how to carry weight without complaint, how to hold the center when circumstances pressed in. Those instincts were solid and honestly forged. Yet over time I sensed that presence alone, however faithful, was not always enough. What had steadied me could still leave others guessing; silence, even when protective, could ask too much of those who needed clarity. Endurance maintained order, but it did not always translate into reassurance.

So, I began to choose translation over assumption.

This choice did not come naturally. Speaking what had never been spoken felt exposed, as though naming reassurance might weaken authority or articulating care might dilute seriousness. I had inherited a belief—unspoken but deeply embedded—that strength was proven through endurance rather than expression, feelings carried aloud signaled fragility, and composure meant keeping language restrained. Speaking, I believed, risked the ground beneath me. But courage, I slowly came to understand, is not only the ability to withstand pressure; it is the willingness to clarify what pressure conceals.

There were moments with my wife when the familiar impulse rose to absorb rather than articulate, to solve quietly, to hold without explaining. Silence had always felt like competence. Restraint felt responsible. And yet, in those moments, I learned to pause and ask not what I could endure, but what the other person needed to feel secure. More often than not, what they needed was not additional stability, but visibility; not more strength, but naming.

So, I spoke.

I named reassurance even when nothing was wrong. I said 'I love you' not as punctuation or habit, but as orientation. I explained disappointment without allowing it to harden into distance, and I allowed vulnerability to sit beside steadiness without forcing a choice between them. This was not softness replacing strength; it was strength expanding—learning a language that had never been taught.

Breaking silence did not mean breaking fidelity to my father's way of loving. It meant extending it. Translating action into meaning. Pairing presence with clarity so love did not have to be inferred or earned through guessing. And in the process, I discovered something unexpected. Speaking did not make me weaker. It made me more grounded. Language did not erode authority; it deepened trust. My wife did not become less resilient because reassurance was named; she became freer to be herself without wondering where she stood. The structure held—and the space inside it widened.

This, I now believe, is the work of the next generation—not to reject silent love, but to translate it; not to dismantle endurance, but to add articulation; not to abandon restraint, but to ensure it does not obscure connection. Fidelity is not proven by repetition alone, but by discernment.

There is courage in saying what was never said to you. In offering what you once had to infer. In choosing clarity where you learned to be strong. This courage does not dishonor what came before; it honors it by refusing to let devotion stop where it once had to.

My father showed me how to stand. My task is to stand—and speak.

Slowly and sometimes reluctantly, I came to see that loving more fully than I had been loved did not require rejecting what I received. It required finishing a sentence that had been left incomplete. My father's love had given me posture, steadiness, and endurance. It did not always give me translation. And the responsibility of my generation, I began to understand, was not to dismantle the structure we inherited, but to inhabit it differently—to let presence remain, while allowing language to enter.

Choosing translation over assumption became an act of responsibility rather than rebellion. It meant refusing to let silence do all the work simply because it always had. It meant recognizing that what once protected could now unintentionally obscure, and that strength expressed only through containment could limit connection even as it preserved order. I was not being asked to become someone else. I was being asked to become more legible.

This realization showed up first in small, unremarkable moments. Moments when nothing was wrong, and yet something could be named. Moments when I felt the familiar instinct to absorb tension quietly, to move past discomfort without slowing down the room, to carry concern internally rather than risk unsettling anyone else. For years, that instinct had felt like maturity. Now, it began to feel incomplete.

So, I learned to pause instead of absorbing automatically, and to ask whether silence was actually serving the moment or merely preserving habit. I learned to notice when reassurance was needed not because stability was absent, but because clarity was. I learned that naming care does not create dependency; it creates orientation. People function better when they know where they stand, especially those who are still learning how to locate themselves in the world.

Speaking love did not come easily. It felt unnatural at first, almost indulgent, as though articulation might cheapen what had always been proven through action. A part of me believed words should be reserved for moments of necessity, that emotional expression risked becoming performative, that seriousness required restraint. But I began to see that withholding language was no longer an act of protection. It was a missed opportunity for connection.

So, I practiced saying what I felt before it had to be inferred. I practiced naming reassurance before doubt had a chance to grow roots. I practiced allowing tenderness to exist alongside steadiness, rather than assuming one diminished the other. I learned to say "I love you" not only in moments of intensity or repair, but in ordinary spaces where love might otherwise be assumed and therefore left vulnerable to misinterpretation. I still continue to practice yet, I am far from mastering the craft.

This practice did not erode strength. It clarified it. The steadiness remained, but it became more visible. Authority did not weaken; it softened into trust. Presence did not disappear; it became relational rather than merely structural. I offered my family not a different kind of love, but a more complete one— love could feel without having to decipher it.

Breaking silence, I discovered, did not mean breaking fidelity to my father. It meant honoring him by extending what he had built. His way of loving had been shaped by necessity, history, and survival. Mine could be shaped by discernment. I did not need to carry forward the limits that had once been required to protect. I could carry forward the devotion and allow it to speak.

There were moments when vulnerability felt risky, when naming fear or uncertainty stirred the old instinct to retreat inward and manage alone. But each time I chose articulation instead of absorption, something subtle shifted. Connection deepened. Misunderstanding lessened. Emotional weight redistributed itself rather than accumulating silently. I was no longer the sole container of what could be shared.

What surprised me most was how natural this began to feel over time. Language stopped feeling like exposure and started feeling like alignment. I was not abandoning endurance; I was pairing it with clarity. I was not dismantling restraint; I was ensuring it did not stand alone as the only proof of love. Strength was no longer measured solely by how much I could carry without speaking. It was measured by how wisely I could decide when speaking mattered more than holding.

This is the courage that arrives after endurance has done its work. Not the courage to survive without complaint, but the courage to remain present and articulate once survival is no longer the only goal. It is the courage to believe that saying what was never said does not erase what was done, and that naming love does not diminish the sacrifices that made life possible.

The next generation's task, I now see, is not to reject silent love, but to translate it. To take what was lived faithfully and make it intelligible to those who come next. To ensure that devotion does not remain hidden behind restraint, and that presence is accompanied by words capable of anchoring it securely in the hearts of those who receive it.

My father taught me how to endure. I am learning how to endure—and speak.

There comes a moment when presence, no matter how faithful, begins to feel unfinished. Not insufficient, not wrong, but incomplete—like a structure that has held for decades and now asks for windows. The walls did their work. They protected. They endured storms. But what once needed enclosure now needs light. This is the moment when love, having proven its reliability, is invited to learn how to speak.

Silence had served us well. It absorbed fear, contained volatility, and kept life from splintering when conditions were unforgiving. In those earlier years, restraint was not avoidance; it was wisdom shaped by necessity. Not everything could be named without cost. Not every truth could be spoken without destabilizing what little margin existed. Survival required discretion, and discretion became habit. Silence did its work.

But time changes the work required.

What once needed protection no longer does. What once would have burdened now could heal. And love, if it is to mature rather than merely persist, must respond to the present rather than remain loyal only to the past. This is not betrayal of what was necessary then. It is fidelity to what is needed now.

I began to sense this most clearly in moments of stillness, when the urgency of endurance loosened its grip and something quieter surfaced. The questions were not dramatic. They did not arrive as accusations. They came as invitations. What remains unsaid that no longer needs to be guarded? What has silence preserved that language could now restore? What does love require in this season—not as memory, but as living practice?

Presence can hold a life together. It can provide safety, continuity, and trust. But presence alone cannot always mend what has been strained or misunderstood. It cannot always repair the inner narratives formed in the absence of explanation. It cannot always release what has been carried too long without relief. For that, words are required—not many, not ornate, but honest and timely.

I began to see how silence, even when born of care, can outlive its usefulness. What once prevented chaos can later prevent closeness. What once protected dignity can later obscure tenderness. Silence that is never revisited becomes less a shelter and more a boundary, one that keeps others from entering fully even when the danger has passed.

This realization did not diminish the power of presence. It completed it.

Love that learns to speak does not abandon restraint; it refines it. It chooses words not to explain everything, but to clarify what matters most. It understands that articulation is not indulgence, but stewardship. That naming care does not weaken authority; it grounds it in trust. That healing often requires language precisely because pain was once managed without it.

There are things that can be healed only once they are spoken—not loudly, not repeatedly, but truthfully. Reassurance that must be named because it was once assumed. Gratitude that must be voiced because it was once expressed only through duty. Even sorrow must be acknowledged, not to reopen wounds, but to let them finally breathe.

This is where reconciliation begins—not with confrontation, but with permission. Permission to speak what no longer needs to be carried alone.

Permission to let love expand beyond the forms it once required to survive. Permission to believe that strength can include vulnerability without surrendering its center.

Presence holds. It always has. But words heal because they make meaning shared rather than solitary.

And healing, unlike survival, asks not only that we remain standing, but that we become reachable.

This is the work that comes next. Not the undoing of what endured, but its release into fuller expression. Not the rejection of silence, but its integration. Because love that has carried weight faithfully for years deserves the chance to speak—not to justify itself, but to complete what it began.

What must be said now is not what could not be said then. It is what love, having endured, is finally ready to offer.

And in that offering, something long held begins, at last, to loosen.

Silent love did its work first, building something load-bearing and reliable, a structure strong enough to carry a family through years that demanded more endurance than explanation. What my father gave through presence, restraint, and steadiness was not incomplete; it was foundational. Without it, nothing else could have stood.

But foundations are not the finish. What is built to survive must eventually be lived in, and what is lived in must eventually be named. Strength that never learns tenderness risks becoming only functional, and love that is never articulated can remain faithful while still feeling unfinished. This does not diminish what came before; it reveals what it was quietly preparing for.

I no longer see silence and speech as opposites, but as movements within the same life. Silence carried us when language would have been too fragile to hold weight. Words arrive when strength is no longer threatened by being known. One protected; the other heals. Together, they make love whole.

This is not a rejection of endurance but its fulfillment. Strength is not diminished by tenderness; it is completed by it. To speak love after years of holding it is not weakness, but maturity—the courage that follows survival, when the task is no longer to brace, but to open.

What my father taught me through presence gave me a place to stand. I have since had to learn how to let others stand with me, how to share what was once carried alone, and how to trust that love grows stronger, not softer, when it is named.

The movement now changes—from endurance to expression, from holding to sharing, from protection to communion. The chapters ahead turn toward love lived in daylight, where what was once carried silently is woven into ordinary moments, spoken naturally, and offered without fear of collapse. Not love proved through strain, but love worn gently into daily life.

He taught me how to stand. I had to learn how to speak.

SACRED WAYPOINTS

Love Spoken Less Than Lived

I can count on one hand how many times I heard, "I love you," growing up, not because love was absent, but because it was rarely verbalized. Presence did the speaking, and endurance carried the meaning—until I realized a child shouldn't have to decode love to feel secure.

- Where have you been asking someone to 'interpret' your love instead of receiving it clearly?
- What sentence would steady the most vulnerable person in the room?

Sit with this truth: What goes unnamed often gets filled in by fear.

When Protection Didn't Become Connection

My father kept the storm out, but there were moments when I needed him to arrive differently—not bigger, not louder, just nearer in a way that named what his presence already meant.

- Where are you protecting someone when they're really asking to be understood?
- What would it look like to lean forward instead of standing guard?

Ask for courage: "Lord, teach me to connect, not only contain."

The Limits He Set Without Withdrawing Love

Back-to-school shopping taught me something fast. My brother wanted something he liked, but didn't need, and my father calmly drew the line. He said,—"If you don't need it, put it back"—a boundary on provision, not a boundary on love.

- Where do you confuse limits with rejection, in yourself or others?
- What boundary could actually make love clearer, not colder?

Sit with this truth: Love can be firm without becoming distant.

The Park Where His Smile Translated Everything

Some of my clearest memories are simple ones—KFC, the local park, my brother and me playing while the stress fell off my dad for a moment and a small smile or laugh appeared. That was his tenderness, unannounced but real.

- Where have you overlooked the quiet ways someone has loved you well?
- What ordinary rhythm could become a healing place for your family now?

Ask for gratitude: "Lord, help me recognize love that didn't know how to speak."

The Strength I Inherited and the
Silence I Mistook for Maturity

I learned to be 'strong enough' by watching what survived, and I carried needs privately because it felt responsible. Only later did I see that self-containment can look like strength while quietly becoming loneliness.

- What have you trained yourself not to need?
- Where are you carrying weight that was never meant to be carried alone?

Sit with this truth: Endurance is not the same as intimacy.

Compassion Without Condemnation

My father's silence was shaped by history, culture, survival, and necessity. Emotional language is learned, and he loved with the tools he had—faithful, real, and limited in ways that deserve honesty without blame.

- What limitation in someone you love needs compassion instead of critique?
- Where can grief and gratitude be held together without rushing to resolve?

Ask for mercy: "Lord, let me see the whole story, not just its effects on me."

The Courage to Translate What Was Never Spoken

I inherited the belief that saying how you feel is weakness, then learned the reversal—articulation is strength when it keeps love from being guessed at. Speaking didn't replace what my father built; it completed it.

- What love do you need to say out loud, even if it feels unfamiliar?
- Where is silence done serving—and ready to be released?

Ask for help: Teach me, Lord, to pair presence with words that heal.

Presence That Holds, Words That Heal

Silent love built the structure, but spoken love turns shelter into home. The next movement isn't abandoning endurance; it's letting tenderness finish what strength began.

- What must be said now that no longer needs to be protected?
- What would change if love became legible instead of implied?

Sit with this truth: Presence holds, but words heal.

ANCHORS OF THE WORD 

The Strength That Is Assumed

"For who is God besides the Lord? And who is the Rock except our God?" (Psalm 18:31 NIV)

Strength that endures rarely draws attention to itself. When something holds consistently, it becomes assumed rather than examined. My father's steadiness was trusted not because it was explained, but because it never failed. Only later did I see how much weight he had absorbed quietly so others could stand without fear.

Reflection: What in your life is trusted simply because it has never given way?

Quiet Security

"The fruit of that righteousness will be peace; its effect will be quietness and confidence forever." (Isaiah 32:17 NIV)

Our home was not silent; it was alive, loud with passion and movement. Yet beneath that energy was containment. Worry existed, but it was bounded. Fear surfaced, but it was never allowed to rule. That quiet confidence did not come from ease—it came from someone holding the center.

Reflection: Where has your faith created security for others without being named?

Integrity That Carries Others

"The righteous lead blameless lives; blessed are their children after them." (Proverbs 20:7 NIV)

Integrity does not announce itself. It reveals itself through consistency over time. My father's restraint, reliability, and refusal to abandon responsibility created a path others could walk without knowing who cleared it. His steadiness became a blessing long before it was recognized as one.

Reflection: Who is standing more securely today because of the way you walk?

The Weight Beneath the Work

"Unless the LORD builds the house, the builders labor in vain. Unless the LORD watches over the city, the guards stand watch in vain. In vain you rise early and stay up late, toiling for food to eat— for he grants sleep to those he loves." (Psalm 127:1-2)

What lasts is rarely the result of only effort. Beneath my father's labor—his provision, endurance, and silence—was a deeper support he never named but never left. The house stood not because he carried everything alone, but because something unseen carried him.

Reflection: What unseen ground is supporting the work you do each day?

Endurance Without Display

"Be joyful in hope, patient in affliction, faithful in prayer." (Romans 12:12 NIV)

Faithfulness does not always sound like prayer; sometimes it looks like return. Return to obligation. Return to steadiness. Return to what must be done when nothing improves. My father's faith rarely spoke, but it never left.

Reflection: Where is faith being practiced in your life without words?

When What Held Must Be Examined

"There is a time for everything, and a season for every activity under the heavens." (Ecclesiastes 3:1 NIV)

What was necessary in one season can become incomplete in another. The strength that once protected must eventually be understood, softened, and shared. Discernment does not dishonor the past; it prepares the future.

Reflection: What strength has served you well—and what might it be asking to become next?

LEGACY NOTES

ELEVEN

Love Worn Into the Rhythm of Ordinary Days

"The place God calls you to is the place where your deep gladness and the world's deep hunger meet."

— Frederick Buechner (1926–2022),
American theologian, Presbyterian minister, and novelist

Some loves arrive like revelations. Others arrive like routines—and stay. Frederick Buechner once suggested that the life of faith is found not in moments of intensity, but in the long obedience of ordinary days, and I have come to recognize that love works the same way. After the conversation ends, after the words have finally been spoken aloud, something quieter begins. The air does not crackle with resolution. There is no closing ceremony. Love simply returns to its place in the day and asks to be lived.

When the necessary words are said—when reassurance is named, when silence loosens its grip—there is often an expectation that something dramatic should follow. A sense of arrival. A visible shift. But what comes next is usually far less cinematic. Love does not announce itself again. It settles. It takes off its coat. It moves into the rhythms that were already there and begins, slowly, to inhabit them differently.

Speech opens the door. Practice keeps it open.

I learned this not in moments of emotional clarity, but in repetition. In mornings that did not feel resolved, but still needed breakfast made. In evenings that were not especially intimate, but still required presence. In days when nothing profound was said, yet something meaningful was done. Healing, I began to see, rarely arrives as a turning point. It arrives as a pattern. It makes itself known not by how intensely it is felt, but by how consistently it returns.

What is said once must be lived many times.

After words find their way into a relationship, they do not replace what came before. They ask to be joined to it. Love that has learned to speak must now learn to endure differently—not by holding more, but by showing up again and again with less fanfare. The work becomes quieter. Less explanatory. More faithful. What once needed emphasis now needs embodiment.

This is where love matures.

It stops asking to be noticed and begins asking to be trusted. It no longer needs to clarify itself because it has become predictable in the best sense of the word. Not rigid, not stale, but reliable. Love reveals its depth not by intensity, but by its willingness to repeat itself without resentment. To keep choosing the same care on days that feel unremarkable. To remain present when nothing seems to be at stake.

There is a particular humility in this stage of love. A letting go of performance. A refusal to dramatize progress. After the conversation, love does not demand that everything feel different. It simply asks to be lived differently. It asks to be folded into the ordinary—the shared meals, the errands, the routines that once carried silence and now carry meaning.

This is where the real courage lies. Not in saying what was once unsayable, but in allowing those words to shape behavior when no one is watching. Not in the relief of articulation, but in the patience of integration. Love, once spoken, becomes less about expression and more about rhythm. Less about declaration and more about fidelity. It begins to wear itself into the fabric of daily life, thread by thread, until it is no longer remarkable—and no longer fragile.

The conversations mattered. They were necessary. They opened space that had been closed for a long time. But they were never the destination. They were the threshold. What comes after is slower, quieter, and more demanding. Love now asks not to be explained, but to be practiced. Not to be proven, but to be repeated.

And in that repetition—unnoticed, uncelebrated, deeply human—love finally becomes what it was always meant to be.

Love does not retreat after the conversation; it descends. It moves downward into the places that do not sparkle, into the hours that will never be remembered individually, into the tasks that feel interchangeable until one day they are not. This is where love assumes its most serious form —not dramatic, not declarative, but weight-bearing. It begins to live where life actually happens.

The sacred weight of the ordinary is easy to overlook because it rarely asks for interpretation. It simply repeats. Breakfast appears again. The calendar fills itself. Dishes return to the sink. Someone needs to be driven, listened to briefly, waited for without comment. Nothing about these moments feels decisive, and yet they are. They are the ground where love proves whether it was sincere when it spoke.

This is where love becomes believable.

Care, when it is real, does not rely on urgency. It does not require a crisis to justify its presence. It shows up when nothing is wrong, when no one is watching, when the act itself seems too small to matter. And yet, over time, these small acts accumulate a gravity that cannot be manufactured any other way. They begin to signal something essential—: You are not alone in this life, even when nothing is being said about it.

Faithfulness is rarely impressive, but it is always formative. It forms trust not through explanation, but through return. It teaches the nervous system what to expect. It tells the body, before the mind ever catches up, that care is not contingent on mood, performance, or gratitude. It arrives again tomorrow, not because it feels inspired, but because it has decided to belong here.

I began to recognize this form of love not in exceptional gestures, but in the quiet reliability of presence that did not need to announce itself. Meals prepared without commentary. Schedules adjusted without complaint. Attention given without urgency. These moments carried no obvious emotional payoff, and yet they provided something deeper than reassurance. They established continuity. They made love durable.

There is a particular holiness to this kind of showing up, precisely because it does not feel holy while it is happening. It does not feel like sacrifice. It feels like responsibility. Like maintenance. Like choosing to stay engaged when disengagement would be easier and unnoticed. Love, in this form, is not energized by recognition. It is sustained by commitment.

I slowly learned slowly that repetition does not dilute devotion; it deepens it. Doing the same loving thing again and again is not evidence of stagnation, but of seriousness. It means love no longer depends on emotional weather. It has learned how to survive ordinary days, which is the only way it ever survives a lifetime.

Intensity can be intoxicating, but it is consistency that convinces.

A child does not remember every meal, but they remember that meals always came. A partner may not recall every conversation, but they remember that someone returned at the end of the day. Love becomes trustworthy not because it is constantly affirmed, but because it is consistently enacted. Over time, the ordinary becomes the place where love stops needing to prove itself and begins simply to be relied upon.

This is where devotion sheds its drama.

There is no applause for folding laundry or asking how a day went when the answer is predictable. There is no visible transformation in choosing patience over efficiency, or attentiveness over distraction. And yet these choices quietly shape the emotional climate of a life. They tell others, without needing to say so, that they matter enough to be tended to even when nothing is at stake.

Choosing presence when no affirmation follows is one of love's most honest tests. It reveals whether love is transactional or covenantal, whether it requires response or simply offers itself. In the ordinary, there is often no feedback loop. No gratitude. No visible result. Love must decide whether it will continue anyway. This is where it either matures or retreats.

I began to see that the love I admired most was not the love that spoke beautifully, but the love that kept returning quietly. Love that did not escalate to be noticed. Love that did not withdraw when uncelebrated. Love that trusted the slow accumulation of care to do its work without supervision.

This kind of love does not hurry healing. It does not force resolution. It understands that most wounds do not close through intensity, but through safety sustained over time. It creates an environment where people can exhale without explaining themselves, where trust grows not because it is demanded, but because it is experienced repeatedly.

The ordinary is where love learns restraint of a different kind—not the restraint of silence, but the restraint of humility. It accepts that it will not always feel meaningful in the moment. It agrees to be faithful without being memorable. And in doing so, it becomes something far more powerful than memory. It becomes rhythm.

Rhythm carries life forward when meaning feels thin. It steadies when emotion fluctuates. It holds when clarity fades. It keeps love intact on days when nothing profound can be said. And it is here, in these repeated acts of care, that love wears itself into the shape of daily life—not as a performance, but as a presence that no longer needs emphasis.

Love that lasts learns how to live quietly. It learns how to show up without insisting on significance. How to be attentive without urgency. How to remain faithful when nothing dramatic is happening. This is not lesser love. It is love that has survived the need to be remarkable.

And in time, this quiet love becomes the most convincing testimony of all—not because it announces itself, but because it never leaves.

As the years added distance and perspective, I began to notice that my father's love had never been absent from daily life—it had simply chosen a different grammar. It did not arrive in explanation or emphasis. It arrived in rhythm. In patterns repeated so faithfully that they disappeared into normalcy, which is often where devotion hides best.

He loved us by making life livable.

Morning followed night with reassuring predictability. Work was returned to. Bills were paid. Meals appeared. The house held its shape. Nothing about this felt sentimental at the time. It felt ordinary, even inevitable. And yet that inevitability was earned. Someone had decided—again and again—that the basic structures of life would not be left to chance or mood. Responsibility was not episodic; it was rhythmic. And rhythm, repeated long enough, becomes trust.

There is a particular tenderness embedded in predictability, though it rarely gets named as such. Knowing what tomorrow will look like does not eliminate fear, but it gives fear boundaries. It tells the nervous system where the edges are. It says, quietly, that even if difficulty arrives, it will arrive inside something that holds. My father did not promise ease. He promised continuity. And continuity, I came to understand, was his way of loving.

The rituals were not ceremonial, but they were consistent. Leaving for work at the same time. Returning home without needing to be summoned. Sitting in the same place. Attending to the same responsibilities with minimal commentary. These patterns did not sparkle, but they steadied. They created an emotional architecture in which life could unfold without constant recalibration. We did not have to wonder whether the ground would shift overnight. It rarely did.

And yet, within that steadiness, there were moments when something unexpected appeared—not announced, not dramatized, but quietly placed inside the rhythm. One Christmas morning, without explanation or buildup, a rod hockey game sat beneath the tree. No speech accompanied it. No justification. Just the object itself, unmistakably chosen because my father knew my brother and I wanted it. It did not interrupt the rhythm; it emerged from it. The surprise was not the gift alone, but the recognition it represented—that beneath the predictability, someone had been paying attention all along.

That, too, was his way.

This steadiness reduced fear not by denying difficulty, but by refusing to dramatize it. Problems were addressed, not announced. Worry was present, but contained. There was space to struggle without the additional burden of instability. Even when circumstances tightened, the rhythm held. And because it held, we could keep moving forward without constantly checking whether we were about to fall through something unseen.

This is the difference between emotional distance and rhythmic devotion. Distance withdraws. Rhythm remains. Distance leaves gaps that must be filled with speculation. Rhythm fills space with reliability. My father did not always lean in emotionally, but he never stepped away structurally. He stayed inside the pattern. And staying, repeated enough times, became its own language.

Love, in this form, does not ask to be interpreted in the moment. It asks to be trusted over time.

I did not always feel emotionally met, but I rarely felt abandoned to uncertainty. There was comfort in knowing how the day would unfold, in knowing which responsibilities were covered, in knowing that someone was quietly tracking what needed to be done without requiring acknowledgment. That kind of attentiveness does not feel expressive, but it is deeply protective. It lowers the ambient anxiety of a household. It makes room for children to be children, even if they do not yet understand why they feel safe.

Looking back, I can see how much of my own sense of order was formed inside these rhythms. The predictability trained me to expect continuity rather than volatility, response rather than reaction. It taught me that care does not always announce itself, and that love can be trusted even when it does not explain itself. I learned that showing up matters more than saying you will, and that repetition is not indifference—it is investment.

He did not erase difficulty. He made it manageable.

There were hard seasons. Illness, fatigue, constraint, and worry were never fully absent. But because the rhythm remained intact, those difficulties did not become defining. They were events within a larger continuity, not forces that reorganized everything. The structure absorbed the strain so others did not have to carry it all at once. That is a form of love that does not draw attention to itself, but without it, everything else becomes heavier.

I understand now that this was not accidental. Rhythm requires discipline. It requires returning when novelty has worn off, when gratitude is inconsistent, when no one is watching. It requires choosing the unremarkable over the impressive, the dependable over the expressive. My father chose that repeatedly, not as strategy, but as instinct. It was how he knew to love.

And because he did not name it, it was easy to miss.

Only later did I recognize how much safety had been built into those patterns, how much fear had been quietly neutralized by the simple fact that life kept its shape. That is no small gift. To make life livable, day after day, without demanding recognition, is a form of devotion that does not announce itself because it assumes its work will eventually speak.

It did.

His love did not rely on intensity. It relied on return. It did not seek to be felt in moments, but to be trusted across years. And while it may not have always reached me emotionally in the way I later learned to need, it gave me something just as enduring — a sense that the world could be inhabited without constant bracing, that tomorrow would arrive inside something stable, that care did not disappear when nothing dramatic was happening.

This was the rhythm he modeled without naming.

And now, standing far enough away to see it clearly, I can say this without hesitation—: He did not love us loudly, but he loved us thoroughly. He loved us by making life possible to live inside, by returning to the same responsibilities until they became invisible, and by choosing steadiness so often that it eventually felt like safety itself.

That kind of love does not dazzle. It endures. And in the long arc of a life, endurance quietly becomes one of love's most persuasive forms.

There comes a moment—quiet and almost imperceptible—when love stops reaching for proof and simply takes up residence, not because effort is no longer required, but because effort is no longer the point. The posture shifts from showing to being, from sustaining to inhabiting. And love no longer asks whether it has done enough, trusting instead that it is already present.

This moment does not arrive dramatically or announce itself with clarity or relief. It tends to emerge after years of faithful repetition, when the nervous system finally recognizes that it is no longer under review, that the work has been done, the ground is sound, and nothing more needs to be demonstrated for love to remain.

For much of my life, I felt that love had to be carried forward actively, even vigilantly. Care was expressed through attentiveness, anticipation, and the constant monitoring of what might fall through the cracks. So loving well meant staying alert, proving reliability, remaining useful, and allowing love to show itself primarily through doing.

Over time, however, something softened.

I began to notice moments when care did not require explanation or reinforcement, when presence no longer felt like vigilance, and when simply being together—without agenda, improvement, or narrative—was enough.

These moments were not empty; they were full in a different way, filled not with intention but with trust.

This is where love matures.

Mature love does not withdraw effort so much as it releases the need for constant demonstration, understanding that care, once established, does not need to reintroduce itself every day. It allows affection to exist without achievement and no longer treats closeness as something that must be earned through attentiveness or maintained through performance.

There is a particular rest that arrives when love stops auditioning.

In that rest, silence changes its character. It no longer asks to be interpreted or decoded. It becomes spacious rather than ambiguous, so that being quiet together no longer feels like something missing, but like something settled. Silence no longer has to do the work of love, because love is already there.

This form of rest was not foreign to my father's way of loving, though I did not recognize it as such at the time. His love had always been more inhabiting than expressive, more present than persuasive, and what changed for me was not his love but my capacity to receive it without needing it to perform. I no longer required evidence in the form of effort; I could allow his presence to be enough.

That shift mattered.

When love is no longer required to prove itself, it becomes gentler without becoming weak. It can release the impulse to over-explain care, to narrate intention, or to reassure preemptively, because it trusts the shared ground, assumes continuity, and rests inside what has already been built.

This does not make love passive; it makes it secure.

I noticed this security most clearly in simple, unremarkable moments— sitting in the same room without speaking and feeling no pressure to fill the space, sharing time without shaping it, letting the day pass without extracting meaning from it. These moments did not feel significant in the way milestones do, yet they carried a deeper signal — nothing needed to be added for love to remain intact.

For someone formed inside endurance, rest can feel like risk, and letting go of effort can resemble neglect. Yet mature love teaches a different truth, showing that care does not disappear when effort relaxes and often becomes more visible when freed from performance, allowing affection to surface naturally, without urgency or defense.

Rest, I came to understand, is not withdrawal but trust.

It is the confidence that love does not require constant maintenance to stay alive. It is the belief that care woven into the fabric of daily life can be relied upon rather than reenacted, and it is the willingness to stop managing perception and simply inhabit connection.

This is where love begins to feel like home rather than obligation.

In this space, affection no longer needs justification or proof, nor does it arrive with explanation. It exists quietly, asking nothing of the moment, where being together is enough, sharing space is enough, and the absence of effort is not the absence of care but evidence of security.

I can see now that my father's love always pointed in this direction, even if I did not yet know how to follow it there. His steadiness created the conditions for rest long before I understood how to enter it, and what once felt like distance now reveals itself as trust—trust that love did not need to keep announcing itself to stay.

Mature love does not insist. It inhabits, living in the shared air of ordinary days, in the comfort of not having to perform, in the freedom to be present without explanation. It settles into rhythm and remains, and when love reaches this place, it no longer asks whether it is enough, because it already knows.

There is a kind of repair that does not arrive through conversation, not because conversation is unwelcome, but because words are no longer the most faithful instrument for the work that needs to be done. It happens indirectly, while attention is focused elsewhere, carried forward not by explanation but by experience, unfolding slowly enough that you often recognize it only after it has already taken hold.

This was the repair that surprised me most.

Nothing was formally resolved, and there were no decisive moments of reckoning or conversations where everything unsaid was finally gathered and placed in order. Life simply continued, and within that continuation something subtle began to soften. Time was shared without agenda, ordinary interactions accumulated, and the tone shifted before the story ever did. Ease returned quietly, without asking permission or offering explanation.

I noticed it first in laughter—not careful or polite laughter, but the unguarded kind that interrupts itself, arrives unexpectedly, and leaves a lightness behind. We laughed again without needing to name what had changed or why it now came more easily. That laughter mattered more than any explanation could have, because it signaled that vigilance had loosened its grip and the space between us had become less charged.

Trust was not restored through reassurance, but through repetition. Through the steady experience of nothing going wrong, of being together without consequence, of time passing without needing to be managed. This is how many wounds actually heal—not by being reopened and addressed directly, but by being surrounded long enough by safety that they no longer require protection.

When love keeps showing up consistently, without demand or insistence, the nervous system updates its expectations. It learns, gradually and often unconsciously, that bracing is no longer required, the danger it once anticipated does not arrive, and the ground remains steady even when no one is watching it.

Ease returned this way—not all at once and not evenly, but in small increments that could easily be missed if I had been searching for progress instead of presence. A conversation that felt lighter, a silence that no longer carried weight, time spent together that did not require preparation or recovery. These were not breakthroughs so much as signs of a system recalibrating itself toward trust.

What surprised me was how little needed to be said for this to happen. Shared life itself did the work. Meals, errands, familiar rhythms revisited without tension, sitting in the same space and allowing the moment to remain ordinary—all of it accumulated quietly, forming a counter-narrative stronger than memory or analysis. The body learned what the mind could not reason itself into believing.

Repair, in this form, does not feel like fixing; it feels like relief. The quiet relief of no longer scanning for disappointment, of no longer anticipating distance, of no longer preparing internally for misalignment. It is the relief of discovering that you can arrive as you are and remain there without consequence, that nothing needs to be corrected for connection to hold.

This kind of healing does not erase the past, but it renders it less determinative. What once felt unresolved loses urgency when the present consistently contradicts the old expectation. Love, enacted faithfully over time, begins to rewrite what was once internalized as permanent. The question is no longer whether something was missed, but whether it still governs how you move now.

For me, the answer arrived quietly. I realized I was no longer bracing, no longer measuring my words as carefully, no longer managing my presence for fear of misstep, no longer holding back parts of myself that once felt safer kept inside. Trust had returned, not because every injury had been revisited, but because nothing new had reinforced the old ones.

This is the wisdom of repair that happens sideways. It understands that some wounds heal best when they are no longer the center of attention, when love is allowed to surround them rather than interrogate them, and when shared life becomes the medium through which trust is restored. It respects the truth that not all healing requires articulation, and that some forms of reconciliation are built not through resolution, but through reliability.

Love kept showing up—without commentary, without agenda, without requiring recognition for its persistence. It showed up in the decision to remain present, to keep returning, to allow the ordinary to be enough. And in doing so, it restored something essential, not by repairing the past, but by making the present livable without fear.

Some things heal because they are named. Others heal because they are no longer alone. This was one of those.

There comes a moment when love no longer feels obligated to explain itself, when it stops answering questions that no longer need to be asked and releases the quiet tension of justification that once followed it everywhere. The need to measure, interpret, or defend what love looks like begins to fall away, not because the past has been resolved into neat conclusions, but because the present has proven itself trustworthy enough to stand on its own.

I began to notice this shift not through insight, but through ease. The absence of vigilance. The quiet recognition that I was no longer comparing what was given to what might have been missing, no longer translating every gesture into evidence, no longer scanning for signs that love might withdraw or need to be earned again. Peace arrived not as certainty, but as permission—the permission to let love be what it is now without holding it accountable to what it once could not be.

This did not require a reckoning with the past or a final accounting of what was done well and what fell short. Gratitude no longer needed grief to balance it, and appreciation no longer felt obligated to explain itself carefully so it would not sound naïve or disloyal to earlier truths. I could honor the love that existed without rehearsing its history, and I could stand inside it rather than circling it with evaluation. That posture changed everything. Love no longer felt like something I had to understand to accept. It simply became something I could inhabit.

I came to see that love evolves not by rejecting its earlier forms, but by outgrowing the conditions that once shaped them. What was once expressed through endurance alone had expanded into something quieter and more spacious, not because it had been corrected, but because it had been lived long enough to soften. Growth did not diminish what came before; it absorbed it. And in that absorption, love became sufficient without needing to be impressive, adequate without needing to be defended, and real without needing to be explained.

There is a particular freedom that comes when love is allowed to exist without apology, when it is no longer required to justify its shape or prove its legitimacy. The arguments dissolve. The comparisons fade. What remains is a steady awareness that love, as it stands now, is enough. Not perfect, not complete in every way, but settled. And that settledness brings peace not because all questions have been answered, but because love has stopped insisting that it must.

This is where endurance finally gives way to rest, where affection no longer feels like effort or evidence, and where the deepest trust emerges—not in love's ability to explain itself, but in its willingness to remain. Love endures best, I have learned, when it is no longer busy defending its past or forecasting its future, but is simply allowed to be present, whole, and sufficient where it stands.

As urgency recedes, something quieter takes its place, and love begins to reveal what it looks like when it is no longer summoned by necessity. There is a difference between love that is required and love that remains, between presence demanded by circumstance and presence that stays because it no longer has anywhere else it needs to be. When the work slows and the constant readiness to respond is no longer essential, love is freed from its former posture of vigilance and allowed to rest into something gentler.

I noticed this change not as an event, but as an atmosphere. The absence of hurry. The easing of the internal clock that had once measured days by what still needed to be done. Love no longer arrived braced for impact or oriented toward problem-solving. It arrived as availability, unguarded and unambitious, content to share space without needing to justify its usefulness. What once carried weight now carried calm, and that calm felt earned rather than accidental.

There is an intimacy that emerges only when protection is no longer the primary task, when strength is not being tested and endurance is not being asked to prove itself again. In those moments, presence softens. It listens more than it anticipates. It allows silence without feeling responsible for filling it. Being together no longer serves a function beyond itself, and that is precisely what makes it meaningful. Nothing needs to be accomplished. Nothing needs to be explained. The relationship is not moving toward anything except continued being.

This is where love matures toward gentleness, not because gentleness replaces strength, but because strength has finally done enough work to step back. Endurance, having carried what it needed to carry, yields to availability. The vigilance that once held everything together loosens its grip, and in that loosening there is relief rather than risk. Love is no longer busy holding the line. It is simply present, attentive without urgency, faithful without effort.

In this space, companionship takes on a different quality. Conversations wander without destination. Shared stillness feels complete rather than empty. Time stretches without pressure, and the absence of agenda becomes its own quiet gift. Love no longer needs to demonstrate its reliability because it has already done so across years of return. What remains is trust, settled and unremarkable, woven into the ease of being side by side.

There is something deeply reassuring about love that does not need to intervene, correct, or prepare. It suggests that enough has been done, the structure will hold without constant reinforcement, and presence can now exist for its own sake. This is not withdrawal, but fulfillment. Not the end of love's work, but the completion of a long season of effort. What is offered now is not protection or proof, but peace.

I have come to believe that this is love's final generosity. After carrying weight, absorbing strain, and remaining steadfast through years that required strength, love offers calm as its closing gift. It does not announce itself or ask to be recognized. It simply remains, unhurried and unburdened, allowing those within it to rest. Love that once carried weight now carries peace, and in that peace, something in all of us finally learns how to be still.

By the time love reaches this stage, it has already done its hardest work. It has held through silence when words were unavailable, clarified itself when language finally arrived, and learned how to live inside ordinary days without needing to be proven again. What remains is not effort or explanation, but presence that endures because it no longer has anything left to secure.

Each movement mattered. Silent love built the structure when endurance was required more than articulation. Spoken love clarified what had always been there, lifting the burden of guessing and allowing connection to deepen without weakening the ground beneath it. Ordinary love, repeated without drama, sustained everything that followed, not through intensity, but through faithfulness woven into daily rhythm.

This is how love outlives speech. Not by returning to silence, but by no longer needing to justify itself.

When love has been spoken honestly and lived consistently, it stops striving to be understood. It trusts that what has been given will remain recognizable even in quiet seasons. There is no need to revisit old reckonings or restate devotion. Love rests because it has endured.

This is not the absence of care, but care that has finished insisting.

In this space, love becomes generous in a new way. It loosens its grip without withdrawing, allows others to stand on their own footing without fear of abandonment, and trusts the ground it has already laid. What once held everything together no longer needs to hold so tightly, and that easing feels like grace rather than loss.

This is not love diminishing, but love completing itself. Love does not disappear when its work is done; it changes posture. It becomes less about holding and more about allowing, less about guarding and more about trusting. It remains present without needing to remain central.

This is where legacy begins to take shape, not as instruction or inheritance alone, but as atmosphere. What is carried forward is not only what was said or withheld, but what was lived faithfully long enough to become trustworthy. Love that has endured does not cling to relevance. It blesses what comes next.

And so, the story turns again. Toward aging, where strength is no longer measured by how much can be carried. Toward reconciliation, where presence replaces explanation. Toward letting go, where love no longer needs to hold everything in place to remain real.

What love looks like then is quieter still, not because it has faded, but because it has finished its work. It waits without anxiety. It releases without fear. It trusts that what was built will stand.

In the end, love did not need to be louder. It needed to be lived.

SACRED WAYPOINTS

Love That Stayed After the Words

Love did not end when it was finally spoken. It softened. It settled. What had once required effort became habit, and what had once needed explanation became assumed. Love proved itself not through repetition of language, but through continued return.

- Where has love in your life moved from declaration into quiet consistency?
- What no longer needs to be said because it has been lived long enough to be trusted?

Sit with this truth: Love matures when it no longer needs emphasis.

The Holiness of the Unremarkable

Meals prepared. Schedules kept. Work returned to. Days that did not announce themselves as meaningful, yet formed the texture of belonging. Love endured not by intensity, but by attention given when nothing special was happening.

- What ordinary acts carry more meaning than you realized at the time?
- Where might faithfulness be hiding in routines you overlook?

Ask for eyes to see: "Lord, teach me to recognize devotion where nothing is dramatic."

Rhythm That Became Safety

Predictability did not erase hardship, but it gave hardship edges. Knowing what tomorrow would look like allowed fear to rest inside boundaries rather than roam unchecked. Love showed itself by keeping life livable.

- Where has rhythm reduced anxiety without being named as care?
- What patterns in your life quietly communicate, "You are safe here?"

Hold this insight: Consistency is a form of tenderness.

Repair That Arrived Sideways

Not every wound required confrontation. Some softened because laughter returned. Ease reappeared. The body stopped bracing before the mind understood why. Love repaired trust by continuing to show up while attention was elsewhere.

- What has healed in your life without ever being discussed?
- Where has safety returned before explanation followed?

Remember: Some things mend because love stays close.

Love That No Longer Explained Itself

There came a time when love stopped defending its form. It did not need to justify the past or prove the present. Peace arrived when love was allowed to be sufficient as it was, not as it once needed to be.

- Where are you still asking love to explain itself?
- What might happen if you allowed love to rest instead?

Release this need: Love does not owe an apology.

When Strength Became Gentleness

Endurance gave way to availability. Protection relaxed into companionship. Love no longer needed to hold everything together; it learned how to sit quietly without agenda.

- What are you still carrying that no longer needs to be held so tightly?
- Where might gentleness now be the truest form of strength?

Breathe into this truth: Love's final gift is calm.

The Faithfulness That Outlived Speech

What endured was not what was said or withheld, but how love stayed. Silent love built the structure. Spoken love clarified it. Ordinary love sustained it. And then, quietly, love finished its work.

- What love in your life has already done what it came to do?
- What remains when nothing is urgent anymore?

Sit with this ending: Love, once spoken, learns how to rest.

ANCHORS OF THE WORD 

Love That Returns

"Whatever you do, work at it with all your heart, as working for the Lord, not for human masters." (Colossians 3:23 NIV)

Much of the most faithful love is expressed without audience or applause. My father's devotion lived in return—returning to work, to responsibility, to care—long after novelty faded. Love proved itself not through intensity, but through staying power.

Reflection: Where are you being invited to love through return rather than recognition?

Mercy in Repetition

"Because of the LORD's great love we are not consumed, for his compassions never fail. They are new every morning; great is your faithfulness." (Lamentations 3:22-23 NIV)

Healing does not always arrive dramatically. Often it arrives quietly, morning after morning, through the simple fact that love keeps showing up. The ordinary becomes sacred when mercy repeats itself faithfully.

Reflection: What mercy in your life has been renewing itself quietly without being noticed?

The Inheritance of Integrity

"The righteous lead blameless lives; blessed are their children after them." (Proverbs 20:7 NIV)

The greatest gift my father gave was not instruction, but steadiness. Integrity, lived daily and without explanation, became an inheritance that shaped my sense of safety long before I understood it.

Reflection: What patterns are you passing on simply by how you live each day?

Faithfulness Without Display

"He has shown you, O mortal, what is good. And what does the LORD require of you?

To act justly and to love mercy and to walk humbly with your God." (Micah 6:8 NIV)

This is faith lived without spectacle. Love expressed through humility, consistency, and care that does not need to announce itself. My father walked this way instinctively, teaching me that devotion does not need to be impressive to be enduring.

Reflection: Where might humility be the truest expression of love right now?

Love at Rest

"But I have calmed and quieted myself, I am like a weaned child with its mother; like a weaned child I am content." (Psalm 131:2 NIV)

There comes a season when love no longer strives or proves. It rests. Strength softens into availability, and presence no longer needs to hold everything together. What remains is peace.

Reflection: Where in your life is love inviting you to rest rather than carry?

LEGACY NOTES

TWELVE

The Leaving That Taught
Me How to Stay

"The greatest thing a father can do for his children is to love their mother."

— Theodore Hesburgh (1917-2015),
Catholic priest and former President of the University of Notre Dame

---

Love, I came to understand, is not proven only by how long someone stays, but by what they are willing to stay with. That truth sits quietly inside Theodore Hesburgh's words—that the greatest thing a father can do for his children is to love their mother—not as sentiment, but as lived cost. My father did not love my mother abstractly or conveniently. He loved her by remaining when leaving would have been easier for him, though devastating for her and for us.

For years, he stayed beside her as bipolar disorder reshaped daily life and scleroderma steadily narrowed her body and her world. There were seasons when illness spoke louder than reason, when unpredictability became routine, when tenderness required stamina rather than feeling. He did not romanticize this faithfulness. He did not narrate it. He simply stayed. Not because it was noble, but because it was his. Not because it made him stronger, but because love sometimes demands endurance long after comfort has disappeared.

I once thought leaving would feel like loss. I imagined it would hollow out what had been held together for so long. Instead, it clarified what had already been given. Watching my father stay taught me more about love than any speech ever could. He showed me that fidelity is not measured by ease, but by presence under strain, and that the deepest instruction often comes from what someone refuses to abandon.

There was nothing dramatic about how this devotion unfolded. It happened in appointments kept, medications managed, moods endured, and dignity preserved when circumstances stripped so much else away. His staying was not loud. It was patient. And patience, repeated over years, became the atmosphere we lived inside. Long before I had words for covenant or commitment, I had watched it practiced daily in a life that chose responsibility over relief.

When my mother died, the meaning of leaving changed again. This time, it was not a release into trust, but an abrupt solitude. The woman my father had oriented his days around for more than fifty years, protected, and remained faithful to was gone. And with her absence came a loneliness that no structure could fully contain. He went from sharing that assisted-living apartment with my mother to inhabiting the same space alone—surrounded by people, yet unmistakably solitary. Days stretched without the familiar work of caring for her, without the quiet purpose that had once organized his endurance.

This was a different kind of staying. Staying with memory. Staying with grief. Staying with a silence that no longer needed to protect anyone else. He bore that loneliness without bitterness, but not without cost. I saw it in the way time began to loosen its grip on him, in the way wine became a more frequent companion to the evenings, less as escape than as anesthesia, a softening of hours that now stretched unfilled. I saw it, too, in his growing reliance on my brother—nearby, familiar, steady—as his cognitive edges dulled and decisions that once required no thought now asked for help.

His strength, which had once moved outward in work and vigilance, had fewer places to go. And in that narrowing, there was an ache—not of regret, but of displacement. A life that had given itself so completely now had little to hold onto except love remembered, presence recalled, and the quiet fidelity of having stayed until there was no one left to stay for.

And still, even then, he did not retreat into himself. He remained gentle. He remained grateful. He remained oriented toward others, even as his world grew smaller. His fidelity outlived usefulness. It outlived necessity. It endured beyond the point where staying offered him anything in return.

This is where leaving becomes its own form of instruction. My father had stayed when love demanded endurance. Now he stayed when endurance no longer had an object. And in that long, quiet season, I began to understand that his life had been preparing me not just to survive devotion, but to carry it forward when circumstances no longer reward it.

When God finally took him home, I felt not only grief, but a strange sense of completion. The loneliness that had marked his final years was answered, not by explanation, but by reunion. The man who had loved my mother through illness and absence was finally released from staying alone. Whatever mystery surrounds death, I trust this much:—Love that endures so faithfully is not dismissed when the work is done.

Leaving, I now see, was never abandonment in his life. It was always preceded by staying longer than required, more deeply than expected, and more quietly than most would choose. What remained after his leaving was not emptiness, but instruction fully received. I did not lose his presence when he stepped back. I inherited his posture.

This chapter, and this book, begin to close here. Not with answers neatly tied, but with a call to live what has been shown. To stay where love asks for endurance. To release when love asks for trust. To recognize that some of the greatest lessons arrive not when someone explains themselves, but when they give their life faithfully to another, and then, when the time comes, let go.

I thought leaving would teach me how to say goodbye. Instead, through his staying, his loneliness, and his final release, it taught me how to remain—faithful to love, steady in loss, and willing to carry forward what was given until my own work, too, is finished.

Strength did not leave him all at once. It softened first, almost imperceptibly, the way vigilance does when it has been kept too long. What had once been reflexive began to require intention. What had once been carried without notice now asked for pacing, then pause, then assistance. There was no announcement of decline, no dramatic surrender. Just a gradual easing, as though his body and mind were quietly renegotiating the terms of what they could still hold.

I noticed it in small ways before I allowed myself to name it. Fatigue that lingered longer than it used to. Decisions that were deferred rather than asserted, not from confusion, but from a growing awareness that certainty no longer needed to lead every moment. His posture changed, too—not collapsing, but settling, as though the constant readiness that had once defined him was no longer required to be at full alert.

This was not weakness. It was transition.

Leadership, I learned, changes shape before it disappears. It moves from command to consent, from direction to presence, from holding everything together to allowing others to take their turn at the center. My father did not resist this shift, but neither did he romanticize it. He accepted help without commentary. He allowed my brother's proximity to matter more. He trusted others with tasks he once would have handled himself, not because he could not do them, but because he no longer needed to prove that he could.

That trust was not loud. It was offered quietly, the way everything important in his life had been.

There was discomfort in watching this unfold, not because it was sudden, but because it was unfamiliar. The man who had absorbed pressure so others would not have to was now letting pressure redistribute. The steadiness I had leaned on was still present, but it no longer insisted on being load-bearing.

And in that shift, I felt the first real inversion of roles—not dramatic, not explicit, but undeniable.

Endurance, I came to see, is not meant to be permanent. It is seasonal, like all forms of strength that arise in response to need. My father's endurance had been necessary when life demanded constant vigilance, when illness required monitoring, when provision required relentless consistency. As those demands changed, so did the expression of his strength. What remained was not the ability to carry everything, but the wisdom to stop carrying what no longer needed to be held.

His silence changed with this season as well. Where it had once functioned as containment, it now felt more like acceptance. Not resignation, but a settled awareness that some things no longer required management. He spoke less not because he had nothing to say, but because the urgency to explain had faded. There was a gentleness in that quiet, a kind of permission given to the moment to be what it was without correction.

Letting go, I realized, begins long before departure. It starts when strength loosens its grip without fear of collapse, when leadership trusts that what it formed can now stand on its own, when vigilance gives way to watchfulness rather than control. My father had spent a lifetime holding the line. Now, he was learning how to rest within it.

Watching this was both grounding and unsettling. Grounding because it revealed a deeper layer of his character, one that did not depend on capacity. Unsettling because it required me to adjust my understanding of what strength looks like when it is no longer required to prove itself daily. I was being asked, quietly, to recognize that what I had relied on was changing— not disappearing, but yielding.

And in that yielding, there was instruction.

Strength teaches most, not when it is at its peak, but when it knows how to loosen without bitterness, how to release without collapse, and how to remain present, even as its form changes. My father did not cling to who he had been at full capacity. He allowed himself to become who the season required, trusting that what mattered most had already been given.

That trust, more than any display of endurance, marked the beginning of his leaving—not as abandonment, but as preparation.

The space did not arrive as emptiness. It arrived as permission.

There were no declarations, no handoffs marked by ceremony or explanation. Responsibility simply began to rest elsewhere, first in small decisions, then in larger ones, until I realized that what I was carrying had once been his. He did not announce this transfer. He allowed it. And in allowing it, he trusted that what he had formed could now bear weight without his constant presence.

This is how love steps back without leaving.

At first, I noticed it in practical matters. Questions he would once have answered decisively were left open, not because he was unable, but because he was no longer compelled to occupy every center. Tasks that had been his domain were now met with a pause, an invitation rather than an instruction. The absence of direction was not indifference. It was restraint practiced differently.

Emotional space opened the same way, gradually and without drama. He listened more than he corrected. He allowed silence to remain unfilled. Where he once would have stabilized through intervention, he now stabilized through trust. I could feel the weight of that trust, not as pressure, but as responsibility freely given.

Carrying it changed me.

I began to notice how often I checked myself before reaching for him, how instinctively I stepped forward when I once would have waited. The shift was subtle, but cumulative. I was no longer acting in his stead. I was acting from what he had already placed within me. The space he left was not a void. It was an opening shaped by years of modeling, discipline, and quiet instruction.

There is a difference between absence and space. Absence creates anxiety and demands explanation. Space creates room and assumes readiness. My father offered the latter. He was still present, still attentive, but no longer positioning himself as the primary holder of every outcome. Staying, in this season, meant stepping aside without withdrawing care.

I felt the weight of this transition, but I did not resent it. The responsibility was real, but it was not abrupt or unfair. It felt earned, not imposed. The ground did not shift beneath me. It widened.

Handling decisions he once handled brought with it a deeper awareness of how much had been absorbed on my behalf over the years. I understood, perhaps for the first time, the cost of being the one who always stands at the center, absorbing consequence so others can move freely. Now that some of that weight rested with me, it did not feel like burden. It felt like inheritance.

He did not correct every misstep. He did not hover or reclaim authority when I faltered. That restraint required its own kind of strength, one that does not cling to relevance or demand recognition. Trust, when practiced honestly, always carries risk. My father accepted that risk without commentary.

In doing so, he taught me something he had never said aloud. Staying does not always mean holding everything together. Sometimes it means stepping back so others can discover their footing without fear of collapse. Space, offered with care, becomes one of the clearest forms of love.

Only later did I recognize how intentional this was. What looked like absence was actually design. What felt like loss was, in truth, a widening. He was preparing me not for his presence, but for his eventual leaving, and he did so without urgency, without drama, and without making his departure the center of the story.

He taught me how to stay by trusting me with space. And in that space, I did not feel abandoned. I felt invited to become.

The leaving clarified what had already been given.

As his presence softened and space widened, I began to notice how little actually went with him. The rooms changed. The routines shifted. But the formation remained intact, not as memory alone, but as instinct. I did not reach for him in every decision because, without realizing it, I was already reaching from him.

This is the quiet permanence of formation.

There were moments when I heard his voice without hearing it, not as instruction, but as orientation. A pause before reacting. A refusal to dramatize. A steady return to what needed to be done next. I recognized these movements not because I had been told to practice them, but because they had been lived into me over years of proximity and repetition.

What is embodied does not require presence to persist.

I noticed it in how I handled uncertainty, in how I resisted the urge to escalate, in how I chose steadiness over spectacle even when urgency tempted me otherwise. These were not conscious imitations. They surfaced naturally, like muscle memory, revealing themselves only when pressure arrived. His way of standing in the world had been transferred not through words or expectation, but through faithful exposure.

Legacy, I began to understand, is not handed over at the end. It is formed long before leaving becomes necessary.

As I faced decisions, I realized I was not asking what he would do. I was doing what he had taught me to do without ever framing it as instruction. I returned to the center rather than fleeing the discomfort. I absorbed what could be absorbed and released what could not be controlled. I stayed with the work instead of chasing relief. In these moments, his influence was not sentimental. It was structural.

I also saw his steadiness surface in my reactions, particularly in moments that carried emotional charge. Where I might once have sought reassurance or clarity, I found myself creating it. Where uncertainty pressed in, I did not rush to fill the space with noise. I allowed it to remain until the next right step emerged. This was not detachment. It was containment learned through example.

Formation outlives presence because it does not depend on proximity.

I realized, sometimes with a quiet astonishment, how often I returned the way he did. Not physically, but internally. To composure. To responsibility. To restraint that was not avoidance, but care for the larger system. These returns were not nostalgic. They were practical. They allowed life to keep moving without fracture, even when conditions were less forgiving.

What stayed with me was not his voice, but his posture. Not his opinions, but his orientation. Not his strength as display, but his steadiness as practice. These things could not leave because they had already been integrated. They had become part of how I occupied space, made decisions, and carried others without naming it as sacrifice.

This is the inheritance that does not announce itself.

He did not take with him the habits that had been shaped through years of responsibility, the instincts that surfaced under strain, or the capacity to remain present without needing to be central. Those remained, quietly operational, continuing their work without requiring attribution. I could trace them back to him, but I did not need him to authorize them.

When he stepped back, nothing essential collapsed.

That realization brought a particular kind of peace. Not because the loss was insignificant, but because what mattered most had already been given. He had not left behind gaps that only he could fill. He had left behind a way of standing that could be carried forward without him.

He left nothing unfinished that required his presence to survive.

And in that truth, I understood that leaving, when done faithfully, does not remove what matters. It reveals what was already there, waiting to be lived.

What surprised me most was not the weight of responsibility, but the quietness with which it arrived. There was no formal handoff, no moment when authority changed hands or expectations were clearly redrawn. One day I simply realized that I was making decisions he once made, carrying concerns he once absorbed, and choosing restraint without imagining how it would be received. The absence of supervision did not feel like abandonment. It felt like trust that had been extended long before it was tested.

This is what maturity looks like when formation has done its work.

I did not need his eyes on me to behave with care, nor did I require his approval to choose the harder, steadier path. The discipline he modeled had settled inward, becoming less about compliance and more about alignment. I acted rightly not because someone might notice, but because the alternative felt misaligned with who I had been shaped to become. Integrity, I learned, does not need an audience when it has been rehearsed quietly over years.

There were moments when restraint would have been easy to relax and, no consequence seemed likely. And no one would have known. Those moments were revealing, not because they tempted me toward failure, but because they showed me how little supervision I required to remain anchored. I found myself choosing consistency even when convenience offered an easier route, choosing patience when reaction would have felt justified, and choosing steadiness without the comfort of being seen or affirmed. These choices did not feel heroic. They felt normal, which is perhaps the truest sign of formation.

Responsibility, once internalized, does not ask to be witnessed.

I also noticed how little resentment accompanied this weight. I was not bracing against it or tallying its cost. I carried what needed carrying because the moment required it, not because I was trying to prove anything or fulfill an inherited role. The work did not feel imposed. It felt appropriate. That distinction mattered. It meant I was no longer reacting to expectation, but responding from conviction.

Staying, I came to understand, is not enforced from the outside. It is an internal posture that remains even when external structures fall away.

There were days when I felt the loneliness of leadership, the quiet solitude that comes from holding things others may never see. In those moments, I recognized the shape of his life reflected back at me, not as burden, but as continuity. I was not repeating his sacrifices out of obligation. I was inhabiting a way of being offered to me through example rather than instruction.

What once required oversight now required discernment.

I learned to listen inwardly, to pause before acting, to measure my response not against immediate relief but against long-term coherence. The absence of his supervision did not leave me unmoored. It revealed that the anchor had been placed within reach all along. I did not need someone to tell me how to stay. I had learned, slowly and thoroughly, how staying felt when it was done well.

This kind of faithfulness is quiet and largely invisible. It does not draw attention or invite praise. It simply continues, even when no one is watching, even when no reward is offered, and even when the work feels repetitive or unacknowledged. And yet, it is precisely this unseen fidelity that holds life together once instruction has ended and presence has receded.

My father taught me how to stay not by controlling my steps, but by shaping my posture.

Now, standing without supervision, I can see the depth of that gift. I am able to remain faithful to what matters, not because someone demands it, but because I no longer need to be told. Staying has become less about endurance and more about identity, less about proving loyalty and more about living in alignment with what was formed over time.

This is the quiet competence that follows faithful formation.

And it is here, in this unsupervised staying, that I finally understand what his leaving made possible.

What became clear only in hindsight was how little he ever tried to hold me in place. There was no guilt layered into his love, no emotional accounting that kept track of what he had given or what might be owed in return. He did not rehearse his sacrifices or frame them as leverage. His love did not tighten when distance appeared, nor did it sharpen when independence grew. He allowed movement without interpreting it as rejection, and he released without retreating.

That restraint was not indifference. It was confidence.

When paths diverged, he did not ask to be followed or feared being left behind. He did not require constant proximity to feel secure in belonging. Love, for him, did not need to be guarded through grasping. It trusted what had already been built. Because the foundation was sound, he did not panic when others stepped away from it. He understood that staying cannot be coerced and that fidelity loses its meaning when it is enforced.

There was dignity in the way he let go.

He did not bargain emotionally or remind us of what he had endured. He did not use memory as a tether or obligation as a hook. Even as his own world narrowed, he resisted the temptation to tighten his hold on ours. He accepted that our lives would move forward differently than his had, and he did so without resentment. That acceptance carried its own quiet generosity. It said, without words, that love's purpose is not possession but preparation.

I see now how rare that is.

Attachment often disguises itself as care, especially when loss is near. It tightens language, sharpens expectations, and subtly asks others to stay close enough to ease fear. My father did none of that. He allowed absence without accusation and change without protest. He trusted that what mattered most would remain, not because it was demanded, but because it had been formed honestly.

Letting go, in this way, was not a withdrawal of love. It was its refinement.

He did not confuse closeness with control or loyalty with proximity. He understood that people must be free for love to be real. When independence grew, he did not interpret it as ingratitude. When others carried on without him at the center, he did not ask to be reinserted. His love did not insist on being remembered loudly or frequently. It assumed that what had shaped us would speak on its own.

This kind of love does not cling because it does not fear erasure.

It trusts that presence, once truly given, does not disappear when distance grows. It believes that relationship can endure even when roles change and seasons close. It knows that the measure of devotion is not how tightly one holds, but how freely one releases.

In allowing us to leave without emotional cost, he taught me something I did not recognize at the time. Love that is confident does not need to tether. Love that has done its work does not demand to be proven again. And love that trusts its own impact can afford to open its hands.

That is not loss. It is assurance.

His refusal to cling was one of the final ways he stayed faithful. Not by keeping us close, but by letting us go without fear. Not by tightening his grip, but by trusting the ground he had already laid.

Love that trusts does not need to hold tightly.

In the end, there was no turn toward drama. No gathering of words meant to summarize a life or secure its meaning. He did not shift into instruction, nor did he reach for final clarity. What unfolded instead was continuity. The way he left was recognizably his, shaped by the same restraint and fidelity that had governed how he stayed.

His presence did not vanish so much as thin, gradually loosening its grip on the center of things. Conversations shortened. Decisions slowed. The vigilance that once scanned rooms and days softened into something quieter, less directive. He remained attentive, but without urgency, as though the work of holding had been largely completed and no longer required his full weight.

There were no speeches, no parting wisdom framed as legacy. He did not gather us to explain what mattered most or attempt to tie together what had already been lived. That kind of summation had never been his way. He trusted that meaning did not need to be narrated to endure, and that explanation was not required for faithfulness to be real.

What remained was ordinary interaction, understated and familiar. A greeting. A question asked without insistence. Time shared without agenda. Nothing about these moments announced itself as final, and perhaps that was the point. He did not mark the ending because he did not experience it as rupture. Life had been lived steadily, and it would be released the same way.

Faithful lives rarely conclude with clarity offered on demand.

They end the way they were lived, through pattern rather than proclamation. Meaning lingers not because it was explained, but because it was embodied long enough to be trusted. My father did not seek closure, and he did not require it. He allowed things to remain unresolved where resolution would have been artificial, and he did not force coherence onto a life that had already proven its integrity through consistency.

As his strength receded, there was no bitterness layered into the letting go. He did not rehearse grievances or name disappointments that might have been justified. He did not frame his leaving as sacrifice or loss. What he carried, he carried quietly. What he released, he released without commentary. His departure did not ask to be witnessed in any particular way.

Presence tapered into peace. Not the peace of completion or certainty, but the peace of trust. Trust that what had been given was enough. Trust that what remained did not require his supervision. Trust that love, once lived faithfully, could endure without reinforcement.

There was no final lesson offered because the lesson had already been lived. No closing statement because the pattern had spoken clearly enough. He left behind no dramatic absence, only the steady realization that nothing essential had gone missing.

Love remained intact, even without words. That, too, was consistent. His love had never relied on explanation, and it did not require it at the end. What mattered had already been transferred, not through instruction, but through years of repetition, restraint, and return. The exit did not disrupt that transfer. It confirmed it.

He left the way he lived, without spectacle and without fear, trusting that what had been formed would hold when he no longer could. And in that trust, his leaving became one final act of love, quiet and faithful, offering peace not by declaring it, but by embodying it.

After he was gone, the room filled. Not with explanations. With stories.

They came from people I did not expect and from places I had never seen him occupy publicly. Coworkers spoke of fairness that never needed enforcement. Neighbors remembered quiet help offered without announcement. Friends recalled reliability more than charm, presence more than persuasion. No one told a dramatic story. No one reached for spectacle. The accounts were steady, consistent, and strikingly aligned, as though they had all been watching the same life from different angles and had come away with the same conclusion.

He had been trustworthy.

Listening, I realized something I had not fully understood while he was alive. His life had translated itself. Not through speeches or confessions, but through accumulation. What people remembered was not what he said, or even what he did in any single moment, but how he showed up over time. The stories fit together because his life had fit together. There were no contradictions to reconcile, no versions to explain away. The man they described was the man I knew.

That is a rare ending.

It felt honorable not because it was polished, but because it was coherent. The life being remembered did not require interpretation or defense. It stood on its own. And standing there, hearing how his quiet fidelity had traveled farther than he ever intended, I understood that his influence had never been confined to our home. It had simply never announced itself.

This is what staying had produced.

He taught endurance through presence, by returning when it would have been easier to retreat. He taught articulation through silence, by showing how much can be carried without needing to be named. And he taught staying by knowing when to leave, releasing responsibility without resentment and allowing what had been formed to stand on its own.

Nothing about his life asked to be preserved loudly. Nothing demanded replication. What he left behind was not instruction, but orientation. A way of standing in the world that could be inhabited rather than imitated. A posture sturdy enough to support others without requiring them to remain dependent on it.

In the end, his leaving clarified what mattered.

What endured was not control, but trust. Not authority, but formation. Not words, but a life lived consistently enough to be remembered clearly. The stories told at his funeral did not inflate him. They revealed him. And in that revelation, I felt no pressure to add anything, correct anything, or defend anything.

The work was finished.

Now the invitation turns outward.

Each of us carries something forward, whether we choose it consciously or not. Patterns. Postures. Ways of loving learned before we had language for them. The question is not whether we will inherit, but how we will steward what we have received. What we will honor. What we will refine. What we will finally set down because it was never meant to be permanent.

His life gives permission for that discernment.

He did not cling. He did not demand. He did not linger beyond what was required. He trusted that what he had given was enough, and that trust made room for the rest of us to live forward rather than backward.

I do not feel his absence as loss alone. I feel it as direction.

What he left behind was not emptiness, but alignment. Not silence, but clarity. Not a void to be filled, but a way to stay present without being tethered to the past.

He taught me how to leave without abandoning, and how to stay without clinging.

In leaving, he finally showed me how to stay.

SACRED WAYPOINTS

Staying When Leaving Would Have Been Easier

My father stayed when departure might have relieved him—through illness, unpredictability, and years when love required endurance more than affection. His staying was not dramatic. It was chosen daily, without witnesses, or guarantees. In doing so, he taught me that fidelity is not measured by comfort, but by presence when the cost is real.

- Where are you staying simply because it is right, not because it is rewarded?
- What form of faithfulness are you living that no one applauds?

Sit with this truth: Staying is sometimes the bravest form of love.

The Loneliness That Followed Faithfulness

After my mother's death, his world grew quieter. Strength had fewer places to go. Companionship thinned. Some comforts crept in, not as escape, but as relief from long evenings and longer memories. He bore that loneliness without bitterness, but not without cost. Love does not disappear when its object is gone—it changes shape.

- What losses have changed how you move through your days?

- Where are you coping quietly rather than being held?

Sit with this truth: Loneliness does not negate devotion; it reveals its depth.

Space Given Is Love Trusted

As his strength softened, he did not cling to authority or relevance. He allowed space to open—emotionally and practically—and trusted others to step into it. What felt like absence at first was, in time, revealed to be confidence. Staying sometimes means stepping aside so others can grow.

- Where are you still holding space that no longer needs your grip?
- Who are you trusting by letting go?

Sit with this truth: Love that trusts does not tighten when it is threatened.

What Remains When Someone Is Gone

At his funeral, the stories told did not magnify him; they clarified him. No grand gestures. No hidden contradictions. Just a life that held its shape across decades. He left behind habits, instincts, and a way of standing that did not require his supervision to endure.

- What part of you was formed long before you chose it?
- What legacy are you already living, not planning?

Sit with this truth: What is embodied cannot be taken away.

Learning to Stay After the Leaving

His final gift was not instruction, but orientation. He showed me how to remain faithful without being rigid, how to love without clinging, and how to leave without abandoning. In his absence, I did not feel untethered. I felt aligned.

- What are you now free to carry forward?
- What are you finally free to release?

Sit with this truth: In leaving, he taught me how to stay.

ANCHORS OF THE WORD 

Staying When Leaving Would Have Been Easier

"But Ruth replied, 'Don't urge me to leave you or to turn back from you. Where you go I will go, and where you stay I will stay. Your people will be my people and your God my God.'" (Ruth 1:16 NIV)

My father's staying was not sentimental; it was costly. He remained when illness complicated love, when loneliness followed loss, and when departure would have eased his burden but deepened someone else's. His faithfulness was quiet and sustained, chosen daily rather than declared once.

Reflection: Where in your life is staying an act of courage rather than convenience?

Knowing the Season of Strength

"There is a time for everything, and a season for every activity under the heavens." (Ecclesiastes 3:1 NIV)

I learned that strength is not permanent; it is seasonal. My father did not resist the softening of his capacities or cling to authority past its season. He allowed leadership to change shape before it disappeared, teaching me that wisdom includes knowing when to loosen.

Reflection: What season are you in now—and what strength is being asked to change form?

What Remains After a Life Is Lived

"The righteous lead blameless lives; blessed are their children after them." (Proverbs 20:7 NIV)

At my father's funeral, the stories were consistent. No contradictions surfaced. No hidden lives were revealed. What remained was coherence—a life that had held its shape across decades. He left behind formation, not instruction; orientation, not control.

Reflection: If your life were told in stories rather than summaries, what would endure?

Love That Does Not Cling

"Greater love has no one than this: to lay down one's life for one's friends." (John 15:13 NIV)

My father did not tighten his grip as life narrowed. He did not bargain emotionally or rehearse sacrifice. He released with dignity, trusting that love does not need to cling to remain present.

Reflection: Where might love in your life be asking to loosen rather than hold?

A Faithful Exit

"I have fought the good fight, I have finished the race, I have kept the faith." (2 Timothy 4:7 NIV)

My father did not leave with speeches or summation. His presence simply tapered into peace, consistent with how he had lived. His departure did not feel unfinished. It felt complete.

Reflection: What would it mean for you to finish faithfully, without explanation?

What Does Not Fade

"Surely the righteous will never be shaken; they will be remembered forever." (Psalm 112:6 NIV)

What he left behind was not absence, but orientation. His way of standing remains in me—in restraint, responsibility, and steadiness. He is gone, but nothing essential collapsed.

Reflection: What in you has been shaped so deeply it no longer requires supervision?

LEGACY NOTES

The Story He Lived

*"To know even one life has breathed easier because you lived
—this is to have succeeded."*

— Ralph Waldo Emerson (1803-1882), American essayist, lecturer, and poet

To know that even one life has breathed easier because you lived is, I now understand, not a slogan or an aspiration but a quiet description of success itself, one my father never named and never needed to pursue because he embodied it without comment or calculation.

This book has not been an effort to elevate him into something symbolic or extraordinary, nor has it been to polish a life into a lesson that feels larger than it truly was. It has been an attempt to see clearly what already existed—a life shaped by responsibility rather than recognition, by endurance rather than explanation, and by love expressed so consistently it became the background against which others learned how to live without fear.

My father did not wonder how he would be remembered. He did not manage meaning or narrate his own significance. He paid attention to what needed to be done next, to where weight had to be absorbed so others could remain upright, to when staying was required and to when stepping back would better serve love. He trusted, perhaps without realizing it, that fidelity lived daily would speak more clearly than anything said aloud.

And in the end, it did.

The stories told about him were not dramatic or embellished, but they were unmistakably aligned, marked by the same themes of reliability, dignity, and presence that had shaped his life for decades. There were no competing versions of who he was and, no late discoveries that required reinterpretation. Only the quiet coherence of a man whose inner life and outer conduct had long since reached agreement. What people remembered matched what they had lived beside, and that congruence was itself his legacy.

He lived the story he wanted others to tell without ever telling it himself.

I have come to see, slowly and with more humility than confidence, that the deepest moral of a life is not found in its declarations, but in what it makes normal—what it steadies, what it protects, and what it quietly insists upon through repetition. My father normalized responsibility without complaint, restraint without coldness, and staying without drama. In doing so, he taught me that integrity is less about intensity than orientation and, less about what you claim than where you return when no one is watching.

This book is not asking you to become someone else, or adopt a life that does not fit your own conditions. It is an invitation to notice what your presence teaches before you ever speak, what patterns you pass down simply by the way you move through difficulty, and what kind of world forms around you because you remain. Every life leaves a story behind; the only real question is whether it will be clear.

My father did not give me answers to carry forward. He gave me posture. He did not explain love; he enacted it. He did not argue for faith; he stood on it. He did not teach me how to stay by insisting I do so, but by knowing when to release without abandoning what mattered.

And now his life leaves me with a responsibility that feels both sobering and liberating—not to preserve him in memory, but to live in a way that allows others to breathe easier because I was here, to speak where he was silent without diminishing his restraint, to rest where he endured without forgetting what that endurance made possible, and to carry forward what was faithful while setting down what no longer needs to be borne.

This is how legacies remain alive—not by being repeated unchanged, but by being lived forward with discernment, gratitude, and courage.

My father lived a story worth telling.

My work now is quieter, and more demanding.

To live one that is worth passing on.

ACKNOWLEDGMENTS

This book began long before I ever put words to paper. It began in the quiet sacrifices of two people who crossed an ocean with nothing but courage, devotion, and the belief that their labor would mean something long after they were gone. To my mother and father—this book is, in every way, an inheritance from your lives. Thank you for showing me that strength does not need volume, love does not require speeches, and faith is often lived more powerfully through presence than proclamation. Everything I know about endurance, responsibility, and purpose began with you.

To my brother, who shared the early winters, the cramped rooms, the warmth of familiarity in unfamiliar places—thank you for walking with me through the first chapters of our shared story. You were part of the architecture of those early years, and I am grateful for the bond that shaped us both.

To my extended family—especially my uncles and aunts whose own journeys of leaving and becoming helped build the foundation we all now stand upon— thank you. Your courage, your humor, your stories told around kitchen tables, and your quiet resilience formed the backdrop of my childhood and the moral geography of my life.

To the friends, mentors, and colleagues who encouraged me to write this book—thank you for seeing value in a story that unfolds not through dramatic moments but through the slow, steady accumulation of faith and duty. Many of you reminded me, often without knowing it, that the lessons we inherit from those who came before us continue to speak, even when their voices have long gone silent.

To those who helped shape this manuscript—readers who offered feedback, conversations that clarified themes, and people who reminded me to keep going when the writing felt heavier than expected, I am deeply grateful. Your insights refined the message and your kindness lightened the work.

To my wife, whose patience, encouragement, and belief in this project gave me the freedom to write honestly and fully—thank you for standing beside me through every chapter, both written and lived. Your love is the quiet constancy that steadies my life, much like the presence I describe in these pages.

And finally, to the reader—thank you for opening these pages and entering a story that may echo parts of your own. If something here reminds you of the people who shaped you, strengthened you, or loved you in ways they never had words for, then this book has fulfilled its purpose. Legacy is not measured only in what is said, but in what is lived—and in what continues long after the story's first chapter ends.

— Don P. Martone

ABOUT THE AUTHOR

Don P. Martone is the son of Italian immigrants whose quiet sacrifices, unwavering faith, and steadfast devotion shaped the truest architecture of his life. Born in Canada to parents who arrived with little more than hope and endurance, he grew up watching a father who spoke few words but communicated everything through presence, and a mother whose prayers carried the family through seasons of uncertainty. Their example formed the moral and spiritual foundation on which his life and work would be built.

Before becoming an advisor to leaders navigating high-stakes personal and professional transitions, Martone spent nearly three decades inside the plastics, petrochemical, and downstream energy sectors. Working alongside other engineers, operators, and executives, he developed a profound respect for the unseen burdens people carry—the weight of responsibility, the cost of providing for others, and the continuous grind of decision-making that shapes both companies and families. These years taught him what his father had modeled long before that real leadership is measured not by titles, but by steadiness, integrity, and the willingness to stay when the work is hard.

In time, Martone shifted his career toward guiding individuals and families through major life changes. His work is grounded in deep listening, strategic clarity, and a belief that meaningful transitions require both courage and compassion. Known for blending technical insight with human understanding, he helps people move from one chapter of life to the next with intention — honoring the past while shaping a legacy that endures.

Words Not Required is Martone's most personal writing project to date. It is a tribute to his father's quiet strength, his mother's resilience, and the generations whose sacrifices often remain unspoken but are never unfelt. Through this book, he offers readers not only a family story, but a universal truth: Legacy is forged not in extraordinary moments, but in the faithful repetition of ordinary acts.

Outside his professional work, Martone is a devoted husband, a student of faith, and an observer of the small, steady rituals that give life its meaning. He believes in the transformative power of gratitude, the moral clarity found in honest work, and the enduring truth that legacy is not measured by what we say, but by what we build through the lives we touch.

He lives with his wife and Samoyed "children" in the United States, where he continues to write, teach, and help others navigate the journey of creating their own stories they want others to tell.

LEGACY NOTES TO CARRY FORWARD